MODERN JEWISH ETHICS

Modern Jewish Ethics

THEORY AND PRACTICE

Edited by Marvin Fox

OHIO STATE UNIVERSITY PRESS

All quotations from Yigel Lev, *Ha-Milhamah Ohevet Ge-varim Tzeirim* [War Likes Young Men] are used by permission of Bitan Publishers, Tel Aviv. The translation is by Meir Pa'il.

LIBRARY OF CONGRESS CATALOGING IN PUBLICATION DATA

Institute for Judaism and Contemporary Thought.
  Modern Jewish ethics, theory and practice.

  Primarily papers presented at the 1972 meeting
of the Institute.
  Includes bibliographical references and index.
  1. Ethics, Jewish—Congresses 2. Jewish law—
Congresses. 3. Philosophy, Jewish—Congresses.
I. Fox, Marvin, ed. II. Title.
BJ1279.I57   1975   296.3'85   74-28395
  ISBN 0-8142-0192-X

Manufactured in the United States of America

Contents

CONTENTS

PREFACE

THE PAPERS IN THIS VOLUME were first presented at meetings of the Institute for Judaism and Contemporary Thought in Israel. The institute was founded in 1971 at the initiative of a group of professors from Bar-Ilan University in Israel under the chairmanship of Professor Harold Fisch, who was then rector of the university. The executive committee was subsequently expanded to include scholars from the United States, Canada, and South Africa in addition to the Israeli members. The purpose of the institute is to explore in depth the ways in which classical Judaism and contemporary thought may illuminate and fructify each other. The participants in the meetings of the institute represent a wide variety of Jewish positions and life-styles, ranging from orthodoxy to secularism and from total religious observance to very little or none at all. What unites them is the strong conviction that Judaism is an intellectually live and significant option for contemporary men, and the equally strong conviction that a living Judaism must be in touch with and responsive to the best in contemporary thought. In addition to the theoretical concerns and interests that unite the participants in the institute, they are also united by a common practical concern with contemporary Jewish affairs and with the ways in which scholars and thinkers may influence those affairs. The papers in this volume reflect this combination of theoretical and practical interests and are a fair sample of the discussions that take place at the annual summer meetings of the institute.

With the exception of the introductory paper by the editor all the papers in this volume were presented at the meeting of July 1972 at Bar-Ilan University and at Nir Etzion, Israel. The editor's introductory paper was presented as one of the opening public lectures of the 1971 institute in a session held at Bar-Ilan University. The papers have undergone some revision from their original form, and in some cases incorporate the author's responses to points that were raised in the discussion. It should be noted that this 1972 meeting took place more than a year before the renewal of the war between Israel and its Arab neighbors in the autumn of 1973. Some of the papers that deal directly with issues concerning Israeli society may therefore appear to be dated. It seems clear, however, that although the authors may have misread the political and military future, their work continues to be of interest, for they confront the perennial moral issues that face a society that has military power and still seeks to live with regard for its Jewish heritage.

The papers are divided between theoretical and practical concerns, though even the latter are not without theoretical interest. The introductory paper by the editor attempts to set a general methodological foundation for the kind of inquiry that is carried on under the auspices of the institute. That foundation is not restricted to the topic of the present volume, but it is included here as a general introduction both to the volume and to the intellectual stance of the institute. It should be added, of course, that though the editor is confident he is expressing the views of a substantial portion of the participants in the institute, he is in no sense their official spokesman, nor is there any assurance that they would all subscribe to the views expressed in his opening paper. The remaining papers are divided among those which are devoted to topics that search out the theoretical foundations of Jewish ethics, particularly in relationship to Jewish law, those that are concerned with general philosophical questions and their relationship to Jewish ethics, and those that are directed to practical moral issues both in Israel and in the Diaspora.

I should like to express my gratitude to the contributors to this volume who were kind enough to participate in our institute meetings and to make their papers available to us for publication, and to Judith A. Berlin, who prepared the index with great skill. My special thanks go to Arthur Lesley and Sanford Ames who did a labor of love in preparing an English translation of the paper by Emmanuel Levinas, to Nancy Riddle who typed the manuscript with rare skill and good humor, though she was at times working with copy that was barely legible, and to Mrs. Elizabeth Hellinger, executive secretary of the Ohio State University Department of Philosophy, who generously provided technical help and counsel. Above all, my appreciation must be expressed to my wife, June T. Fox, who is both an ideal Jewish woman and a scholar of impeccable intellectual taste. There is no way to give adequate expression to the debt I owe her for her share in all my work.

Marvin Fox

ACKNOWLEDGMENTS

THE WORK OF THE Institute for Judaism and Contemporary Thought has been made possible through the generous support of a group of concerned individuals and institutions. We are deeply grateful to each of them for their interest in our work and their faith in the significance of our enterprise. We record here our debt for continuing support to: I. Meier and Henrietta Segals, and H. Jerome Sisselman. Support for the 1972 institute program was also provided by: Ludwig Jesselson, Jacob Lowy, Dr. Y. Mirelman, and Rabbi Elio Toaff (chief rabbi of Rome). We are particularly indebted for both material and moral support to the following agencies: Bar-Ilan University, the Israel Ministry of Education and Culture, the Jewish Agency, and the Society for Justice, Ethics and Morals of South Africa and Israel.

It is with special sorrow that we record the death of Dr. Arie Toeg, a member of our 1972 summer institute, who gave his life in defense of his country during the Yom Kippur war of October 1974. He was a brilliant young scholar, a faithful Jew, and a model of those virtues that our institute seeks to encourage. He will be sorely missed by all of us who worked with him and benefitted from his learning and insight.

The committee that carries the continuing responsibility for planning and executing the programs of the Institute for Judaism and Contemporary Thought is composed of: Professor

ACKNOWLEDGMENTS

Harold Fisch, Bar-Ilan University, chairman; Professor Morton W. Bloomfield, Harvard University; Mr. Adi Cohen, Tel-Aviv; Dr. Gabriel Cohen, Bar-Ilan University; Professor Marvin Fox, Brandeis University; Professor Moshe Goshen-Gottstein, the Hebrew University of Jerusalem; Professor Ephraim Katzir, the Weizmann Institute of Science, President of the State of Israel; Mrs. Rebecca Katz, Bar-Ilan University; Professor Aharon Kirschenbaum, Tel-Aviv University; Professor Charles S. Liebman, Bar-Ilan University; Dr. Stefan Moses, the Hebrew University of Jerusalem; Professor Jakob Petuchowski, Hebrew Union College-Jewish Institute of Religion; Professor Yehoshua Schächter, Bar-Ilan University; Professor Moshe Schwarcz, Bar-Ilan University; Dr. Uriel Simon, Bar-Ilan University; Rabbi Adin Steinsaltz, Jerusalem; Dr. Aaron Streiter, Bar-Ilan University; Professor Abner Weiss, University of Natal. We also acknowledge with much appreciation the services of Dr. Aaron Streiter, who served as secretary for the meetings of 1971 and 1972, and of Dr. Aaron Skaist, who served as secretary for the meetings of 1973 and 1974.

Part One

INTRODUCTION

MARVIN FOX

Judaism, Secularism
And Textual Interpretation

IN THIS INTRODUCTORY ESSAY I shall not deal
directly with questions of Jewish ethics. My purpose is rather to
set forth what I understand to be the basic methodological principles that underlie the common efforts of the participants in
this volume to understand and interpret important aspects of
Judaism. The Institute of Judaism and Contemporary Thought,
under whose auspices these papers were originally presented,
was established by a group of people who share the conviction
that "Judaism" and "contemporary thought" are not mutually
exclusive. On the contrary, we are convinced that one of the
great strengths of Judaism is the fact that it has a method for
remaining true to itself while absorbing, or, at least, fruitfully
confronting, various aspects of non-Jewish thought. In every
age, including our own, Jewish thinkers have had a vital need to
come to terms with the insights of the science, philosophy, and
morality of their time. They have been forced to accept or reject, absorb or shun, ideas and doctrines whose initial source is
not within the Jewish tradition. Judaism itself provides a
method for carrying on this intellectual-spiritual confrontation.
It is a method by which the boundaries between the Jewish and
non-Jewish worlds are sometimes erased, and are at other times
drawn sharply. Some outside teachings are accepted, natu-
ralized, and given a home within the Jewish fold. Others are rejected and excluded from any claim to Jewish legitimacy.

This method, an instrument of intellectual honesty and spiritual survival, is necessary because Judaism, as it has sometimes been described, is a "book-religion," that is, a religion that bases itself on texts that are considered sacred and that are canonized. These texts include the Bible, the Talmud, the later rabbinic writings, the codes, and similar works. It is well known that these works have been, almost from their first appearance, the subject of continuous exegesis, for Jews were hardly ever satisfied with a bare text without commentaries. The process of exegesis did not come to an end at some specified time, but continues down to the present. When the text of the Bible was fixed, the activities of biblical interpretation were centered in the Talmud and the Midrashim. When the Talmud was closed and its text set, the processes of interpretation were carried forth in the Geonic literature and in the commentaries. In fact, the commentaries are normally treated by students as if they were a part of the text itself. The textual commentaries generated super-commentaries, and the process of interpretation went on. If, as Jewish tradition teaches, the oral law was given at Sinai together with the written text, it would appear that the practice of treating the text as always requiring interpretation began at Sinai and has continued down to the present. Inside the Jewish tradition, an uninterpreted text is practically an unknown phenomenon.

What I shall argue in this paper is that this process of exegesis and interpretation is the most important device that Jewish tradition used in order to be able to stand simultaneously in the classical tradition of Judaism and in the contemporary world. Each age, living in its particular cultural and intellectual milieu, had fashioned its way of being faithful to the teachings of Judaism while accommodating itself to the best of contemporary scientific and philosophic doctrine. The integrity of the texts on which Judaism rests is respected, while, by the process of exegesis, their openness to the contemporary world of ideas is assured.

One of the greatest dangers to Jewish faith and Jewish

thought is the fundamentalist tendency that occasionally mani-
fests itself (in our own time, as in others) and that seeks to
freeze doctrine at a particular point. Such fundamentalism,
which often claims to rest on a literal reading of the texts, is
alien to the dominant tendencies of Jewish intellectual history.
It ignores the obvious fact that we have no literal uninterpreted
texts, and seeks to arrogate to a position of authoritative permanence particular views that are themselves only one more interpretation of Jewish doctrine. In denying to Judaism the flexibility to retain its essential nature while at the same time using
the freedom of interpretation to come to terms with the world
of contemporary ideas, this fundamentalism is not only unfaithful to the whole tenor of Jewish thought but also poses a
serious threat to the ability of Judaism to survive.

Religious fundamentalism has as its counterpart a kind of
secularist fundamentalism that is equally insensitive to the fact
that we are always dependent on and involved in processes of interpretation. This secularist fundamentalism sometimes mas-
querades under the guise of being purely scientific in character.
It is, in fact, a caricature of science, just as Jewish fundamentalism is a caricature of historic Judaism. It stems from a desire
for the perfect security that it hopes will come to us if we are
able to reduce all human knowledge to a single plane and to
restrict ourselves to a single authorized method for pursuing
and establishing all claims to knowledge. This goal was
brilliantly expounded and defended in the seventeenth century
by the great philosopher-mathematician Gottfried Wilhelm
Leibniz. In a youthful essay, one of many that he wrote on the
subject, Leibniz set forth his general plan for a universal system
of notation in which all subject matters could be adequately expressed. This system was to be mathematical in character, so
that all differences of opinion about any matter whatsoever
would be subject to resolution by mathematical means. Leibniz
assures us that when the universal characteristic has been in-
vented, and when we learn to apply it with proper skill, there
will no longer be room or occasion for the interminable disputes

5

to which we are accustomed among thinkers in the various fields of human inquiry. A dispute between philosophers, he says, will become simply a dispute between bookkeepers, or, to read him more literally and with admiration at his prophetic foresight, a dispute between computers. The parties who have a complex issue about which they differ "will only have to take pens in hand, seat themselves at their counting-boards, and say to each other, 'Let us calculate.'"[1] Although Leibniz himself was extremely interested in the advancement of religion, metaphysics, and ethics as well as logic, mathematics, and the natural sciences, he nevertheless left us a heritage that set monistic reductionism as its intellectual ideal. At its worst, that reductionism has taken the form of a scientistic fundamentalism that claims to know the world with certainty. This kind of science ignores the extent to which it engages in more than pure observation and forgets that there are no uninterpreted data. It denies all exegesis, or what amounts to the same, recognizes only one official authorized interpretation of the data available to us. As such, it claims, in effect, to be in exclusive possession of the truth, or, at least, of the only way to truth, and denies the possibility or legitimacy of alternate ways.

All responsible scientific thought is aware that, in fact, there is no more possibility of dispensing with exegesis in the sciences than there is in the treatment of religious texts. For the true scientist the world is a text that needs both to be discovered and interpreted, and often the discovery is the interpretation. Like his counterparts in the world of religious thought, he works with a combination of tradition and freedom. Were he to cut himself off totally from the established ways of scientific thought and understanding, he would lack an operating framework. Were he to insist on a fundamentalist literalism that makes the framework of his time permanently fixed, he would prevent his science from developing and from speaking meaningfully to its own age. As one of the most distinguished contemporary historians of science expresses it:

6

Observation and experience can and must drastically restrict the range of admissible scientific belief, else there would be no science. But they cannot alone determine a particular body of such belief. An apparently arbitrary element, compounded of personal and historical accident, is always a formative ingredient of the beliefs espoused by a given scientific community at a given time.[2]

He goes on to argue that all scientific research is affected by the professional education of the scientist in question. That education has provided him with certain modes of thought and understanding that Thomas Kuhn calls "normal research activity." He describes this as a

strenuous and devoted attempt to force nature into the conceptual boxes supplied by professional education. . . . We shall wonder whether research could proceed without such boxes, whatever the element of arbitrariness in their historic origins, and, occasionally, in their subsequent development. . . . Normal science, for example, often suppresses fundamental novelties because they are necessarily subversive of its basic commitments. Nevertheless, so long as those commitments retain an element of the arbitrary, the very nature of normal research ensures that novelty shall not be suppressed for very long.[3]

A slavishly conservative adherence to the currently established ways of viewing things would end all scientific progress. A total rejection of all that is currently held to be known would paralyze all efforts at understanding. Science, as we know it today, moves from the established to the novel, using its own techniques of interpretation and discovery. Judaism, I shall argue, does precisely the same with its materials, and it is by the use of the various modes of textual interpretation that Judaism retains its power to be faithful to its past while, at the same time, coming to terms with the secular world in which it lives. It is in this way that it becomes possible for Jewish faith and

7

secular science to live together in harmony. Each rests, in part, on the legitimacy and inescapable necessity of exegesis and interpretation.

As a first step we must see whether Jewish teaching recognizes as legitimate and proper an independent secular realm. In particular, we must ask what status and authority Judaism gives to knowledge that we gain through reason alone or through scientific inquiry. We must, however, begin with a caveat. The richness and diversity of views that have emerged over many centuries of Jewish tradition are so great that it is irresponsible to speak of what Judaism teaches. All we claim to do is to establish that within the official literature some of the most respected and recognized rabbinic teachers of various periods of Jewish history have affirmed the propriety of accepting as true what we learn through the natural sciences. Though other opposed views could be cited, my contention is that those which I shall present are widely held and are a thoroughly legitimate version of Jewish doctrine.

There were some eminent talmudic sages who did not hesitate to affirm the truth of scientific claims although they contradicted the then accepted Jewish views. Their position seems to have been that in such matters the best evidence must be accepted, whatever its source. The Talmud records, for example, a discussion concerning an astronomical question on which the Jewish authorities held a different view from that current among the non-Jewish astronomers. Our printed texts record that Rabbi Judah the Prince sought to defend the standard Jewish view but that he failed. In a reading that we no longer have, but that was available to Maimonides, the text says explicitly, "The gentile sages vanquished the sages of Israel." In another reading, that of Rabbi Isaac Arama in his *Akedat Yizhak,* the passage says, "The sages of Israel admitted their error." Later in that same talmudic passage there is a second discussion of a similar question, now concerning the course of the sun, and this time all the texts carry the statement that Rabbi Judah the Prince said, "Their view is preferable to

8

ours."[4] It would appear that they did not consider such matters open to purely internal Jewish resolution, but rather held that the best evidence and the most persuasive arguments must prevail.

This openness to scientific knowledge, whatever its source, has not been the universal Jewish attitude. At a later time there were Jewish authorities who simply could not accept the idea that there could be non-Jewish doctrines even on such scientific matters that were true while the teachings of the sages of Israel were in error. Rabbenu Tam (c. 1100–1171), the grandson of Rashi, is reported to have explained the talmudic passage that we cited above in the following way. "Though, at the time, the gentile scholars prevailed over the sages of Israel, this was only a rhetorical victory which stemmed from the fact that they offered superior arguments [which the Jewish scholars did not know how to refute]. However, the truth of the matter is still that which was taught by the sages of Israel."[5]

In contrast with this strong feeling that even on scientific matters Jews must seek their own internal truth, Maimonides sees in the talmudic passage in question a model case for the principle that we should be controlled only by the best arguments and the best evidence, not by any respect for eminent Jewish figures and their revered traditions. "For everyone who argues in speculative matters," he says, "does this according to the conclusions to which he was led by his speculation. Hence the conclusion whose demonstration is correct is believed."[6] In a later passage he affirms even more explicitly that in astronomy we have no obligation to accept any traditional Jewish teachings. The sages of Israel, we now know, were mistaken in some of their views about astronomy. This is due, Maimonides believes, to the fact that the general development of mathematics was in a fairly primitive state in talmudic times, hence, they lacked an essential tool for achieving sound astronomical knowledge. We should not be troubled or ill at ease when we are forced to reject talmudic teaching concerning scientific issues, since when the Rabbis dealt with such questions, "they did not speak about this as transmitters of dicta of the prophets, but rather because in those times they were men of knowledge in these fields or because they had heard these dicta from the men of knowledge who lived in those times."[7] For Maimonides, there is no authoritative prophetic teaching about the natural world that we must view as binding on faithful Jews. On the contrary, when the sages of Israel made scientific judgments it was not in their role as the official transmitters of prophetic teaching but only as men of science or the pupils of men of science. As such, their only claim to authority is the evidence they can marshal in behalf of their doctrines. If at any time their evidence is superseded by superior evidence and argument, we are, of course, bound to accept that view for which the best evidence is offered, no matter who its author. As Maimonides puts it in an early work, "One should accept the truth from whatever source it proceeds."[8]

The extent to which Maimonides succeeded in establishing his principle is eloquently clear when we see that a nineteenth-century orthodox Bible commentator approached Maimonides' science with exactly the same critical attitude that Maimonides evinced toward the science of the ancient Jewish sages. Rabbi Meir Loeb Malbim opens his commentary on the Book of Ezekiel with a brief introduction in which he explains that we can no longer accept Maimonides' interpretation of the Chariot Vision because it is based on a natural science and philosophy that are outdated. Maimonides bases his conclusions, says Malbim, on principles that "have all been undermined by developments in scientific research in recent times. This research has given us an astronomy and other natural sciences which rest on foundations which are both stronger and more reliable." Here we have an instance of a recent exegetical work, fully accepted in the most orthodox Jewish circles, which acknowledges that even in the case of so sensitive a text we must adjust our religious understanding to the best scientific information we have, rather than the reverse.

Although trust in the independence of rational inquiry and

scientific research experienced varying fortunes in Jewish intellectual history, its strongest support came from the philosophers. In the philosophic literature we consistently find reason defended and praised as a sound independent source of human knowledge. Though this defense is often coupled with the assurance that religious teaching is in accord with the dictates of reason, it still lays great stress on the duty to pursue rational inquiry. A typical statement is that of Saadia Gaon, who assures us that "the Bible is not the sole basis of our religion, for in addition to it we have two other bases. One of these is anterior to it; namely, the fountain of reason. The second is posterior to it; namely, the source of tradition. Whatever, therefore, we may not find in the Bible, we can find in the two other sources."[9] Saadia's belief in the primacy of reason is cited with approval by Bahya ibn Paquda in the introduction to his *Hovot Ha-Levavot* and is echoed also in the *Kuzari* of Judah Halevi.[10] It is surely reasonable to suppose that these thinkers, and others like them, would have the same confidence in natural science, if they were living today, that they had in the powers of reason in their own time. It is equally reasonable to suppose that they would be sensitive, as well, to the limitations of science, and would recognize the extent to which the sciences themselves depend on interpretation.

The accepted methods for accommodating the Torah to a diversity of doctrinal positions are exegesis and interpretation. The range of interpretation often seems virtually unlimited, especially when we are dealing with narrative or aggadic passages, with matters of doctrine rather than with questions of practical law. A Midrash compares the interpretation of Torah texts to the interpretation of dreams. "Behold, it says, 'A dream carries much implication' (Eccles. 5:2). Now by using the method of *kal vahomer* we may reason: If the contents of dreams which have no effect may yield a multitude of interpretations, how much more then should the important contents of the Torah imply many interpretations in every verse."[11] This principle is based on the biblical verse, "Is not my

11

word like as fire, saith the Lord; and like a hammer that breaketh the rock in pieces?" (Jer. 23:29). The Rabbis interpreted this to mean that just as the hammer breaks the rock into many pieces, so is the Torah (God's word) open to a multiplicity of interpretations.[12] Especially in the realm of Aggada, though not exclusively there, Jewish tradition kept the gates of interpretation wide open.

A few specific examples, chosen from the very many that are readily available, will show us to what extent free interpretation is normal Jewish practice. It is widely taken for granted in the tradition that the locus classicus that provides us with the ideological and juridical model for conversion to the Jewish faith is the case of Ruth. In the standard interpretation of the events, Ruth, a pagan Moabite woman, was married to the Jew, Mahlon. She remained a pagan until after her husband's death when she chose to accompany her mother-in-law, Naomi, back to the land of Israel. At that time she was formally converted to Judaism. Ruth's declaration of adherence to the faith and people of Naomi was, in the view of the Rabbis, a model of proper religious conversion. Ruth pleads with Naomi to be allowed to accompany her, and declares, "For whither thou goest, I will go; and where thou lodgest, I will lodge; thy people shall be my people, and thy God my God" (Ruth 1:16). In the Talmud this is interpreted as pointing to the various detailed steps involved in the process of becoming converted to the Jewish faith.[13] That talmudic interpretation is rarely disputed in the traditional literature. Yet, no less a figure than Abraham ibn Ezra categorically rejects this line of interpretation. According to ibn Ezra, despite what the Talmud has to say, Ruth and Orpah were both converted before they married Mahlon and Chilion. For, says ibn Ezra, it is unthinkable that Jews of such distinguished position would have married unconverted gentile women. "It is not possible that Mahlon and Chilion married these women before they were converted."[14] His case rests, initially, on his own understanding of the facts, and he then proceeds to read the verses in the text to conform with his

12

view. Thus, he construes Orpah's leaving as an abandonment of her Jewish faith, and Ruth's moving declaration as a reaffirmation of that Jewish faith which she had accepted prior to her marriage. Ibn Ezra feels no need to apologize for or to justify his rejection of a standard talmudic-midrashic tradition, for the gates of interpretation and exegesis are open.

We find similar diversity in the case of the identity of the Cushite woman whom Moses married.[15] Now the explanation of what took place in this episode is not to be treated lightly. It is of high importance since it has to do with the life story, the personal behavior, and the moral standards of the supreme prophet, Moses. We need to know what seeming impropriety in his behavior evoked both the open criticism by his brother, Aaron, and his sister, Miriam, and God's high praise and fierce defense of him. One might have expected that about so grave a matter there would be a single fixed tradition. Instead, there are at least two lines of interpretation, very different in character and with very different moral implications. One line holds that the reference to the Cushite woman simply is another way of speaking of Zipporah, the wife of Moses, whom we know from the Bible. She is called Cushite, either because she was in fact dark-skinned, or else because she was so beautiful that she was referred to euphemistically by an opposite term, just as Job's wife urges him to "Bless God and die," when she means, "Curse God and die."[16] In this case, Moses is accused of having abandoned his wife, who is both virtuous and beautiful, so that he might devote himself completely to his career as prophet, without being encumbered by family responsibilities. Moreover, there is the suggestion that he is motivated by a desire to emphasize his special holiness and purity, a kind of posing that Miriam and Aaron find offensive. A second line of interpretation bases itself on a legend that Moses served as king of Ethiopia for forty years, during the period after his flight from Egypt and before he appeared in Midian. In Ethiopia he was given a royal wife, who is the "Cushite woman whom he married."[17] Miriam and Aaron speak against him for reasons

13

that are connected with this Ethiopian woman, but we are not told precisely what their complaint is.

Our understanding of the charge against Moses, which is never made explicit in the Bible itself, depends on which of the two versions we accept. Though we are dealing with the life of the supreme prophet, there is no attempt to limit our interpretation to a single authorized version. On the contrary, the two versions literally live side by side in the various editions of the *Mikraot Gedolot*. There are three Targum versions of the text in the standard printed editions. The first, Onkelos, translates "Cushite woman" as "beautiful woman," with no further comment. Targum Yerushalmi I (Pseudo-Jonathan) construes the passage as referring specifically to Zipporah, but Targum Yerushalmi II construes it as referring to the Ethiopian queen whom Moses is supposed to have married. Ibn Ezra mentions this last view, but rejects it. Rashi interprets the passage as referring to only Zipporah, but his grandson Rashbam insists that only the Ethiopian queen could possibly be intended here and those who hold that the Cushite woman is Zipporah (and his grandfather Rashi is among them) are simply in error. All this can be found on a single page of the standard Pentateuch with commentaries regularly used by pious Jews to this day. What is instructive is the fact that such opposed ways of understanding the text can and do live side by side without generating any tension or uneasiness. This is possible only because of the deeply rooted principle in the Jewish tradition that there is no single fixed way of understanding the text. The gates of interpretation are open and it is fully proper to go through various gates, at different times and for different purposes.

Lest it be thought that the cases we have cited deal with matters of little practical consequence and only for that reason are they open to a variety of interpretations, let us consider another case that is unquestionably of major practical importance in determining the way in which a Jew should live his life. Does Judaism approve, perhaps even require, ascetic self-denial, does it permit it grudgingly, or does it condemn such a life pattern? The model case is that of the Nazirite, whose vows include among other restrictions, abstinence from "wine and strong drink."[18] How does the Jewish tradition regard his abstinence? Because he has voluntarily denied himself that which is permitted is he a man of superior virtue, or is he a sinner? Should we imitate him, or should we shun his ways? Now it should be made clear that so far as the practical laws of the Nazirite are concerned there is no problem. Once he has made his vow the law is clear as to what he may and may not do, what the standard term of his vow is, what offerings he must bring and under what circumstances. Yet, with respect to the wider question of what value we should put on his asceticism there is deep disagreement. In a familiar passage in the Talmud the asceticism of the Nazirite is severely condemned. "R. Elazar ha-Kappar, Berabbi, said: Why does Scripture say, 'And make atonement for him, for that he sinned by reason of the soul' (Num. 6:11). Against what 'soul' did he then sin? It can only be because he denied himself wine. If then this man who denied himself only wine is termed a sinner, how much more does one sin who is an ascetic in all things!"[19] For this reason, it is held, a Nazirite who becomes impure must bring a special sin-offering, since he is now required to extend the term of his abstinence. The Tosafot comment that he is guilty because he "extends the fixed period of his suffering during which he suffers the pain of abstinence from wine."[20] Asceticism is clearly condemned here as undesirable self-denial that is contrary to good Jewish practice. The ascetic is judged guilty of sin, and the more he extends his asceticism the greater his sin. Some contemporary scholars are so certain that this negative attitude toward asceticism is normative that they simply declare without qualification that, "The Nazirite was severely discouraged by the rabbis since asceticism was against the spirit of Judaism."[21]

Yet, in the Talmud itself there is also a quite different view of asceticism. In another passage where the same statement of Rabbi Elazar ha-Kappar is cited, there follows a disagreement. The other view holds that the Nazirite is called "holy" in

15

Scripture because his self-denial is a mark of special piety. Asceticism is represented as an ideal to be imitated and admired, for, "If this man who denied himself only wine is termed holy, how much more so he who denies himself the enjoyment of ever so many things."[22] The one qualification seems to be that he who takes the vows of an ascetic must be confident that he has the capacity successfully to endure his self-affliction, otherwise he might well turn into a violator of his vows or even a bitter denier of God. This praise of ascetic self-denial as a state of superior holiness is taken up by certain medieval authorities. Maimonides, for example, ends his codification of the laws of the Nazirite with high praise for one who makes Nazirite vows with complete sincerity. Such a man rises, in Maimonides' view, to a special level of holiness, and has merit equal to that of a prophet.[23] In his philosophic work Maimonides maintains the same position. He praises the Nazirite for abstaining from wine, "which has caused the ruin of the ancients and the moderns. Whoever avoids it is called holy and is put in the same rank as a High Priest as far as holiness is concerned."[24] Nahmanides, in his commentary on the Pentateuch, explains that the sin-offering that the Nazirite is required to bring when he completes the term of his vow is an atonement for the fact that his period of abstinence has come to an end. Directly contradicting Tosafot, Nahmanides says that ideally he should remain in the ascetic state of Nazirite holiness permanently. When at the end of his fixed time as a Nazirite, he reverts to an ordinary nonascetic pattern of life, he is considered a sinner who must offer a sin-offering as atonement. Here we have a case where practical consequences ensue from general attitudes. Yet, even in this case, different patterns of interpretation are permitted, and with them the different practical ideals they imply.

There were important rabbinic authorities who evinced deep opposition to the openness of interpretation that we have described. They directed their attack in particular against the Aggada, because they saw that with respect to the interpretation of aggadic texts only a very low degree of control is possible. Despite the long history of differing decisions and rulings with respect to the practical law, the law does tend to become fixed and crystallized. On the other hand, the Aggada tends to have almost unlimited flexibility, and in the interpretation of any given text it accommodates an astounding variety of doctrines, attitudes, and ideals. There were those who saw in this openness a danger to sound doctrine and the possibility of both intellectual and spiritual corruption. They were fierce in their expressions of opposition to those who occupied themselves with Aggada. In one passage the danger of Aggada is established by showing that by its methods it is possible to interpret a single biblical verse in directly contradictory ways. Rabbi Zeira concludes that the Aggada is unstructured, that it turns true teaching upside down, and that one cannot extract sound doctrine from it. For that reason he strongly advises his son to give up all study of Aggada and devote himself rather to the Halakha, which is alone sound and reliable.[25] In another such passage, we are warned that dire consequences and a divine curse await those who occupy themselves with the Aggada.[26]

Notwithstanding these instances of intense opposition to preoccupation with the Aggada, throughout most of the Jewish tradition the principle of free exegesis, especially of aggadic materials, prevails. Perhaps the tone and mood that dominates Jewish tradition is best expressed in a Midrash on the verse, "The voice of the Lord is according to the strength"(Ps. 29:4). The Midrash stresses the point that the verse reads, "according to *the* strength" and not "according to *His* strength." Had it contained the latter reading, we might conclude that God speaks to all men in a single voice and in a single language. If that were the case, only those who could hear and understand would know Him, whereas those who could not hear or failed to understand would be cut off from Him. The Midrash teaches that, on the contrary, God addresses us in such way that each individual may hear him in accordance with his own particular capacity. Even at Sinai "the divine voice went forth to all Israel

17

and was assimilated by each person in accordance with his particular capacity—the elders in their own way, the youth in their
own way, the children in their own way, the sucklings in their
own way, the women in their own way, and also Moses in his
own way. . . . For this reason it is written, 'The voice of the Lord
is according to *the* strength' and not 'according to *His* strength'
to teach us that each one grasps His message according to his
own particular power and capacity."[27] This conviction that the
one divine truth may be apprehended and expressed in a variety
of ways runs very deep in the Jewish tradition. It serves as the
ground on which freedom of interpretation rests.

The joining together of respect for secular knowledge and
open exegesis leads often to new, sometimes even startling,
readings of the biblical text itself. Perhaps most striking is the
introduction into Judaism of the doctrine that God is absolutely
incorporeal, a doctrine that appears to run directly counter to a
simple literal reading of the Bible. It is true that the Bible appears to be ambiguous on the subject of God's corporeality. On
the one hand, there is the very strong prohibition against any
representation of the divine in a physical form. There is no need
to cite the numerous passages, in the Ten Commandments and
elsewhere, that express revulsion at the very idea of a statue or
picture of God. At the same time, it can hardly be denied that
the Bible does speak of God anthropomorphically and anthro-
popathically. Although some of the biblical writers are engaged
in a struggle against actual idolaters or those who attempt to
represent the true God by way of a physical form, the later
Jewish generations have to come to terms not with actual
idolatry, but with the language of the Bible. One can discern a
steady movement from earlier periods with their relatively mild
attempts to interpret the anthropomorphisms in ways that
blunt their offensive uses to the totally unrestrained attack that
the medieval philosophers unleashed on any attempt to read the
anthropomorphic passages literally.

In the case of the philosophic interpretations, which have
since become normative in Jewish religious thought, we see a

18

model of how secular learning and the biblical text were brought together through the devices of textual interpretation. Unlike the earlier Jewish teachers, who objected to literalizing the anthropomorphisms on purely religious grounds, the medieval philosophers based their objections primarily on the grounds of purely secular philosophic knowledge. They held that reason teaches that God is incorporeal, and this secular source of knowledge was decisive for them. Given their conviction that rational argument establishes beyond all question the fact of God's incorporeality, they read the Bible mindful of a secular doctrine that controlled their interpretation. For these Jewish thinkers it was axiomatic that if the Bible is to be accepted as a source of truth, then it must conform to the principles of reason. If it seems to contradict the truths of reason, then we must read it in such way as to make it harmonize, for only by way of such a nonliteral reading will we be able to uncover the true teaching of Scripture. Saadia Gaon expressed the point with complete clarity when he said, "For all divine attributes pertaining to either substance or accident that are encountered in the books of the prophets it is necessary to find in the language of Scripture nonanthropomorphic meanings that would be in keeping with the requirements of reason."[28] What should be especially noted is his explicit statement that Scripture must be read in accordance "with the requirements of reason." That is to say, the sacred text and secular knowledge are brought into harmony by interpreting the text so that it will conform to the results of rational reflection. The text is not to be construed as meaning what it literally says, for it simply cannot mean what it appears to say. Nonliteral interpretation is not only permitted; it is mandatory. In the most extreme case we have the legal ruling of Maimonides that one who reads such texts literally, and thus attributes to God corporeal qualities, is guilty of heresy. "Five classes are termed heretics [minim] . . . He who says there is one Supreme Being but that He is a body and has a shape."[29] Despite the outcry of Rabad, contained in his gloss on this passage, that those who hold such a view cannot be called

19

heretics because they are simply following a literal reading of Scripture and Aggada, the bulk of opinion would tend to support Maimonides. Even Rabad, while defending them from charges of heresy, explains the views of these people as resulting from their dependence on *dibre ha-aggadot ha-meshabbeshot et ha-de'ot,* "the words of the *aggadot* which confuse (or corrupt) sound beliefs."[30] Though he is reluctant to go to the extreme of excluding such people from the community of the faithful, Rabad recognizes that they are misled into holding a false doctrine because they read the texts literally, rather than interpreting them in accordance with the teachings that are set down by reason. Even he accepts the principle that we must interpret texts in a nonliteral way if that is required by sound rational doctrine.

Let us consider a final case that will show how deeply committed Jewish tradition is to the processes of textual interpretation as a way of bringing together the worlds of secular learning and the teachings of religious faith. If we examine briefly the treatments of the problem of creation, that is, whether God created the world *ex nihilo* or out of a prime matter that is eternal, we can see how the secular and the sacred are brought together. The scriptural text is ambiguous on this point. It simply announces that God created the world, but it tells us nothing about the process of creation. We are only informed that it took place by divine fiat. Yet, by rabbinic times the doctrine of creation out of nothing was very deeply rooted in Jewish thought. E. E. Urbach holds that there is no suggestion among the Tannaim of the doctrine that the world was created from an eternal prime matter.[31] Whether the propagation of the doctrine of *creatio ex nihilo* was part of a polemic against gnosticism, whether it had its roots in some other source or motive, is a problem that lies beyond the limits of the present discussion. What is clear, however, is that, with minor exceptions, it became a standard Jewish doctrine, and the biblical texts were interpreted in accordance with this doctrine.

When we turn to the philosophers, and I refer, of course, only to philosophers who are recognized as Jewish authorities, we find a rather different situation. Saadia stays firmly within the rabbinic tradition. He holds that the doctrine of creation out of nothing is fully established by a set of sound philosophic arguments. When the philosophic evidence is added to the force of the tradition that also supports this doctrine, he is left with no doubt that all the scriptural texts teach only this view. In Scripture "our Lord, exalted be He, made it known to us that all things were created and that He had created them out of nothing. Thus Scripture says: In the beginning God created the heaven and the earth (Gen. 1:1). . . . Besides that, all this was verified for us by Him by means of miracles and marvels, so that we accepted it as true."[32] (We should note that the evidence about miracles is itself derived only from Scripture.) For Saadia, the scriptural verses are to be understood in only one particular way, despite their patent ambiguity, because both the tradition and reason require it. This being the case, we must then interpret any biblical passage that seems to cast doubt on creation out of nothing in such way that it conforms with this doctrine. And that is exactly what Saadia does.

Later philosophers were far less certain than Saadia that the philosophic issue was settled. They were aware that alternate lines of philosophic reasoning were possible, and that it was difficult to provide definitive proof of the doctrine of creation out of nothing. Thus, Judah Halevi held a far less fixed position. He recognized that there were no decisive philosophic arguments that could settle the question as to whether the world was created or eternal. Consequently, though for himself he accepted the traditional view, he did not read out of the faith or accuse of irreparable error those Jews who believed in the eternity of matter. As he puts it:

> The question of eternity and creation is obscure, whilst the arguments are evenly balanced. The theory of creation derives greater weight from the prophetic tradition of Adam, Noah, and Moses, which is more deserving of credence than conclusions

21

reached only by speculation. Nevertheless, if a follower of the Torah finds himself compelled to believe by rational argument that there is an eternal matter and that many worlds preceded our present world, this would not constitute a major defect in his faith, since he could still believe that the present world was created at a particular time and that Adam and Noah were among the first men.[33]

Tradition teaches us one way to understand the scriptural passages concerning creation, and philosophical speculation suggests another possible way. Halevi inclines toward tradition, since the philosophic arguments are not demonstratively certain. At the same time, he accepts the legitimacy of the non-traditional view, and by implication admits that Scripture could be interpreted to conform with it.

The classic statement of this position was set forth by Maimonides. He examined all the arguments for creation and for eternity, and concluded that none was decisive. Since there were no compelling rational grounds for choosing between opposed views, he held that it was legitimate to make a decision on other grounds. Because other aspects of religious faith would be deeply and adversely affected by the acceptance of the eternity of matter, Maimonides opts for the theory of creation out of nothing. However, he makes a strong and explicit point of saying that were there any decisive philosophic-scientific evidence for the eternity of matter, he would accept it without hesitation, and would be able with no difficulty to interpret Scripture accordingly. He assures his readers "that our shunning the affirmation of the eternity of the world is not due to a text figuring in the Torah according to which the world has been produced in time. For the texts indicating that the world has been produced in time are not more numerous than those indicating that the deity is a body. Nor are the gates of figurative interpretation shut in our faces or impossible of access to us regarding the subject of the creation of the world in time. For we could interpret them as figurative, as we have done when denying His corporeality."[34] Here the point is made openly and

22

without any ambiguity. Secular knowledge, if it is based on sound evidence such as should properly persuade any rational man, must command our assent. Whenever we have such knowledge we must proceed to understand Scripture so as to conform to it, and it is our right, perhaps even our duty, to interpret Scripture in such way that it accords with philosophic understanding and scientific knowledge.

The issue becomes even more pointed when we come to Gersonides in the fourteenth century. He openly affirms the Platonic theory of creation, which asserts that there is an eternal unformed prime matter out of which the world is formed by God. Though he runs counter to the vast bulk of the rabbinic tradition as well as to the Jewish philosophic tradition, Gersonides feels no hesitation about affirming his view. Moreover, he assures us that a correct interpretation of Scripture will support the claim that this is the doctrine of creation that is taught in the Bible. How could it be otherwise, since this theory of creation, Gersonides believes, is shown to be true for science and philosophy, and the Torah neither teaches nor requires us to believe that which is false.[35] It follows, therefore, that having discovered through science and philosophy a doctrine that we are convinced is demonstratively certain, we are justified in our confidence that any sound interpretation of Scripture will construe it so as to show that it accords with such doctrine.

The various essays in this volume exemplify the principle that we have set forth and explicated here. They approach problems of Jewish ethics with full respect for the tradition, and yet with confidence that the tradition is responsive to values and knowledge that come to it from outside its own boundaries. Like Jewish thinkers and teachers of all ages they rely on the devices of exegesis and interpretation to bring together the ideas and values of the contemporary world and the world of classical Judaism. Free exegesis serves as the bridge that connects the fixed tradition with changing ideas, with different times, different places, and different ways of understanding the world.

23

If we had no regard for Jewish tradition, we would no longer justly claim that our views are authentically Jewish. If we had only a rigidly fixed tradition we could not survive as thinking Jews in a world that grows and changes. It is our aim to remain faithful to our tradition while using its commitment to the openness of interpretation to bring to it the best insights and achievements of the human spirit in our time. Such freedom admittedly involves a serious risk that we may lose our connection with Jewish tradition and fall into a pure secularism to which we wrongly attach the label "Jewish." It is a risk to which we expose ourselves with appropriate concern, but with the conviction that as faithful Jews we have no choice. A Judaism that would demand of us the sacrifice of secular learning or intellectual integrity would betray its own highest principles and could no longer command our loyalty. Whatever the differences of doctrine among the contributors to this volume, all affirm the rabbinic teaching that "The seal of the Holy One, blessed be He, is truth."[36] It is on that ground that we come together to explore from a variety of perspectives the ways in which Judaism and contemporary thought may be joined. Even those of us who are firm in their adherence to Jewish law and consider it to be fixed and binding recognize that there is a very wide range in the ways in which we may legitimately understand Judaism and interpret its fundamental ideas.

1. G. W. Leibnitz, "De Scientia Universali seu Calculo Philosophico," *Opera Philosophica,* ed. J. E. Erdmann (Berlin, 1840), pp. 82–85 (author's translation).

2. Thomas S. Kuhn, *The Structure of Scientific Revolutions* (Chicago, 1962), p. 4.

3. Ibid., p. 5.

4. *Pesahim,* 94b. For the alternate readings see Maimonides, *Guide of the Perplexed,* II:8 and Isaac Arama, *Akedat Yizhak,* Bo, sec. 37. For a discussion of the problem of the alternate readings and of the rabbinic attitude on this question, see *Moreh Nebuchim* (ed. Yehuda ibn Shemuel), II:8, p. 129, fn. 4, where additional references are also given.

5. Cited in *Shita Mekubbezet* to *Ketubot* 13b.

6. Maimonides, *Guide of the Perplexed*, II:8.

7. Ibid., III:14 (end).

8. Maimonides, *Eight Chapters*, ed. Gorfinkle (New York, 1912; repr. 1966), Foreword, p. 36.

9. Saadia Gaon, *The Book of Beliefs and Opinions*, trans. Samuel Rosenblatt (New Haven, 1948), III:10, p. 174.

10. Cf. *Kuzari*, I:67.

11. *Midrash Haggadol Bereshith* (ed. Schechter), p. xxv; ibid. (ed. Margulies), p. 39. Cited in Saul Lieberman, *Hellenism in Jewish Palestine* (New York, 1950), p. 70.

12. Cf. Rashi to Gen. 33:20 and *Shabbat* 88b.

13. *Yebamoth*, 47b. Cf. Targum to Ruth 1:4,5,10, and 16, which explicitly states that they are gentile women and that Ruth was converted after her husband's death.

14. Abraham ibn Ezra, Commentary to Ruth 1:2.

15. Num. 12:1.

16. Job 2:9.

17. For a detailed discussion see Louis Ginzberg, *The Legends of the Jews* (Philadelphia, 1946), vol. 2, pp. 286–89; vol. 5, note 80, pp. 407–10; vol. 6, note 488, p. 90.

18. Num. 6:3.

19. *Nazir*, 19a (Soncino translation).

20. Ibid., *Tosafot*, s.v., *V'hainu Ta'ama*.

21. *Encyclopaedia Judaica*, vol. 12, p. 909.

22. *Ta'anith*, 11b.

23. *MT, Nezirut*, 10:14.

24. *Guide of the Perplexed*, III:48 (end).

25. *P. T. Ma'asrot*, III:10, 51a.

26. *P. T. Shabbat*, XVI:1, 15c. It may be that the stress in this passage is on a prohibition against writing Agadda, as is suggested by the parallel passage in *Soferim*, XVI:2; however, it is clear from the context that beyond a desire to restrict Aggada to an oral form there is also a deep distrust of Agada in general.

27. *Shemot Rabbah*, V:9. Cf. *Mekhilta, Bahodesh* 9 (ed. Horovitz-Rabin), p. 235.

28. Saadia Gaon, *The Book of Beliefs and Opinions*, ed. Rosenblatt (New Haven, 1948), II:8, pp. 111–12; cf. II:3, p. 100. For Saadia's extended discussion of the conditions under which Scripture should be read nonliterally, cf. VII:2, pp. 265–67.

29. *MT, Teshubah*, III:7.

30. *Hassagot ha-Rabad, ad loc.*

31. E. E. Urbach, *Hazal: Pirke Emunot V'Deot* (Jerusalem, 1969), pp. 168–69.

32. *The Book of Beliefs and Opinions,* I:1, p. 40.

33. Judah Halevi, *Kuzari,* I, 67.

34. *Guide of the Perplexed,* II:25.

35. Levi ben Gerson, *Milhamot Ha-Shem,* VI:2,1.

36. *Shabbat,* 55a; *Sanhedrin,* 64a; for a somewhat different, but instructive formulation, cf. *Yoma,* 69b.

Part Two

THE LEGAL BASIS

ERNST SIMON

The Neighbor (*Re'a*)

Whom We Shall Love

A BASIC PRINCIPLE OF JEWISH MORALITY is set forth
in the biblical verse, "You shall not take vengeance or bear a
grudge against your kinsfolk [the children of thy people]. Love
your neighbor as yourself" (Lev. 19:18).[1] The question that
faces us is, who is my neighbor? What does the Bible mean by
neighbor (*re'a*)? How is the term understood in the Jewish
tradition? Whom are we obligated to love as we love ourselves?

There are several avenues of approach to the resolution of
these questions. First, we may subject the term *re'a* to a semantic analysis in the context of biblical usage. Second, we can
study the ways in which the term was understood, on the one
hand, by the major Jewish biblical commentators and exegetes
and, on the other hand, by the halakhic (i.e., legal) authorities.
Third, we can seek an understanding of the term as it is affected
by and reflected in social-psychological attitudes. Finally, we
can consider the meaning of *neighbor* as it emerges in the
realities of contemporary education and morality among Jews
in Israel and in the Diaspora. In the present study we shall give
consideration to each of these four ways of understanding the
biblical commandment.

Let us turn first to the biblical-semantic analysis. An initial
possibility is that the two halves of the verse are parallel. In that
case it would follow that just as the first half is limited to *bene
amekha,* that is, to members of the Jewish people, so is the

second half limited only to other Jews. Read this way, the commandment instructs us not to take vengeance or bear grudges against other Jews, and to love other Jews as we love ourselves. In interpreting such biblical verses, however, there is also a second possibility, namely, that the two parts are not parallel but opposed. In that case, since the first half is explicitly restricted to Jews, the second half can be construed as having a wider nonrestrictive referent. According to this interpretation, our neighbor is every man, and we are commanded to love all men as we love ourselves. If we take this verse in isolation, there seems to be no decisive ground for favoring one interpretation over the other.

We must then seek to clarify the issue by studying the ways in which this term neighbor (*re'a*) and terms that are similar in meaning are used elsewhere in the Bible. Without attempting to examine every instance in which this key term is used, we can, nevertheless, get a reliable picture by studying sample cases. When Moses went out of Pharaoh's palace to his Jewish brothers he found two of them fighting. Turning to the offender, he said, "Why do you strike your fellow [*re'akha*]?"(Exod. 2:13). In this case it is clear that both contenders are Jews so that the term *re'a* refers here only to another Jew. A bit later we find a case where *re'a* refers specifically to a neighbor who is a non-Jew. God instructs Moses to command the Israelites who are about to leave Egypt "that each man shall ask of his neighbor [*re'ehu*] and each woman of her neighbor [*re'utha*], jewels of silver, and jewels of gold"(Exod. 11:2). As the context, and the following verse make unmistakably clear, this is a case in which the *re'a* of both sexes is a non-Jew. In fact, he and she are Egyptians, members of the people who oppressed and enslaved the Israelites. The parallel passages in Exod. 12:35,36 and Exod. 3:21,22 that refer to the same matter, though not using the same term, give the fullest support to the unmistakable conclusion that we have here an instance in which *re'a* is a non-Jew who is living side by side with Jews. However, we find other scriptural passages in which *re'a* can mean only

30

another Jew. With respect to the ownership of real property in the land of Israel, we are told: "You shall not move your neighbor's [re'a] landmarks, set up by previous generations, in the property that will be allotted to you in the land that the Lord your God is giving you to possess"(Deut. 19:14). Since this has to do with the permanent division of the land among the tribes of Israel, neighbor here can only be another Jew. No one else is given such rights or claims on the land.

At the same time we find other instances in the Bible where *re'a* probably, and in some cases certainly, refers to non-Jews, and even cases where the term is used of non-Jews in relation to each other. When Jeremiah chastised the Jewish people for being unfaithful to their God, he said bitterly, "But thou [i.e., the Jews] hast played the harlot with many lovers [*re'im rabbim*], and wouldest though yet return to Me, saith the Lord"(Jer.3:1). The *re'im* after whom the children of Israel went, in violation of their covenant with God, were the idols of the nations around them, idols who are the epitome of all that is non-Jewish, yet are specifically identified as *re'im*.[2] One final instance will show the range of usage for the term *re'a*. In Job 2:11 the three friends of Job who came to comfort him are designated by the term *re'a*. Yet, among the views in the talmudic discussion concerning Job, are the theories that Job was either not a historical figure at all but only a parable or that Job and his friends were even non-Jews.[3] There are, of course, opposing interpretations, but it is sufficient for our purposes to see that there are cases in which the talmudic sages understood the biblical term *re'a* to refer completely to non-Jews in their relationship to each other.

From this survey we can only conclude that the scriptural evidence is by no means decisive. The term *re'a* appears to be used in a variety of ways with no single meaning as its controlling center. It serves as the designation for diverse relationships between and among a variety of persons. There is no fixed usage that makes it possible for us to determine unambiguously what is the essence of a *re'a*, or what is the essential nature of the

31

relationship to a *re'a*. Both the nature of the neighbor and of the relationship to him vary considerably, so much that we might almost conclude that there is a considerable degree of chance and arbitrariness in the biblical use of the term. The one reliable conclusion is that *re'a* is consistently a person who is near to you, and one with whom you may maintain diverse relationships. These relationships, as we have seen, cover a range from intimate friendship to active enmity.[4] The scriptural evidence that we have surveyed is insufficient to tell us with certainty who is my neighbor, whom I am commanded to love as myself.

Before turning to the rabbinic literature we need to examine one more aspect of the biblical verse. In concentrating on the term *re'a* we failed to take notice of other linguistic elements in Lev. 19:18 that may be instructive. The verse reads, *veahavta lere'akha kamokha.* How are we to understand the *l*? Is it a preposition, or does it have the same force as *et,* that is, a marker of the accusative? Is there ground for supposing that there would be a significant difference in the meaning of the verse if the *l* were construed prepositionally rather than accusatively? The best evidence from within the classical exegetic tradition is to be found in the commentary of Nahmanides (1195–ca. 1270) who distinguishes explicitly between the prepositional and accusative readings. In his view, if the text had read you shall love *et re'akha,* it would have meant that there was to be no limit whatsoever on our love and concern for our fellows, just as we put no limit on our love and concern for ourselves. This is an unrealistic demand, according to Nahmanides, and it is, therefore, qualified by the prepositional form. As he interprets the verse, it means that we are commanded to love our neighbor in certain specific and restricted ways, and we must seek his good and welfare within the limits of these restrictions. Another restrictive point is also made by Rashbam (Rabbi Samuel b. Meir, 1080–1158) in his commentary on the Pentateuch. "Love your neighbor" means love him "if he is truly your neighbor, i.e., if he is good; but if he is a wicked man, then fulfil the verse (Prov. 8:13), 'The fear of the

32

Lord is to hate evil.'" Nahmanides supports his case by pointing out the parallel with the later commandment in the same chapter of Leviticus concerning love of the stranger who resides in the land. There the prepositional form is clear, and the text reads *veahavta lo kamokha,* "you shall love him [*lo*] as yourself" (Lev. 19:34). Just as this latter must be understood as a love that has limits, says Nahmanides, so must the former be understood as restricted to specific situations and circumstances.

In making this parallel, Nahmanides generates problems rather than solving them. When we turn to Deuteronomy we find the commandment to love the stranger stated in the accusative form. "Love the stranger [*et ha-ger*], for you were strangers in the land of Egypt" (Deut. 10:19). This certainly casts doubt on the effort to justify a limit on the love of one's neighbor through the parallel with the supposed limit on the love of the stranger, both based on the preposition *l.* Initially, one is struck by the fact that, in the previous verse in Deuteronomy, God explicitly identifies Himself as one who loves the stranger. Martin Buber once noted that there is no other case of a class of persons with whom God is identified as their lover. This might lead us to conclude that Scripture commands us to love the stranger in an absolute and unconditional way. Yet, such is the complexity of our problem and such the ambiguity of the biblical text that the very verse to which we look for solution only increases our uncertainty. In Deut. 10:18 we read that "God loves the stranger,[5] providing him with food and clothing." Is the last phrase simply an example of God's absolute and unconditioned love, or is its force restrictive and limiting? Perhaps it means to tell us not that God loves the stranger absolutely and that we must do likewise but rather that God loves even the stranger sufficiently to provide for his essential needs and that in this respect we must imitate Him.

It is evident that Scripture alone does not offer us a satisfactory solution to our problem. Let us, then, turn to the later literature to see how the rabbinic authorities and the exegetes

33

understood the term *re'a*. What is striking is that, with few exceptions, they seem consistently to have construed our moral duties restrictively, giving special status and claims to other Jews, rather than to men in general. This is reflected in the Targum of Onkelos, the canonical Aramaic translation of the Pentateuch. Himself a proselyte, Onkelos (second century, C.E.) translates Deut. 10:19 as follows: "You shall love the proselyte [*ger*], for you were sojourners [*gerim*] in the land of Egypt." Though the term *ger* occurs in both halves of the sentence, Onkelos construes the first, in accordance with the Halakha, as referring specifically to pious converts who fully accept the faith and discipline of Judaism. The second, which has only historical, but not legal, significance, he translates literally. In passing, we might note that Onkelos engaged in the process of demythologizing Scripture millenia before Bultmann made either the activity or the term popular. Our *ger*, Onkelos, ignores completely the literary balance of the verse and the poetic imagination that informs it. Instead he offers us a dry, prosaic, and unsentimental rendition that sacrifices both beauty and inspiration to exact legality and factuality.

Onkelos is consistent in his treatment of this theme. So, for example, in rendering Lev. 19:33,34 he follows the restrictive rule that understands *ger*, not as any stranger who dwells among us but specifically as a convert to Judaism. Thus, "When a stranger resides with you in your land," becomes for him, "When a convert [*ger zedek*] resides with you, etc."; and, "The stranger who resides with you shall be to you as one of your citizens; you shall love him as yourself," is again not just any stranger, in his version, but only *giyora*, the true convert. He reflects rabbinic teaching in this interpretation. Thus, in the *Sifra*, a tannaitic Midrash, we are told that the *ger* is compared in the verse to the *ezrah*, the native Jew. Just as the latter is bound by all of the Torah without exception, so must a *ger* who merits our full love be one who is bound by the entire Torah, that is to say, he must be a true convert.[6] Onkelos even imposes the same limitation on God's love. He renders the verse that

34

tells us that the Almighty is *ohev ger,* that is, He who loves the stranger, as "He who loves the convert," *Rahem giyora*(Deut. 10:18).

The comparison we have drawn between the stranger and neighbor, *ger* and *re'a,* is not arbitrary. For, as we now turn to an examination of the rabbinic literature, we shall see that they are often parallel terms, and both have a restrictive in-group reference. Let us begin with an example from another halakhic Midrash, the *Sifre* to Deuteronomy. With reference to the remission of debts in the sabbatical year, we read, "Every creditor shall remit the due that he claims from his neighbor [*re'ehu*]; he shall not dun his neighbor [*re'ehu*] or kinsman [*ahiv*], for the remission proclaimed is of the Lord. You may dun the foreigner [*nokhri*]" (Deut. 15:2,3). In its comment, the *Sifre* follows the pattern that we have already seen. "His neighbor" is restricted so as to exclude others, that is, non-Jews, and "his kinsman" is restricted to exclude aliens resident in the land of Israel who ceased to be idolators but did not become converts to Judaism.[7] Here we see another clear case in which *re'a* is not any neighbor at all but only a fellow Jew. The Torah itself, in the verses in question, seems to stress this point when it opposes *re'a* to *nokhri* as the neighbor, who is my brother, to the foreigner, who is of another people. However, despite the clarity of the language, this is not a definitive case. The principle of the sabbatical year is connected in special ways with the land of Israel, and, as we have already noted, with respect to the land the Torah grants to Jews special privileges as well as special duties. It may be, therefore, that we can draw no final conclusions from this instance in which *re'a* is treated restrictively.

An instance from the Mishna will help us to see again the general trend of the rabbinic literature in the understanding of who is my neighbor. Scripture teaches: "When a man's ox injures his neighbor's [*re'ehu*] ox and it dies, they shall sell the live ox and divide the price" (Exod. 21:35). The Mishna makes explicit the law that is derived from this verse in the following way: If an ox of an Israelite gored an ox that belonged to the Temple,

35

or an ox that belonged to the Temple gored the ox of an Israelite, the owner is not culpable, for it is written, "The ox of his
neighbor" (Exod. 21:35)—not an ox that belongs to the Temple.
If the ox of an Israelite gored the ox of a gentile, the owner is
not culpable. But if the ox of a gentile gored the ox of an Israelite, the owner must pay full damages.[8] In this Mishna we see
how the term re'a is used restrictively. On the one hand, it excludes the Temple and its property because it is not another
human being and cannot, therefore, fall under a rule that concerns my neighbor. On the other hand, it excludes non-Jews because, though persons, they are not members of the Jewish
people and are, on this ground, not to be considered neighbors.

Maimonides (1135–1204), in his codification of this law,
offers an explanation that justifies the seeming discrimination
against gentiles. The Jew whose ox gores the ox of a gentile is
not held liable, "For heathen do not hold one responsible for
damage caused by one's animals, and their own law is applied to
them."[9] If a gentile's ox gores the ox of a Jew, the owner must
pay full damages. "This," says Maimonides, "is a fine imposed
upon heathens because, being heedless of the scriptural commandments, they do not remove sources of damage. Accordingly, should they not be held liable for damage caused by their
animals, they would not take care of them and thus would inflict
loss on other people's property."[10] If we accept this explanation, which seems to be original with Maimonides, then gentiles are excluded from the category of neighbor in this case, not
because of any intrinsic defect in them but only because it is required for the general social welfare. The law is simply a way to
force them to exercise reasonable responsibility with respect to
their potentially destructive animals. If, however, we follow the
matter out more fully, this explanation will hardly suffice.

In its discussion of this Mishna the Gemara presents us with
a kind of semantic-juridical analysis of the precise meaning of
the term re'a. It seeks to determine whether neighbor is to be
taken in the narrow sense as referring only to a fellow Jew, or
whether the term carries a general meaning and is not restricted

36

to any particular group or class of persons. This might lead us to suppose that the issue is open; however, the law itself shows us how the matter is settled in practice. The law rules that where a Jew claims damages of a gentile, or the reverse, we judge the case by whichever legal system will be to the advantage of the Jew. This latter consideration determines whether we settle the case in accordance with Jewish law or in accordance with the law that governs the gentiles in question. This rule, which seems, at first glance, unjust is explained by Maimonides. In his *Commentary on the Mishna* he reassures those who are astonished and troubled by this law—and we can only rejoice in the fact that there were Jews who were astonished and troubled—that it is based on sound moral and legal principles. His explanation is not very satisfying for us. Maimonides justifies this treatment of the gentile by a harsh comparison. Invoking, as a general principle, the rule that the lower in nature is ordained to serve the higher, he argues that we are, for this reason, permitted to slaughter innocent animals in order to provide food for man. Similarly, those men who are so primitive in their intellectual and moral development that they barely merit the appellation human have as their proper function service to the higher and more fully developed men. This doctrine may, however, be construed in such way that it limits the law of our Mishna only to men so uncivilized that special measures must be invoked against them. This would then be the ground for Maimonides' later explanation in the passage from his *Mishneh Torah,* which we cited earlier. This is, in fact, how the law was usually understood by later authorities, who restricted its application only to those gentiles who were totally lacking even the rudiments of morality and social responsibility.[11]

As we consider another specific treatment of our topic by Maimonides in the twelfth century we confront several questions. In addition to the question of who is our neighbor, we must also ask what, in practice, is the nature of the love we must extend to him. In his *Mishneh Torah,* Maimonides offers us a peculiar instance in which the horizons are both contracted and expanded. After listing a series of acts of human kindness and concern for others, such as visiting the sick, comforting mourners, dowering a needy bride, he adds the following comment. "These constitute deeds of loving kindness performed in person and for which no fixed measure is prescribed. Although all these commands are only on rabbinical authority [and not explicitly enjoined in the Torah], they are implied in the precept: And thou shalt love thy neighbor as thyself; that is, What you would have others do unto you, do unto him who is your brother in the Law [Torah] and in the performance of the commandments."[12] We see here a more severely restrictive interpretation of re'a than we have encountered heretofore. For Maimonides, my neighbor is not even every other Jew, but only a Jew who is meticulous in observing the commandments and who devotes himself to the study of Torah. (It may be the case, though I am not so persuaded, that the expression "your brother in the Torah and in the performance of the commandments" is only an idiomatic phrase designating all fellow Jews.) Yet, although he restricts the range of love of neighbor, he expands in another direction by construing love as involving positive duties rather than negative restrictions. In this, as we shall see, Maimonides goes beyond much of the rabbinic tradition.

With respect to the limits of our obligation to love our neighbor, there is a well-known controversy. "Rabbi Akiba says, 'Thou shalt love thy neighbor as thyself' is a great principle in the Torah. Ben-Azzai says 'This is the book of the generations of Adam' (Gen. 5:1) is an even greater principle."[13] While Rabbi Akiba places very high value on the love of neighbor, the meaning of neighbor in his usage is open to doubt. If we take it, as I presume Rabbi Akiba did, in its technical halakhic sense, then it can only mean another Jew. There are those who attempt to expand the meaning by construing kamokha to mean, "he is like yourself." This interpretation, which is offered by various exegetes from Mendelssohn and Wessely in the eighteenth century to Hermann Cohen in the twentieth,[14] means to expand the reference to all humanity by stressing that every other man is human like yourself, and by virtue of that fact merits your love. This need not be the case, however, since we can easily read "he is like you" to mean he is a Jew like you, and in this respect is your neighbor whom you should love. It can even be read to conform with Maimonides' greater restriction, namely, he is an observant and learned Jew like you and this is the reason that he deserves your love.

Ben-Azzai wanted to avoid all such ambiguities. For that reason he stressed as his primary principle the concern with humanity as such. Consider his proof-text in its entirety. "This is the book of the generations of Adam. In the day that God created man, in the likeness of God made He him"(Gen. 5:1). About this notion of man there can be no debate. He is everyman, for he is like Adam the first man, who is not a Jew. He is, beyond all parochial limits, man created in the image of God.

We should take note of the fact that a distinguished Jewish scholar interprets this controversy in a quite different way. Professor Louis Finkelstein argues[15] that Rabbi Akiba's demand is that we must actively love every man. He tells us that we can properly understand Rabbi Akiba's interpretation of Lev. 19:18 only if, in addition to the sources we have already noted, we give due weight to "the full text found only in *Abot D'Rabbi Nathan*, 'I the Lord have created him; you are required to love him.' "[16] According to Finkelstein, Rabbi Akiba holds that we are commanded to love every man because he is God's creature and we should see in him the divine image. It is Ben-Azzai, says Finkelstein, who holds us to a far more limited objective. Recognizing that to *love* every man is beyond the capacity of most people, Ben-Azzai teaches that though love may be limited to those who are nearest and dearest, we must, at least, "*respect* other people as the creatures of God, bearing his likeness."[17]

However we read the passage, the problem of how truly to love our neighbor confronts us. We noted earlier that various exegetes, among them Nahmanides, make the point that if the commandment is taken literally it makes an impossible demand. Who, except a rare saint, can love another, to say nothing of every other, just as he loves himself? Probably it was this kind of concern that led Hillel to formulate the principle negatively. For a potential convert he summarized the essence of Judaism in the principle, "what is hateful to you, do not to your neighbor [havrakh]; that is the whole Torah, while the rest is the commentary thereof; go and learn it."[18] It is generally agreed that this is a negative formulation of the commandment to love our neighbor. If this is how the commandment is understood, then Rabbi Akiba, like Hillel, overcomes the "impossible" command, by construing it negatively. We are thus only commanded to treat our fellow men with sufficient consideration so that we refrain from doing to him what we would find offensive if it were done to us. It may be relevant support for our interpretation of Rabbi Akiba's stand that a very similar episode to the Hillel story is recorded, and a negative formulation almost identical with that of Hillel is attributed to Rabbi Akiba.[19] We should note that in these stories the person addressed is not just an ordinary gentile. He is an unidentified individual, but certainly a gentile about to be converted, one who wants to learn the Torah, and, in the case of Rabbi Akiba, one who is ready to follow the teachings of the Torah.

If we now return to Maimonides, we can see the force of his position. On the one hand, he rejects the negative formulation and insists on the positive. It is not enough to love our neighbor only by refraining from injuring him. Maimonides interprets love of neighbor positively to mean such acts as caring for the sick, providing for the needy, burying the dead. Yet he accompanies this positive formula with the severe restriction of the concept neighbor to other Jews, and, on one reading, only to observant and learned Jews.

Some modern writers have struggled to defend the negative formulation against the charge that it is morally inferior to the positive commandment of love. Ahad-Ha-Am argued that only in the negative formula is justice preserved. The positive formula, "Do for your neighbor, that which you would like him to do for you," places my neighbor in a superior position to me, says Ahad-Ha-Am. It gives him priority over me, and in so doing it violates an elementary rule of justice. If this were intended, then the commandment would have read, "Love your neighbor more than yourself." This would be both unjust and unrealistic. However, to love him as yourself means to treat him and yourself with complete equality, and this is an essential rule for a just society.[20] Hermann Cohen makes a similar argument. Maimonides, despite his restrictive interpretation of re'a, stands in firm opposition to such views and construes love as setting clear and positive duties for us in relationship to our fellow men.

In considering a final rabbinic passage we shall see the full force of the limitations introduced into the Halakha with respect to who has juridical status as my neighbor. Scripture teaches, "When a man schemes against another [i.e., his neighbor, re'ehu] and kills him treacherously, you shall take him from my very altar to be put to death"(Exod. 21:14). The Mishna in setting forth the specific laws concerning offenders who are liable to the death penalty, states: "And these are they that are to be beheaded. . . . A murderer who slew his fellow [re'ehu] with a stone or an iron instrument."[21] Who is this re'a, this fellowman who is slain and whose murderer suffers the death penalty? Is he any man without exception? Clearly not, if we accept the testimony of the next Mishna where we read, "If he intended to kill a gentile and he killed an Israelite he is not liable." This means that he is free from the death penalty by action of the court, however, he is subject to punishment by God, which may be less severe and is certainly not immediate. This judgment is based on the principle that this particular penalty of death can only be imposed by the courts in accordance with the strict limits set forth in the biblical verse. There we read that a man is liable to this punishment only if he deliberately murders his re'a, his neighbor but not another. We

41

now see that, here again, gentiles are explicitly excluded from the class of re'a and therefore this rule does not apply to offenses against them. The *Mekhilta d'Rabbi Ishmael,* a tannaitic Midrash, expresses this point in its analysis of our scriptural verse, when it says, *"re'ehu,* his neighbor, this is meant to exclude others [i.e., gentiles, who are not considered members of the class of re'a]."[22] Now clearly it is not the intention of this passage to suggest that killing gentiles is permitted. Every murder, no matter who the victim, is an abominable act that is to be condemned. That is why in the same *Mekhilta* passage another teacher asks how this ruling is possible. "Even before the giving of the Torah we were forbidden to shed blood; after the Torah has been given should it have the effect of making the law more lenient rather than stricter?" It is in response to this objection that we are told that murder of gentiles is also forbidden, and that the guilty, though immune to human punishment, will receive their penalty from God.

Maimonides, when he codifies this law, expresses the fullest condemnation for murder, as the most destructive of all human actions. Other transgressions may bring more severe punishment, he says, but "none cause such destruction to civilized society as bloodshed." From the perspective of a strictly dogmatic theology, idolatry, or sexual license, or desecration of the Sabbath may seem worse than murder. Yet, Maimonides rules that bloodshed exceeds all of these in severity. "For these are crimes between man and God, while bloodshed is a crime between man and man. If one has committed this crime he is deemed wholly wicked, and all the meritorious acts he has performed during his lifetime cannot outweigh this crime or save him from judgment."[23] This doctrine, which seems to condemn all murder with equal severity, may also be reflected in the opening section of the same chapter of the *Code* where Maimonides rules, "If one intends to kill A and kills B instead, he is exempt from the penalty of death by the court."[24] We are tempted to read this as a kind of liberalizing tendency in which Maimonides makes no distinction between gentiles and Jewish

42

victims. There is a significant sense in which it is true that Maimonides does support the principle that murder is equally abhorrent whether the victim be Jew or gentile. In the passage that we just cited he abandons the restrictive clause of the Mishna that reads, "If he intended to kill a gentile and killed a Jew, he is not liable." For this, Maimonides, basing himself on other sources, substitutes the general statement, "If one intends to kill A and kills B instead," and eliminates completely the distinction between Jews and gentile. Furthermore, this impression is strengthened by the fact that he opens his discussion of the prohibitions against murder by stating that "If one slays a *human being* [*ben-adam*], he is guilty of transgressing a negative commandment, for Scripture says, 'Thou shalt not murder.' "[25]

Unfortunately, when we pursue the matter further we discover that, although the prohibition against murder is maintained in the strongest way, even in connection with this topic Maimonides still reverts to the exclusive interpretation of *re'a* as referring only to other Jews. Thus, in dealing with the duties of preserving human life, he cites the biblical commandment, "Thou shalt not stand idly by the blood of thy neighbor [*re'ekha*]"(Lev. 19:16), and adds the note that this does not include either persistently sinful Jews, or gentiles, for "none of these is 'thy neighbor.' "[26] This is also why he rules, following the Mishna, that one who kills a gentile is not subject to the death penalty by the judgment of a court, but is only subject to God's punishment. Here, too, the controlling consideration is the scriptural verse that restricts this penalty to the murder of a *re'a*, and this excludes gentiles.[27]

The same restrictive interpretation of the commandment concerning love of neighbor is found in many other authorities. Rabbi Moses of Coucy (thirteenth century) in his *Sefer Mitzvot Gadol* lists the commandment to love one's neighbor as oneself and interprets it to refer to one "who is your fellow [*re'akha*] in Torah and mitzvot," that is, a faithful Jew.[28] In the *Sefer Ha-Hinnukh* the commandment is set forth as involving the duty "to love every Jew with devoted love."[29] Even the recent *Talmudic Encyclopedia* follows this tradition in stating, "It is a positive commandment to love every Jew as one loves oneself, for Scripture says, 'You shall love your neighbor as yourself.' "[30] In these works no separate place is reserved for the love of man as such, but it becomes another term for the brotherly love among Jews.

In some theological writings that are rooted in the rabbinic literature we find the identical conceptions. Here, too, love of neighbor is understood as a commandment restricted only to other Jews. A typical case is that which we find in the *Liqqutei Amarim* of Rabbi Schneur Zalman of Lyady (1747–1812), founder of the Habad (Lubavitsch) hasidic community. He offers a formula for self-training through which one can achieve the capacity to fulfill the commandment of brotherly love "toward every soul of Israel, both great and small." Having restricted the commandment to other Jews, he goes on to refer to the verse, "Have we not all one father" (Mal. 2:10), as evidence that this is why "all Israelites are called real brothers by virtue of the source of their souls in the one God."[31] This interpretation may shock contemporary readers who are accustomed to hearing the words of Malachi cited in sermons as one of the loftiest and most exalted calls to universalism. Perhaps they will be even more shocked to learn that in the view of some standard commentators the verse refers to Jacob, the common father of all the generations of the Jewish people.[32]

In the *Shulhan Arukh* of the same Rabbi Schneur Zalman we find an even sharper and more offensive expression than occurs elsewhere in the literature. In dealing with legal technicalities concerning what constitutes a dwelling with respect to certain laws of the Sabbath, he rules that "the dwelling of a gentile has the legal status of the dwelling of an animal."[33] Now, this is admittedly only a formal-legalistic comparison, not a judgment of the worth of other human beings. Moreover, I can find no other place in any of the codes or their commentaries where this expression is used. Yet, the fact remains that, whatever its technical purpose, this offensively insensitive expression is used and may have some detrimental effect on those who study this code.

In many printed editions of the various codes, in particular the *Tur* and the *Shulhan Arukh,* there is a prefatory comment that is aimed at overcoming the negative impression created by those legal rulings which seem to discriminate against non-Jews. These prefaces affirm vigorously that none of the discriminatory laws are operative today in the civilized countries in which Jews live. In all these lands we are bound by the established civil law, and it is our duty as citizens and also our religious obligation to abide by the law of the land. They then go on to state that the legislation giving special privileges to Jews and the expressions of discrimination against non-Jews are only special measures to protect Jews who live in barbaric societies that are without any true religion and that lack any concept of love of fellowman. It is in those special circumstances that our law is applicable, for it seeks to safeguard Jews against unrestrained barbarism. Pejorative expressions refer only to those heathens who are so primitive that they lack the most elementary moral development.

One hesitates to judge whether these statements are sincere, or whether they are only motivated by fear of the censor's hand. Even if we grant their sincerity, we cannot ignore the fact that the discriminatory language is contained in the rabbinic texts, and that language does have serious negative effects on the student. These are texts that constitute major elements in a classical Jewish education. One hesitates to estimate how they have contributed to the raising of barriers between Jews and non-Jews.

Are there no counterinstances in the rabbinic tradition, no cases in which the distinction between Jew and non-Jew is overcome by concern with their common humanity? There are such instances, though fewer in number than their opposite. They are best understood in the light of the social-psychological approach, which we proposed as our third pattern of analysis. The oldest text I can identify in which the distinction between Jew

45

and non-Jew is completely eliminated is a well-known passage in *Seder Eliahu Rabba* (ca. ninth century C.E.). In this Midrash we find the following remarkable statement: "I call heaven and earth to witness that whether one be gentile or Jew, man or woman, male slave or female slave, in accordance with the merit of his deeds does the Holy Spirit rest on him."[34] Here we seem to be in a different world, one in which all men are truly equal in their humanity and every person is judged meritorious only by virtue of his deeds. Nothing else matters. It seems likely that this open attitude toward the non-Jew is a kind of universalistic humanism that is connected with a positive attitude toward the exile of the Jewish people. In another passage in this same Midrash the exile is praised as the salvation of the Jewish people. God is said to have placed them where they were assured of being saved from destruction.[35] Another version of this teaching is found in the Talmud where Rabbi Oshaia sees positive value in the exile. As he expresses it, "The Holy One, blessed by He, showed righteousness [mercy] to Israel by scattering them among the nations."[36] Once the exile is viewed in positive terms it is easier to view our neighbors in the lands of our exile in equally positive terms.

Perhaps we have here the beginning of Jewish apologetics with respect to traditional teaching concerning relationships with non-Jews. Under the force of the social and economic realities of life in a predominantly non-Jewish environment, Jewish thinkers began to regard gentiles in a new light. They made intense efforts to eliminate most of the discriminatory Jewish legislation as well as the offensive expressions and judgments. The basic technique was that which we already mentioned in the prefatory notes to some editions of the *Shulhan Arukh*. All legislation that seems to discriminate against non-Jews, and all those expressions that are derogatory to non-Jews are now taken to refer exclusively to barbaric idolators. Jews had to protect themselves against the predatory ways of such peoples. They had to erect their own barriers against the absence of law and morality in such societies. However, none of this, it is now held, applies to the enlightened and civilized peoples among whom we live today. Jews are required by their religion to recognize and abide by the just laws of their non-Jewish hosts, and, even more, to love and honor those non-Jews for they are truly our "neighbors."

The most impressive case, and one of great historical importance, is that of Rabbi Menahem Ha-Meiri (1249–1306) who rose to eminence in Provence during the late thirteenth and early fourteenth centuries. Ha-Meiri was a pioneer in developing the juridical and theological structures that transformed the status of gentiles in Jewish law. One of his major contributions was the formulation of a new juridical term and with it a new legal-social status for the gentiles who were his contemporaries, and surely for those of later times. He speaks of *ummot ha-gedurot be-darkhe hadatot,* "nations restricted by the ways of religion." These are, of course, the Christians among whom he lived, and similarly civilized peoples. They are contrasted with those nations whose moral and social patterns are not formed by religion. It was among these latter that Jews were living in talmudic times, and it was with respect to them that discriminatory legislation necessarily existed. However, Ha-Meiri wants to distinguish sharply between those gentiles of talmudic times and the contemporary "nations restricted by the ways of religion." He teaches that Christians are not idolators and the laws concerning relations to idolators do not apply to them or to most other contemporary gentiles, since "now idolatry has disappeared from most places."[37]

Ha-Meiri did not approach the legal rehabilitation of gentiles with a spirit of grudging concession as did some of his predecessors. "Contrary to this, Ha-Meiri is almost glad to notice the obsolescence of the talmudic precepts. 'In our days nobody heeds these things, neither *Gaon,* Rabbi, Disciple, *Hasid,* nor would-be *Hasid'.* . . . In contrast to the other halakhists, who could give their assent to the disregarding of the talmudic precepts with reluctance only, Ha-Meiri could do so whole-heartedly, since in his opinion it was not a concession but a clear case based upon a firm principle."[38]

As a consequence, he is able to remove from Jews the entire moral burden of legislation that either discriminates against gentiles or that prevents normal commercial relations with them. Unlike his predecessors, who were never quite at ease with the practical abolition of this legislation, Ha-Meiri invoked what he believed were sound legal principles. He states explicitly that contemporary gentiles, who are possessed of religious and moral precepts, are not included in this discriminatory legislation. Every such gentile is for legal purposes "to be regarded as a full Jew in respect of all this."[39]

By considering a single concrete case, we can see, in a striking way, how this approach to the gentile world affected the concept of neighbor. Scripture teaches that we are required to watch over and return to its owner any lost article that we happen to find. However, it introduces the familiar limitation, "so shalt thou do with every lost thing of thy brother's"(Deut. 22:3). The Talmud explicitly interprets this as restricting the obligation to "your brother," that is, to fellow Jews, but not to gentiles who do not have the status of brother.[40] Maimonides codifies this ruling, stating that, "the lost property of a gentile may be kept, for Scripture says, 'Lost thing of my brother's,' "[41] and the gentile is not my brother. However, Maimonides, like the Talmud, goes on to find conditions under which it is proper to return the lost article of a gentile. "If one returns it in order to sanctify God's name, thereby causing persons to praise the Israelites and realize that they are honest, he is deemed praiseworthy. In cases involving a profanation of God's name, it is forbidden to keep a gentile's lost property, and it must be returned."[42] Here we have an argument that mandates the return of such property, not out of concern for the gentile but only out of concern for the good name of the Jewish people and their God. When Ha-Meiri deals with this question he is less concerned with external considerations. Instead he rules that the duty to return lost articles applies to "the lost articles of your brother, and everyone who is restricted by the ways of religion is your brother."[43] No longer do we depend on any secondary consideration. We have rather a new and firmly held legal category—"nations restricted by the ways of religion"—and this moves us to recognize all our neighbors as brothers who have full legal and moral status. Through the teaching of Ha-Meiri the barriers that distinguish Jews from gentiles are broken down. The gentile is now seen as truly our brother and thus our neighbor.

This should not lead us to the false conclusion that Ha-Meiri wanted to abolish all the social barriers that separated Jews from their non-Jewish neighbors. While eliminating all forms of legal discrimination against the gentiles of his time and recognizing them as having the juridical status of brother and neighbor, he nevertheless reaffirmed those aspects of Jewish law and custom which were designed to maintain the social barriers that would keep Jews apart from their non-Jewish neighbors. Like almost all his Jewish contemporaries, "Ha-Meiri felt himself attached to the symbols of the Jewish religion and retained, like any other Jew of the Middle Ages, his aversion to the gentile world."[44] Nor did he view Jewish exile as anything other than a calamity. He was influenced in his view of gentiles by the socioeconomic realities with which he was confronted in his own Diaspora experience. In the light of that experience he distinguished sharply between tribes of primitive idolators and the civilized nations of Europe. Yet, despite his remarkable contribution to the removal in Jewish law of all stigma from gentiles, he did not welcome them as desirable companions for his fellow Jews, and he wept over the sins of Israel that condemned them to live out their lives in exile in a predominantly non-Jewish environment.

More recent rabbinic figures, motivated largely by apologetic concerns, have treated the issue of who is my neighbor as if it constituted no problem at all. Thus Rabbi David Hoffman (1843–1921), a prominent leader of German Orthodox Judaism in the latter nineteenth and early twentieth centuries, is content to treat the new legal categories of Ha-Meiri as if they had always been present in Jewish law. In similar fashion, Hanoch Albeck, one of the greatest of contemporary talmudic scholars, also argues that with respect to the status of gentiles Ha-Meiri merely sets forth in systematic fashion the principles that are present in classical Jewish law from early times.

The extent to which the revised attitudes took root can be seen in two nineteenth-century orthodox Bible commentators, Jacob Zvi Mecklenburg (1785–1865) and Meir Loeb ben Yehiel Michael Malbim (1809–79). The former served as rabbi in Koenigsberg, the city of Immanuel Kant, though his tenure in office from 1830 to 1865 was long after Kant's death. The latter spent the last four years of his life as rabbi of the small Orthodox congregation of Russian Jews in Koenigsberg. Malbim, commenting on Lev. 19:18, interprets it as a form of Kant's categorical imperative. His interpretation approximates the version of the categorical imperative that reads, "Act in such a way that you always treat humanity, whether in your own person or in the person of any other, never simply as a means, but always at the same time as an end." Although Malbim does not mention Kant by name, he does refer to "the philosophers" and their ethical principles. Now, as far as I know, Malbim never says directly that *re'a* means every man. In fact, he does not even raise the question. Yet, if we construe the commandment as he does, it means that we must act in such a way that we could universalize the principle of our action. To do so means to take account of all men and to include all men, without exception, equally in the range of my concerns. Thus interpreted the commandment is taken to mean, "Love every man as yourself."[45] Although Malbim introduces this note tacitly, it seems likely that he was aware that he was deviating from the earlier Jewish legal tradition, despite the fact that he is never explicit about the matter. It may well be that he was making use of the considerable freedom open to an exegete, and therefore, did not feel obligated in this case to observe the formal restrictions of

50

halakhic procedure. The same may be true of Mecklenburg, though he is direct and totally unambiguous. He interprets the commandment as meaning that whatever good things a man would like to have done to him by his fellowmen, "he should do to his neighbor [re'ehu], *who is every human being.*"[46] This formula is set forth in so straightforward a fashion that an unwary reader might suppose that there never was, nor could there ever be, any question that this is what Scripture and tradition have always understood as the meaning of *re'a*. The complete turnabout from early times strikes us when we read a comment in the great dictionary of Eliezer ben Yehudah. In his discussion of *re'a* as it is used in Lev. 19:18, he notes with irritation that, "Some non-Jewish scholars have sought, *without any justification whatsoever,* to limit the meaning of the word here only to other Jews."[47] It is as if the Mishna, the Gemara, the Codes did not ever give any justification to the narrower meaning.

Although there is surely some element of apologetics underlying these cases of extreme liberality, that does not seem to be a sufficient explanation for this new tendency. Perhaps it is also symptomatic of the feeling on the part of these morally sensitive men that the Halakha is not sufficient to answer all our needs. They seem to be suggesting, however indirectly, that there is a Jewish ethic that is external to the Halakha, one by which the Halakha itself must be judged and to which it must be made responsive. These men feel the moral pressure to abolish any suggestion of legitimacy in the discrimination against gentiles on the part of faithful or nationalistic Jews. Some, like Albeck and Hoffmann, read their contemporary morality back into the legal literature of Jewish antiquity. Others like Malbim, Mecklenburg, and Eliezer ben Yehudah seemed to forget that there had ever been a problem. And Rabbi Menahem Ha-Meiri, aware of the problem, acted with admirable boldness to introduce new categories and conceptual structures into the law. All, however, were moved in some measure by moral distress with the law as it had been received. So they arrived either at bold apologetics or at bashful and wishful thinking, or at a mixture of both.

We should emulate these great figures, as to their recognition of morality that is above the law, and their readiness to adjust the law to meet the demands of higher moral concern, but not as to their still scholastic way of thinking that tries to keep alive an artificial continuity, rather than admit that some break with the established law has become inevitable. There comes to mind an episode that I witnessed after World War I in Frankfurt. Many Jewish women were left without certain knowledge of the fate or whereabouts of their husbands. According to the Halakha they were *agunot,* abandoned wives who could not be set free to marry again without acceptable legal evidence that their husbands were dead. A group of rabbis, themselves fully orthodox, were struggling to find a solution. They felt moral pressure to release these women from their bonds, but they were unable to find any way to do so within the rule of Halakha. (In this case, it should be noted, the Halakha itself is extremely lenient because it seeks to alleviate needless suffering. Thus, while normally two male witnesses are the minimum requirement for valid testimony, in this case the law rules that if there is *one* person, male or female, who has seen the man dead and who mentions this fact incidentially, this testimony is accepted.) In sorrow the rabbis threw up their hands and said, "What can we do? This is the law." At that point, Bertha Pappenheim, the leader of the Jewish women of Germany, turned to the rabbis with deep moral indignation and spoke words that I shall never forget. "Gentlemen," she said, "When the capitalist economy developed to a point where it was no longer possible to observe the Torah's explicit prohibition against lending money for interest your predecessors managed to find within the halakha an acceptable way to circumvent the law. From your failure to act now, I can only conclude that the halakha, as you interpret it, places higher value on economic concerns than on the human needs and rights of these pathetic and unfortunate women." She was saying that there was a moral obligation to free these

52

women, and that obligation had to take priority over legalistic considerations. The law stands under the judgment of moral principles, and the test of its soundness is in its capacity to adjust itself in order to satisfy higher moral demands. It is a tribute both to the Halakha and to the rabbinic authorities who interpreted it—especially the late Rav Kahane of Warsaw and Rabbi Shlomo Goren—that after World War II ways were found to solve this very problem, and hardly any women were left as *agunot*. It is this same kind of moral concern that we would like to see today as a major force in other areas of Jewish law as well.

This brings us to a brief consideration of love of neighbor as a current issue, as a moral and educational ideal in the context of our own contemporary situation. How well do we contemporary Jews in Israel and in the Diaspora fulfil the biblical commandment? Whom, in reality, do we recognize as our neighbor? In Israel, where there is a growing gap between the rich and the poor we are behaving with something less than brotherly love toward the less fortunate members of our society. The fact that members of the oriental communities have not found a full measure of equality for themselves in our society is painful evidence that we are not fulfilling the commandment even toward our fellow-Jews. Our reluctance to receive new immigrants, particularly those from Soviet Russia, with personal warmth and fellowship is not only of political significance. It is a moral and religious failure as well. We have also been less than perfect in establishing brotherly relations with our Arab neighbors. Whatever may be said in justification of our policies in the occupied territories, can there be any justification for our denial of the right of the Arab residents of Biram and Ikrit to return to their homes? Surely, no interpretation of the commandment to love our neighbor could justify that action. While taking satisfaction when we do behave with love toward all men, we cannot afford to ignore our failures. And if love, apparently, cannot be commanded, we may settle on the duty to honor in each human being God's creature.

53

"Rabbi Simeon bar Yohai taught: The Holy one, blessed be He, said to Israel, 'I am the God of all mankind, but I have chosen only you to bear my name. I am not called the God of the idolators, but only the God of Israel."[48] When we know in the depths of our being that our neighbor is every man, and when we truly honor him as we love ourselves, only then will the Holy One allow Himself to be known as the God of Israel.

1. Use is made of both the old and new Jewish Publication Society translations of the Bible, as well as of our own translations, depending on which gives the clearest rendition for our purposes.

2. Cf. the parallel passage in Hos. 3:1.

3. *Baba Bathra,* 15a, 15b.

4. For an illuminating discussion of this topic see Y. Moriel, "Thou Shalt Love Thy Neighbor as Thyself," *Shematin,* Kislev-Tebet, 5731, 26–36 (in Hebrew).

5. For qualities of God that we are specifically instructed not to imitate, such as hatred, jealously, and so forth, see *Midrash Hag-gadol* to Genesis, 37:1 (ed. Margolith), p. 619; cf. S. Schechter, *Some Aspects of Rabbinic Theology* (New York, 1936), p. 204.

6. *Sifra, Kedoshim,* 8:3 (ed. Sh. Koleditzki Jerusalem, 1961), II, p. 92.

7. *Sifre, Re'eh,* 112:2; ed. Finkelstein, p. 173.

8. *M. Baba Kamma,* IV:3.

9. Maimonides, *Mishneh Torah, Nizke Mamon,* VIII: 5.

10. Ibid.

11. This topic will be more fully discussed below.

12. *Ebel,* XIV: 1.

13. *Sifra, Kedoshim,* 4:12.

14. Hermann Cohen, *Religion der Vernunft aus den Quellen des Judentums* (Leipzig, 1919), pp. 183, 462f.; see especially chap. 8, "Die Entdeckung des Menschen als des Mitmenschen," pp. 131–67, esp. p. 144f. See also, Hermann Cohen, Der *Naechste* (Berlin, 1935), with a Foreword by Martin Buber at whose suggestion these four essays were collected and printed in one small volume.

15. Louis Finkelstein, "The Underlying Concepts of Conservative Judaism," *Conservative Judaism* 26, no. 4, pp. 8–9.

16. In the printed texts this statement is offered anonymously, and not in the name of Rabbi Akiba. However, Finkelstein in his *Mabo le Massektot*

Abot ve-Abot d'Rabbi Natan (New York, 1950), p. 47, presents evidence for his view that the text should be cited in the name of Rabbi Akiba.

17. Finkelstein, "The Underlying Concepts of Conservative Judaism," p. 9. What is surprising is that Finkelstein ignores the rest of the statement that he attributes to Rabbi Akiba in his *Mabo* and that occurs in all the texts. "Indeed, if he acts as thy people do, thou shalt love him; but if not, thou shalt not love him." (Cf., *Aboth de Rabbi Nathan* [ed. Schechter], p. 64. Judah Goldin, ed., *The Fathers According to Rabbi Nathan* [New Haven, 1955], p. 86.) Here we have a restrictive interpretation that seems to negate the universalism that Finkelstein reads into the passage.

18. *Shabbat*, 31a.

19. *Aboth de Rabbi Nathan* (ed Schechter), B version, chap. 26, p. 53.

20. *Al Parashath Derakhim*, 2d ed. (Berlin, 1921), vol. 4, pp. 38–56.

21. *M. Sanhedrin*, IX:1.

22. *Mekhilta d'Rabbi Ishmael*, Mishpatim, 4 (ed. Horovitz-Rabin), p. 263.

23. *Rozeah*, IV:9.

24. Ibid., IV:1.

25. Ibid., I:1 (italics added).

26. Ibid., IV:11.

27. Ibid., II:11.

28. Positive Commandment No. 9.

29. Ed. Chavel, Commandment No. 219.

30. Vol. I, 98a.

31. *Liqqutei Amarim*, chap. 32.

32. Cf., the commentaries of Rabbi Abraham ibn Ezra and Rabbi David Kimhi, *ad loc.*, *Yalkut Shimoni*, I:835 and I:925; *Seder Eliyahu Zuta*, chap. 3.

33. *Shabbat*, 342, sec. 1.

34. *Seder Eliahu Rabba* (ed. M. Friedmann), chap. 10, p. 48.

35. Ibid., chap. 11, p. 54.

36. *Pesahim*, 87b.

37. Jacob Katz, *Exclusiveness and Tolerance* (Oxford, 1961), p. 116. The discussion in chapter ten of this book is devoted primarily to Ha-Meiri and is our source for most of our treatment of this subject.

38. Ibid.

39. Ibid., p. 118.

40. *Baba Kamma*, 113b.

41. *Gezelah va-Abedah*, XI:3.

42. Ibid.

43. Quoted in the Hebrew version of Katz's book, *Ben Yehudim l'Goyim*, pp. 119–20, fn. 21.

44. Katz, *Exclusiveness and Tolerance*, p. 127.
45. Cf. his commentary on the Torah, *ad loc*.
46. *Ha-Ketav ve-ha-Kabbalah, ad loc.* (italics added).
47. Vol. 12, p. 6635, fn. 3.
48. *Shemot Rabba,* 29.

HAROLD FISCH

A Response to Ernst Simon

"AND THOU SHALT LOVE THY NEIGHBOR AS
thyself" (Lev. 19:18). Professor Ernst Simon convincingly
demonstrated that in the standard Jewish interpretation this
commandment applies only to one's fellow Israelite. Since this
does not satisfy his ethical sense, he calls for the acceptance of
an extra-halakhic ethical norm to cover our relations with the
non-Jew. In his words, "The Halakha cannot satisfy all our
needs."[1]

My objections to this may be expressed in the form of five
antitheses, which I should like to nail, as it were, on the door of
the Institute for Judaism and Contemporary Thought. (1) The
demand to *love* one's fellow is a demand so unique that it places
on our moral and emotional organism an almost superhuman
burden. We find it extraordinarily difficult in practice to love
even our fellow Jews. Some find it difficult to love German
Jews, others to love Moroccan Jews. I am acquainted with an
ex-German Jew who finds it impossible to love American Jews.
Nevertheless the Torah commands us to overcome these anti-
pathies. And we see that in some measure we in Israel, especially through the operation of the Law of the Return, have
achieved an approximation to this exalted command. We have
gathered in our exiles from all parts of the world in love and
compassion, often in spite of real social and ethnic barriers that
continue to divide us from one another. It is hard to think of a

parallel in the history of any other nation. The command to love our neighbor in the sense of our fellow Jew is in these circumstances a command of the highest difficulty, which we nevertheless, falteringly and with a varying measure of success, obey. We obey it because in spite of its difficulty it is nevertheless within the bounds of the humanly possible. To achieve more than this, that is, to extend the love relation to all and every nation—Germans, Japanese, and Arabs included—is to expect the impossible. And the Torah, though it sets us a high standard—the highest standard even—does not set us an *impossible* standard.

So much for *love*. (2) There are of course other forms of human relation, founded on esteem for our fellowman simply because he is a human being created in the divine image. But these are not covered by the formula: "And thou shalt love thy neighbor as thyself." To cover our relations with other nations, even hostile or *quondam* hostile nations, we may legitimately adduce such a command as: "Thou shalt not abhor an Edomite for he is thy brother; thou shalt not abhor a Mizrian, because thou wast a stranger in his land"(Deut. 23:8). It will be seen that this is a negative formulation and as such falls short of the commandment to love. Yet it clearly implies a measure of human respect. And without such an ordinance we might allow ourselves to cultivate that hatred and abhorrence which all too often poison international relations. This we are forbidden to do. (3) If we examine the ethical commandment just quoted from Deuteronomy we shall find that, unlike the command to love one's neighbor, it has a *reciprocal* basis. We may not abhor an Edomite because he is our brother, and thus he too may be expected to recognize his kinship with us. Similarly we may not abhor an Egyptian because we own him something. At some time we enjoyed his hospitality. There is a suggestion here of a two-way traffic. This does not apply to the high and almost (as I have said) impossible-to-fulfill exhortation to love our fellow Israelite. Him we are obliged to love whether or not he loves us in return. In fact the Hebrew *ahavah* carries this one-way meaning. Thus in Hos. 3:1., God is said to love Israel (*keahavat*) in spite of her not returning that love. We must find other terms than *ahavah* to cover that esteem which is conditional upon the other side esteeming us in return. Such a term I believe is *hesed,* which generally implies a relation based on reciprocal obligations. *Hesed* is debt to be paid, as in the phrase *gemilut hasadim.* The particular individual concerned may not be in a position to pay back but it is understood that *hesed* applies to acts that bind society together in a relation of mutuality.

Now this *hesed* relation is possible and even mandatory between Israel and other nations, that is, Jew and non-Jew. The world as a whole is said to be built on *hesed* (Ps. 89:3). Thus, Abimelekh addresses Abraham: "According to the *hesed* I have done to thee thou shalt do to me." And Abraham swears accordingly(Gen. 21:23,24). Coming to our own time this represents a high standard of international relationships but it is within the bounds of the humanly possible. To expect us to love our enemies is outside the bounds of the humanly possible. And Judaism does not require it. (4) The specific command, "Thou shalt love thy neighbor as thyself" (Lev. 19:18) has particular reference to the Jewish people. The only other relationship within which *ahavah* is mandatory is in our relation to God. "Thou shalt love the Lord thy God . . . [*veahavta*]" (Deut. 6:5). This too represents an extraordinary moral leap as Professor Simon points out in his paper. It is perhaps the highest demand made of the Jew. The fact that we are expected not only to love but to make such love the basis of our social and religious life-pattern is a sign of Jewish uniqueness, that subsumed under the concept of a covenant people or chosen people. To attempt to widen the concept into a general, and undifferentiated love of mankind after the manner of some impractical ethical humanism is to blur, and ultimately to render meaningless, the particularistic side of Judaism. *Ahavah* is a category that surely belongs to the particularistic dimension of Judaism. Other categories belong to the universalistic dimension. Such a category is *hesed.* It applies both to the internal and to the external rela-

tions of the Jewish people. But we falsify Judaism if we ignore
the boundary between the two realms: the particularistic and
the universalistic. This would be equivalent to ignoring the
boundary between Israel and the nations. (5) In challenging the
rabbis of our time to find ways of satisfying our ethical needs,
Professor Simon referred I believe to the devices created within
the Halakha at different times in order to meet changing circumstances. Such were, for instance, the *Prosbul* (a device of
Hillel for circumventing the cancellation of debts in the sabbatical year) and the *heter iska* (a device for circumventing the
biblical prohibition on charging interest for loans). These were
contrived in order to meet economic exigencies and to ease
social relationships. Similarly, the rabbis nearer our time have
devised methods for all but eliminating the phenomenon of the
aguna (the abandoned wife who, because of the unconfirmed
death of her husband, is unable to remarry). The same degree of
goodwill should now be employed, he says, to solve the problem
of the *mamzer* (the fruit of a forbidden union of the first degree
who as a consequence is unable to contract marriage with an Israelite). This is the position taken by Professor Simon in his
reference to the rabbis of our time.

Elsewhere, however, in his analysis of the command "Thou
shalt love thy neighbor as thyself," Professor Simon comes to
the conclusion that the normative Halakha is inadequate to
satisfy our ethical sense, and therefore he calls for an extra-
halakhic ethical standard to which a contemporary Jew should
adhere. These two positions of Professor Simon seem to me
mutually contradictory. The sense of urgency that led to the
invention of the *Prosbul,* the *heter iska,* and so forth is consistent only with the conviction that no solutions can be found for
such problems outside the Torah itself. Hillel did not say,
"Come, let us leave the law of the sabbatical year on one side
and create an extra-halakhic category which will enable society
to function." He said rather, "Let us find solutions for our
problems within the framework of the Halakha and using principles and mechanisms which the Torah sanctions." Professor

Simon's views on "Love thy neighbor" are not of this kind. He comes to the conclusion (which seems to me incontrovertible) that the Torah does not lead in the direction of the kind of ethical humanism that he requires, and as a consequence he calls for an ethic aside from the Halakha (*lezad haHalakhah*). In this he has led himself into a logically untenable position.

1. This Response is based on the lecture that Professor Simon gave in Hebrew at the opening session of the 1972 meeting of the Institute for Judaism and Contemporary Thought. The final text of that lecture that appears in this volume is not a verbatim transcript. Hence, even though the exact expressions that I quote may not appear in the printed version, the basic ideas are there and are endorsed by Professor Simon.

AHARON LICHTENSTEIN

Does Jewish Tradition Recognize

An Ethic Independent of Halakha?

"DOES THE TRADITION RECOGNIZE AN ETHIC independent of Halakha?" My subject is a simple factual question
presumably calling for a yes-or-no answer. But what kind of
Jew responds to salient questions with unequivocal monosylla-
bles? Certainly not the traditional kind. Moreover, as formulated, this particular query is a studded minefield, every key
term an ill-defined boobytrap. Who or what represents the
tradition? Is the recognition de facto or de jure? How radical is
the independence? Above all, what are the referents of ethic and
Halakha? A qualified reply is obviously required.

Before presenting it in detail, however, I must confess that, at
one level, an unequivocal response could be easily mounted. If
the issue be reduced to natural morality in general, it need
hardly be in doubt. "Rabbi Yohanan stated," says the Gemara
in *Erubin,* "'If the Torah had not been given, we would have
learnt modesty from the cat, [aversion to] robbery from the
ant, chastity from the dove, and [conjugal] manners from the
cock.'"[1] The passage implies, first, that a cluster of logically
ante-halakhic virtues exists; second, that these can be inferred
from natural phenomena; and, probably, third—with Plato and
against the Sophists—that these relate to *physis* rather than
nomos, being not only observable through nature but inherent
within it. Nor does the passage stand alone. The wide-ranging
concept of *derekh eretz*[2]—roughly the equivalent of what

Coventry Patmore called "the traditions of civility"—points in the same direction. Its importance—again, not as descriptively synonymous with conventional conduct but as prescriptive *lex naturalis*—should not be underestimated. The Mishna cites Rabbi Eliezer b. Azaria's view that "without Torah, there is no *derekh eretz,* and without *derekh eretz,* there is no Torah";[3] and the Midrash goes beyond this dialectical reciprocity, stating that *"derekh eretz* preceded Torah."[4] In context, the primary reference is to chronological priority. Nevertheless, one senses that the common tendency—especially prevalent among the *mussar* masters—to include logical if not axiological precedence as well is a response to clearly present undertones; and, in this sense, the two texts are of course closely related. As the Maharal put it, "From this [i.e., the Mishna], we learn that *derekh eretz* is the basis of Torah which is," as explained by the Midrash, "'the way of the tree of life.'"[5] Their link reinforces our awareness of the Rabbis' recognition of natural morality.

There is, however, little need to adduce proof texts. Even if one assumes that the Rabbis' awareness of natural law as an explicit philosophic and historical doctrine was limited—a point that Baer and Lieberman[6] have debated—this would be, for our purposes, quite irrelevant. Indeed, even if one accepts the thesis, recently advanced by Marvin Fox,[7] that the concept of natural law, in its classical and Thomistic sense, is actually inconsistent with rabbinic and *rishonim's* thought, our problem is very little affected. The fact remains that the existence of natural morality is clearly assumed in much that is quite central to our tradition. Discussion of theodicy is predicated upon it. As Benjamin Whichcote,[8] the seventeenth-century Cambridge Platonist pointed out, one cannot ask, "Shall, then, the judge of the whole earth not do justice?"[9] unless one assumes the existence of an unlegislated justice to which, as it were, God Himself is bound; and which, one might add, man can at least apprehend sufficiently to ask the question. Or again, any attempt at rationalizing Halakha—an endeavor already found in *Hazal,* although much more fully elaborated by *rishonim*—presupposes an axiological frame of reference, independent of Halakha, in the light of which it can be interpreted. It makes no sense to say, with Abaye, that "the whole of the Torah . . . is for the purpose of promoting peace,"[10] unless the ethical value of peace can be taken for granted. The same holds true with respect to suggesting reasons for specific *mitzvot*. The intensity of Maimonides' efforts on this front is consistent with the position—advanced by Rav Saadia Gaon[11] and, in broad outline, adopted by Rabbenu Bahya[12] and probably by Maimonides[13]—that, given sufficient time, ability, and interest, the bulk of revealed Torah could have been naturally and logically discovered.

Any supposed traditional rejection of *lex naturalis* cannot mean, therefore, that apart from Halakha—or, to put it in broader perspective, that in the absence of divine commandment—man and the world are amoral. Nor does it entail a total relativism or the view (evidently ascribed to Maimonides by Professor Fox[14]) that social convention and/or utility are the sole criteria for action. At most, the Rabbis rejected natural law, not natural morality. They may conceivably have felt one could not ground specific binding and universal rules in nature but they hardly regarded uncommanded man as ethically neutral. They could have accepted, at the natural plane, the position summarized by Whitehead: "There is no one behaviour-system belonging to the essential character of the universe, as the universal moral ideal. What is universal is the spirit which should permeate any behaviour-system in the circumstances of its adoption. . . . Whether we destroy, or whether we preserve, our action is moral if we have thereby safeguarded the importance of experience so far as it depends on that concrete instance in the world's history."[15] But they would surely have gone no further. One might contend, maximally, that natural morality is contextual rather than formal. It does, however, exist.

Inasmuch as the traditional acceptance of some form of natural morality seems to me beyond doubt, I could, were I literally minded, simply answer our original question in the affirmative and close up shop. I presume, however, that its framers had something more in mind. If I read their concern rightly, the issue is not whether the tradition accords a non-halakhic ethic some theoretical standing by acknowledging its universal validity and provenance. Rather, it is whether now that, in *Hazal*'s phrase, "Torah has been given and Halakha innovated,"[16] that standing is of any practical significance to us; whether, for the contemporary Jew, an ethic independent of Halakha can be at all legitimate and relevant at an operative level.

At this plane, the issue resolves itself, in turn, into the problem both historical and analytic, of the relation of the pre- and post-Sinai orders, something akin to the question of the relation of nature and grace that has exercised so much Christian theology. On this score, traditional thought has focused upon two complementary points. The first is that natural morality establishes a standard below which the demands of revelation could not possibly fall. Thus, in proving that the killing of a gentile constitutes proscribed murder (although the Torah at one point speaks of a man killing "his fellow" [Exod. 21:14], i.e., a Jew), the *Mekhilta* explains: "Issi b. Akiba states: Prior to the giving of the Torah, we were enjoined with respect to bloodshed. After the giving of the Torah, instead of [our obligation's] becoming more rigorous [is it conceivable] that it became less so?"[17] Moreover, this limit does not just reflect a general attitude but constitutes a definitive legal principle to be applied to specific situations. "Is there, then, anything," the Gemara asks, "which is permitted to the Jew but prohibited to the Gentile?"[18] And it uses the implicit rhetorical denial to clinch a fine point in the course of intricate discussion.

The second point is most familiarly associated with a statement—frequently quoted and never, to the best of my knowledge, seriously challenged—made by Maimonides in his *Commentary on the Mishna*. Taking his cue from a Mishna in *Hullin* concerning the prohibition against eating the sciatic nerve (*gid hanashe*), he goes on to postulate a general principle: "And pay attention to this great principle conveyed by this *mishna* as it states that it [i.e., the sciatic nerve] was 'proscribed from Sinai.' What you must know is that [as regards] anything from which we abstain or which we do today, we do this solely because of God's commandment, conveyed through Moses, not because God had commanded thus to prophets who had preceded him. For instance . . . we do not circumcise because Abraham circumcised himself and the members of his household but because God commanded us, through Moses, to become circumcised as had Abraham. . . . Take note of their [i.e., the Rabbis'] remark, '613 *mitzvot* were stated to Moses at Sinai'—and all of these are among those *mitzvot*."[19] On this view, although the substance of natural morality may have been incorporated as a floor for a halakhic ethic, it has nevertheless, as a sanction, been effectively superseded.

At another level, however, we are confronted by an issue of far wider scope. The question is not what vestiges of natural morality continue to bind the Jew or to what extent receiving the Torah abrogated any antecedent ethic. It is rather whether, quite apart from ground common to natural and halakhic morality, the demands or guidelines of Halakha are both so definitive and so comprehensive as to preclude the necessity for—and therefore, in a sense, the legitimacy of—any other ethic. In translating my assigned topic into these terms (so strikingly familiar to readers of Hooker's *Ecclesiastical Polity*[20]), I am of course taking two things for granted. I assume, first, that Halakha constitutes—or at least contains—an ethical system. This point has sometimes been challenged—most notably, in our day, by Professor Yeshayahu Leibowitz; but I do not think the challenge, albeit grounded in healthy radical monotheism, can be regarded seriously. The extent to which Halakha as a whole is pervaded by an ethical moment or the degree to which a specific *mitzva* is rooted, if at all, in moral considerations are no doubt debatable. If evidence were necessary, we need only remember conflicting interpretations of the Mishna concerning "he who says, may your mercies encompass the bird's nest"[21] and the attendant controversy[22] over the rationalization of *mitzvot* en bloc. As for the outright rejection of the ethical moment, however, I cannot find such quasi-fideistic voluntarism consonant with the main thrust of the tradition. One might cite numerous primary texts by way of rebuttal but a single verse in Jeremiah should suffice: "But let him that glorieth glory in this, that he understandeth and knoweth Me, for I am the Lord who exercise mercy, justice, and righteousness, in the earth; for these I desire, saith the Lord."[23] The ethical element is presented as the reason for seeking knowledge of God, or, at the very least—if we translate *ki ani* as "that I am" rather than "for I am"[24]—as its content. In either case, the religious and the ethical are here inextricably interwoven; and what holds true of religious knowledge holds equally true of religious, that is, halakhic, action. This fusion is central to the whole rabbinic tradition. From its perspective, the divorce of Halakha from morality not only eviscerates but falsifies it.

Second, I assume that, at most, we can only speak of a complement to Halakha, not of an alternative. Any ethic so independent of Halakha as to obviate or override it, clearly lies beyond our pale. There are of course situations in which ethical factors—the preservation of life, the enhancement of human dignity, the quest for communal or domestic peace, or the mitigation of either anxiety or pain—sanction the breach, by preemptive priority or outright violation, of specific norms. However, these factors are themselves halakhic considerations, in the most technical sense of the term, and their deployment entails no rejection of the system whatsoever. Admittedly, advocates of such rejection are no strangers to Jewish history; but they are hardly our present concern. However elastic the term *tradition* to some, it does have its limits, and antinomianism, which for our purposes includes the rejection of Torah law, lies beyond them. As a prescriptive category, the currently popular notion of *averah lishmah* (idealistic transgression) has no halakhic standing whatsoever.[25]

Essentially, then, the question is whether Halakha is self-sufficient. Its comprehensiveness and self-sufficiency are notions many of us cherish in our more pietistic or publicistic moments. For certain purposes, it would be comfortable if we could accept Professor Kahana's statement "that in Jewish civil law there is no separation of law and morals and that there is no distinction between what the law *is* and what the law *ought* to be."[26] If, however, we equate Halakha with the *din;* if we mean that everything can be looked up, every moral dilemma resolved by reference to code or canon, the notion is both palpably naive and patently false. The *Hazon Ish,* for one—and both his saintliness and his rigorous halakhic commitment are legend—had no such illusions. "Moral duties," he once wrote, "sometimes constitute one corpus with Halakhic rulings, and it is Halakha which defines the proscribed and permitted of ethical thought."[27] Sometimes—but not, evidently, always. There are moments when one must seek independent counsels. Recognition of this element rests upon both textual and practical evidence. In this setting, I presume little need be said with reference to the latter. Which of us has not, at times, been made painfully aware of the ethical paucity of his legal resources? Who has not found that the fulfillment of explicit halakhic duty could fall well short of exhausting clearly felt moral responsibility? The point to be emphasized, however—although this too, may be obvious—is that the deficiency is not merely the result of silence or ambiguity on the part of the sources. That may of course be a factor, requiring, as it does, recourse to inference and analogy to deal with the multitude of situations that, almost a priori, have not been covered by basic texts. The critical point, however, is that even the full discharge of one's whole formal duty as defined by the *din* often appears palpably insufficient.[28]

Lest this judgment appear excessively severe, let me hasten to add that it is precisely this point that is stressed by the second source of evidence: the textual. "Rav Yohanan said," the Gemara in *Baba Mezia* cites, "'Jerusalem was but destroyed because they [i.e., its inhabitants] judged [in accordance with] Torah law within it.' Well, should they rather have followed the law of the Magians?! Say, rather, because they based their judgments solely upon Torah law and did not act *lifnim mishurat hadin* [i.e., beyond the line of the law]."[29] Nahmanides was even more outspoken. In a celebrated passage, he explains that the general command, "Ye shall be holy" was issued because, the scope of the Torah's injunctions regarding personal conduct notwithstanding, a lustful sybarite could observe them to the letter and yet remain "a scoundrel with Torah license." The same holds true, he continues, with respect to social ethics. Hence, there, too, the Torah has formulated a broad injunction: "And this is the Torah's mode: to detail and [then] to generalize in a similar vein. For after the admonition about the details of civil law and all interpersonal dealings . . . it says generally, 'And thou shalt do the right and the good,' as it includes under this positive command justice and accommodation and all *lifnim mishurat hadin* in order to oblige one's fellow."[30] This position is further elaborated in Nahmanides' explication of the phrase, "the right and the good." He suggests, initially, that it may refer to the collective body of specific *mitzvot,* but then presents an alternative:

> And our Rabbis[31] have a fine interpretation of this. They said: "This refers to compromise and *lifnim mishurat hadin.*"[32] The intent of this is that, initially,[33] He had said that you should observe the laws and statutes which He had commanded you. Now He says that, with respect to what He has not commanded, you should likewise take heed to do the good and the right in His eyes, for He loves the good and the right. And this is a great matter. For it is impossible to mention in the Torah all of a person's actions toward his neighbors and acquaintances, all of his commercial activity, and all social and political institutions. So after He had mentioned many of them such as, "Thou shalt

69

not go about as a tale-bearer," "Thou shalt not take vengeance
nor bear any grudge," "Thou shalt not stand idly by the blood of
thy fellow," "Thou shalt not curse the deaf," "Thou shalt rise up
before age,"[34] and the like, He resumes to say generally that one
should do the good and the right in all matters, to the point that
there are included in this compromise, lifnim mishurat hadin,
and [matters] similar to that which they [i.e., the Rabbis] mentioned concerning the law of the abutter[35]—even that which they
said, "whose youth had been unblemished,"[36] or, "He converses
with people gently,"[37] so that he is regarded as perfect and right
in all matters.[38]

These passages contain strong and explicit language and they
answer our question plainly enough. Or do they? Just how independent of Halakha is the ethic that ennobles us above the
"scoundrel with Torah license?" If we regard din and Halakha
as coextensive, very independent. If, however, we recognize that
Halakha is multiplanar and many dimensional; that, properly
conceived, it includes much more than is explicitly required or
permitted by specific rules, we shall realize that the ethical
moment we are seeking is itself an aspect of Halakha. The demand or, if you will, the impetus for transcending the din is itself part of the halakhic corpus. This point emerges quite
clearly from the primary rabbinic source for the concept of
lifnim mishurat hadin:

"'And thou shalt show them the way'—this is the study of
Torah; 'and the action they should take'—good conduct"—
these are the words of Rabbi Yehoshua. Rabbi Eleazar of
Modi'im says: "'And thou shalt show them'—teach them their
life's course; 'the way'—this alludes to visiting the sick; 'they
shall walk'—to burying the dead; 'therein'—to exercising
kindness; 'and the action'—to din proper; 'which they shall do'—
to lifnim mishurat hadin."[39]

Regardless of whether we accept Rabbi Yehoshua's generalization or Rabbi Eleazar's more specific catalogue, the conjunction of either "good conduct" or lifnim mishurat hadin with

thoroughly mandatory elements clearly indicates it is no mere option.

The obligatory character of *lifnim mishurat hadin* stands revealed in the verses Nahmanides saw as related to it—"And thou shalt do the right and the good" and "Ye shall be holy." Neither was expressed in the indicative or the optative. With respect to the degree of obligation, however, *rishonim* admittedly held different views. Perhaps the most rigorous was held by one of the Tosafists, Rabbi Isaac of Corbeille. In his *Sefer Mitzvot Katan,* one of the many medieval compendia summarizing and enumerating *mitzvot,* he lists "to act *lifnim mishurat hadin,* as it is written, 'which they shall do' "[40] as one of the 613 commandments; and he goes on to cite the Gemara in *Baba Mezia* 30b as a proof text. Nahmanides did not go quite this far, as he does not classify *lifnim mishurat hadin* as an independent *mitzva,* as binding as *shofar* or *tefillin.* However, he does clearly posit it as a normative duty, incumbent upon—and expected of—every Jew as part of his basic obligation. Failure to implement "the right and the good" would obviously not be regarded as mere insensitivity to music of spiritual spheres. It is villainy—with the Torah's license—but villainy nonetheless.

Maimonides, however, does apparently treat *lifnim mishurat hadin* within a more rarefied context. After presenting his account of the golden mean in the opening chapter of *Hilkhot De'ot,* he concludes: "And the early pietists would incline their traits from the median path toward either extreme. One trait they would incline toward the farther extreme, another toward the nearer; and this is *lifnim mishurat hadin.*"[41] On this view, supralegal conduct appears as the hallmark of a small coterie of *hasidim.* Postulated as an aristocratic rather than as a popular ideal, *lifnim mishurat hadin* thus represents a lofty plane whose attainment is a mark of eminence but whose neglect cannot be faulted as reprehensible.

This is, of course, drastically different from Nahmanides and may be construed as indicating—contrary to my earlier statement—that, according to Maimonides, *lifnim mishurat hadin* is

purely optional; that it constitutes a kind of supererogatory
extra-credit morality rather than an obligation, strictly
speaking. Even if the argument is accepted, it would not render
lifnim mishurat hadin wholly voluntary. It would merely shift it,
to use Lon Fuller's[42] distinction, from the "morality of duty" to
the "morality of aspiration." But a Jew is also commanded to
aspire. More important, however, this point has little impact
upon our present broader purposes. The semantics and
substance of the term *lifnim mishurat hadin* aside, Maimonides
most certainly does not regard character development, ethical
sensitivity, or supralegal behavior as non-halakhic, much less as
optional, elements. He simply subsumes them under a different
halakhic rubric, the demand for *imitatio dei.* "And we are commanded," he writes, "to walk in these median paths, and they
are the right and the good paths, as it is written, 'And ye shall
walk in His ways.'"[43] The command refers, of course, to the
golden mean rather than to *lifnim mishurat hadin,*[44] but we are
confronted by the same normative demand for "the right and
the good." The difference in terminology and source is
significant, and were my present subject *lifnim mishurat hadin*
per se I would discuss it in detail. For our purposes, however,
Maimonides' and Nahmanides' views point in the same general
direction: Halakha itself mandates that we go beyond its legal
corpus. Were I to follow Fuller's[45] example and chart a
spectrum running from duty to aspiration, I think that, on
Maimonides' view, so-called non-halakhic ethics would be a
couple of notches higher than for Nahmanides. Even after we
have taken due account of the imperative of pursuing "His
ways," we are still imbued with a sense of striving for an ideal
rather than of satisfying basic demands. Nevertheless, the fundamental similarity remains. The ethic of *imitatio* is not just a
lofty ideal but a pressing obligation. The passage previously
cited from Maimonides explicitly speaks of our being "commanded" (*u'mezuvim anu*) to pursue the golden mean; and subsequent statements are in a similar vein. Thus, he asserts that
Scripture ascribes certain attributes to God "in order to inform

72

[us] that they are good and right ways and [that] a person is obligated [*hayav*] to guide himself by them and to resemble Him to the best of his ability." Or again, he speaks of the attributes as constituting collectively "the median path which we are obligated [*hayavim*] to pursue."[46] Furthermore, it is noteworthy that in describing this ethic, Maimonides uses the very adjectives fastened upon by Nahmanides: "right and good." It can be safely assumed that, in principle, both recognize the imperative character of supralegal conduct.[47]

This exposition is admittedly partial. It rests upon two assumptions: first, that Maimonides recognizes an elitist ethic of the *hasid,* which though grounded in *din* nevertheless transcends it; second, that even the universal median ethic demands much that has not been specifically legislated and that according to Nahmanides' definition would be subsumed under *lifnim mishurat hadin.* I think both points emerge unequivocally from the account in *Mishneh Torah;* but in the earlier *Shemonah Perakim*[48] we do get a distinctly different impression. There, action *lifnim mishurat hadin* is not described as inherently superior to the golden mean but as a propaedeutic technique for attaining it. As in Aristotle's familiar example of straightening the bent stick,[49] one excess is simply used to correct another, this corresponding to standard medical practice. Second, Maimonides suggests that adherence to *din* proper produces the ideal balance so that deviation in any direction— except when dictated by the need to "cure" the opposite deficiency—becomes not only superfluous but undesirable. The brunt of this argument is directed against asceticism, and the excesses decried by Maimonides all concern material self-denial.[50] However, the list of examples adduced to prove the sufficiency of Torah law includes *mitzvot,* which relate to a whole range of virtues and vices: munificence, anger, arrogance, timidity. The net impact of the passage is therefore clearly to diminish somewhat the role of an independent ethic. Nevertheless, I am inclined to regard the later and fuller exposition in *Hilkhot De'ot* as the more definitive. The difference between

Maimonides and Nahmanides, though significant, does not therefore strike me as radical.

The variety of *rishonim's* conceptions of a supralegal ethic may be judged from another perspective—in light of a very practical question: Is *lifnim mishurat hadin* actionable?[51] The Gemara records at least one instance in which it was enforced. It tells a story of some porters who had been working for Rabba the son of Rav Huna and who had broken a barrel of wine while handling it. Inasmuch as they had evidently been somewhat negligent, the strict letter of the law would have held them liable for the damage; and since they had been remiss in performing their assigned task, it would have allowed them no pay. By way of guaranteeing restitution, Rabba held onto their clothes—which had apparently been left in his possession—as surety; whereupon

> they came and told Rav [who in turn], told him, "Return their clothes to them." "Is this the *din?*" he asked. "Yes," he answered, "'That thou mayest walk in the way of good men.'" He then returned their clothes, whereupon they said to him, "We are poor, we have labored all day, and [now] we are hungry and left with nothing!" [So] he said to him, "Go and pay their wages!" "Is this the *din?*" he asked. "Yes," he answered, "'And keep the path of the righteous.'"[52]

Moreover, in a similar passage in the Palestinian Talmud,[53] the story is not told with reference to an *amora*—from whom a higher ethical standard could presumably be exacted—but of an ordinary potter. However, the pathetic circumstances as well as the omission of the term *lifnim mishurat hadin*[54] suggest this may have been an isolated instance. In any event, *rishonim* divided on the issue. The Rosh held that "we do not compel to act *lifnim mishurat hadin*";[55] and inferring *de silentio,* I think it is safe to assume this was the prevalent view of the Spanish school. However, a number of Tosafists—notably, Ravya and Ravan[56]—held such action could indeed by compelled. Of

74

course, such a position could not conceivably be held with reference to all supralegal behavior. *Din* has many ethical levels; and so, of necessity, must *lifnim mishurat hadin*. Surpassing laws grounded in, say, the concept that "the Torah has but spoken vis-a-vis the evil inclination"[57] is hardly comparable to transcending those with a powerful moral thrust. Nevertheless, the fact that some *rishonim* held *lifnim mishurat hadin* to be, in principle, actionable, indicates the extent to which it is part of the fabric of Halakha.

The possibility of such compulsion arises in yet another—and possibly surprising—context. *Hazal* states that *kofin al midat Sodom*, "we coerce over a trait of Sodom."[58] As defined by most *rishonim*, the term refers to an inordinate privatism that leaves one preoccupied with personal concerns to the neglect of the concerns of others; a degree of selfishness so intense that it denies the others at no gain to oneself. There need be no actual spite. Simple indifference may suffice. Nor is *midat Sodom*—despite the severity of the term—confined to what popular morality might regard as nastiness or mindless apathy. One view in the Mishna—the definitive view according to most *rishonim*—subsumed under it the attitude that "mine is mine and yours is yours."[59] It thus broadly denotes obsession with one's private preserve and the consequent erection of excessive legal and psychological barriers between person and person.

This posture the Rabbis both condemned and rendered actionable. To the best of my knowledge, however, *Hazal* nowhere explicitly formulated the basis of this *halakha*. I would therefore conjecture that it is most likely subsumed under *lifnim mishurat hadin;* and if this be so, we have here a striking instance of its scope and force. Admittedly, most of us do not instinctively associate the two concepts. However, this is simply another manifestation of our failure to grasp the full range of supralegal obligation. So long as *lifnim mishurat hadin* is regarded as the sphere of supererogatory extracredit morality, it can hardly include rejection of actions so reprehensible as to earn the opprobrium of *midat Sodom*. However, once we appreciate its true scope—from rigorous obligation to supreme idealism—we should have little difficulty with the association.

The Maharal, at any rate, had none—precisely because he emphasized the centrality and force of *lifnim mishurat hadin*. This emphasis was clearly expressed in the course of his discussion of *gemilut hasadim* (loosely translatable as "benevolent action"). "The anitithesis of this trait," he writes, "is [a person] who does not want to do any good toward another, standing upon the *din* and refusing to act *lifnim mishurat hadin*." This virtual equation of *hesed* and *lifnim mishurat hadin* then becomes the basis for an explanation of the Gemara's comment regarding the destruction of Jerusalem. This was not, the Maharal explains, retributive punishment. It was a natural consequence, as a wholly legalistic community simply cannot exist. Supralegal conduct is the cement of human society. Its absence thus results in disintegration: "Standing upon *din* entails ruin." Likewise, excessive commitment to law invites disaster on a broader scale, for, by correspondence, it both recognizes and enthrones natural law as cosmic sovereign, thus rejecting the providential grace of miracles that deviates from it. Finally, rejection of *lifnim mishurat hadin* is defined as the hallmark of Sodom whose evil, although it issued in corruption, nevertheless was grounded in total fealty to legal nicety: "For this was their nature, to concede nothing, as the Rabbis o.b.m. said, 'Mine is mine and yours is yours—this is the trait of Sodom.' And they have everywhere said, *kofin al midat Sodom*."[60] Identification of *lifnim mishurat hadin* as the source of such coercion is here fairly explicit; and the conjunction of its denial with the biblical apotheosis of malice reflects the importance that the Maharal attached to supralegal conduct.

This exposition is open to two obvious objections. First, if *lifnim mishurat hadin* is indeed obligatory as an integral aspect of Halakha, in what sense is it supralegal? More specifically, on the Ravya's view, what distinguishes its compulsory elements from *din* proper? Secondly, isn't this exposition mere sham? Having conceded, in effect, the inadequacy of the halakhic ethic, it implicitly recognizes the need for a complement, only to attempt to neutralize this admission by claiming the complement had actually been a part of Halakha all along, so that the fiction of halakhic comprehensiveness could be saved after all. Yet, the upshot of this legerdemain does not differ in substance from the view that the tradition does recognize an ethic independent of Halakha—so why not state this openly?

These are sound objections; but they do not undermine the position I have developed. They only stimulate its more precise definition. As regards the first question, a comment made, interestingly, by the Ravya, points toward the solution. In explaining why Rav Nahman had not compelled the finder of a lost object whose owner had despaired of its recovery to return it—legally, he is free to retain it but the Gemara[61] notes that it is returnable, *lifnim mishurat hadin*—he suggests that, in this instance, "perhaps the finder was poor while the object's owner was well-to-do."[62] Within the framework of *din,* this would of course be a startling distinction. Powerful as is the obligation of the affluent to help the relatively disadvantaged, it is a general responsibility to a group and enforceable only through a third party, the community and its *beth din.* Although many *poskim*[63] regard charity as a legal and collectible debt rather than a mere act of grace, an individual pauper certainly has no right—except with respect to one type of *ma'aser ani* (tithe for the poor)[64]—to seize his more affluent neighbor's property. That such a point could be made with reference to *lifnim mishurat hadin* suggests its crucial distinction from *din.* It is less rigorous not only in the sense of being less exacting with respect to the degree and force of obligation—and there are times, as has been noted, when it can be equally demanding—but in the sense of being more flexible, its duty more readily definable in light of the exigencies of particular circumstances. This has nothing to do with the force of obligation. Once it has been determined that, in a given case, realization of "the right and the good" mandates a particular course, its pursuit may conceivably be as imperative as the performance of a *din.* However, the initial determination of what moral duty requires proceeds along different lines in the respective sphere. *Din* consists of a body of statutes, ultimately rooted in fundamental values but which at the moment of decision confront the individual as a set of rules. It is of course highly differentiated, numerous variables making the relevant rule very much a function of the situation. Yet the basic mode is that of formulating and defining directives to be followed in a *class* of cases—it is precisely the quality of generality that constitutes a rule—and applying them to situations marked by the proper cluster of features. Judgments are essentially grounded in deductive, primarily syllogistic reasoning. Metaphors that speak of laws as controlling or governing a case are therefore perfectly accurate.

Lifnim mishurat hadin by contrast, is the sphere of contextual morality. Its basis for decision is paradoxically both more general and more specific. The formalist is guided by a principle or a rule governing a category of cases defined by *n* number of characteristics. The more sensitive and sophisticated the system, the more individuated the categories. Whatever the degree of specificity, however, the modus operandi is the same: action grows out of the application of class rules to a particular case judged to be an instance of that class or of the interaction of several classes, there being, of course principles to govern seemingly hybrid cases as well. The contextualist, by contrast, will have nothing to do with middle-distance guidelines. He is directed, in theory, at least, only by the most universal and the most local of factors—by a minimal number, perhaps as few as one or two, of ultimate values, on the one hand, and by the unique contours of the situation at hand, on the other. Guided by his polestar(s), the contextualist employs his moral sense (to use an outdated but still useful eighteenth-century term) to evaluate and intuit the best way of eliciting maximal good from the existential predicament confronting him. A nominalist in ethics, he does not merely contend that every case is phenomenologically different. That would be a virtual truism. He argues that the differences are generally so crucial that no meaningful directives can be formulated. Only direct ad hoc judgment, usually—although this is logically a wholly separate question—his own, can serve as an operative basis for decision. Between ultimate value and immediate issue, there can be no other midwife.

It goes without saying that Judaism has rejected contextualism as a self-sufficient ethic. Nevertheless, we should recognize equally that it has embraced it as the modus operandi of large tracts of human experience. These lie in the realm of *lifnim mishurat hadin.* In this area, the halakhic norm is itself situational. It speaks in broad terms: "And thou shalt do the right and the good"; "And thou shalt walk in His ways." The metaphors employed to describe it—"the ways of the good" or "the paths of the righteous"—denote purpose and direction rather than definitively prescribed acts. And the distinction from *din* is, finally, subtly recognized in the third source we have noted: "'And the action'—this is the line of *din;* 'that they shall take'—this is *lifnim mishurat hadin*"—the reified static noun being used in relation to one and the open-ended verb in relation to the other. In observing *din,* the Jew rivets his immediate attention upon the specific command addressed to him. His primary response is to the source of his prescribed act. With respect to *lifnim mishurat hadin,* he is, "looking before and after," concerned with results as much as with origins. His focus is axiological and teleological.

Quite apart from the severity of obligation, therefore, there is a fundamental difference between *din* and *lifnim mishurat hadin.* One, at a more minimal level, imposes fixed objective standards. The demands of the other evolve from a specific situation; and, depending upon the circumstances, may vary with the agent.

This point was clearly recognized by a late *rishon,* author of a fourteenth-century commentary on the *Mishneh Torah.* In explaining why Maimonides both expanded and differentiated the concept of *dina debar mezra,* making it legally enforceable in some cases but only obligatory *ante facto* in others,[65] the *Mag-*

gid Mishneh both echoes Nahmanides and goes beyond him. "The point of *dina debar mezra,*" he comments,

> is that our perfect Torah has laid down [general] principles concerning the development of man's character and his conduct in the world; as, in stating, "Ye shall be holy,"[66] meaning, as they [i.e., the Rabbis] said, "Sanctify yourself with respect to that which is permitted you"[67]—that one should not be swept away by the pursuit of lusts. Likewise, it said "And thou shalt do the right and the good," meaning that one's interpersonal conduct should be good and just. With regard to all this, it would not have been proper to command [about] details. For the Torah's commands apply at all times, in every period, and under all circumstances, whereas man's characteristics and his behavior vary, depending upon the time and the individual. The Rabbis [therefore] set down some relevant details subsumed under these principles, some of which they made [the equivalent of] absolute *din* and others [only] *ante facto* and by way of *hasidut*[68]—all [however] ordained by them. And it is with reference to this that they said, "The words of consorts [i.e., the Rabbis] are more beloved than the wine of Torah, as stated, 'For thy love is better than wine.'"[69]

The *Maggid Mishneh* is certainly not espousing an exclusively relativistic or situational ethic. No conscientious halakhist could even countenance the possibility. He is, rather, defining the character of *dina debar mezra,* specifically, and of "the right and the good," generally; and, beyond this, noting that, from a certain perspective, the greater flexibility and latitude that characterize this class of rabbinic legislation gives it an edge, as it were, over the Torah's absolutely rigorous law. The concluding remark is of considerable interest in its own right. Comparisons aside, however, the passage clearly reveals the respective characters of *din* and *lifnim mishurat hadin.*

The second objection—that I am either playing games or stalking a Trojan horse, and possibly both—can likewise be parried. Whether supralegal behavior is regarded as an aspect of—

and in relation to—Halakha does matter considerably. The difference, moreover, concerns not so much the prestige of Halakha as the substance of that behavior. And this in three respects. First, integration within Halakha helps define the specifics of supralegal conduct. One of its principal modes entails the extension of individual *dinim* by (1) refusal to avail oneself of personal exemptions; (2) disregard of technicalities when they exclude from a law situations that morally and substantively are clearly governed by it; and (3) enlarging the scope of a law by applying it to circumstances beyond its legal pale but nevertheless sufficiently similar to share a specific telos. All three, however, constitute, in effect, the penumbra of *mitzvot*. To this end, relation to a fundamental law, which posits frontiers and points a direction, is obviously essential.

Not all supralegal conduct bears this character, however. It may, alternatively, either fill in a moral lacuna at a lower level—*kofin al midat Sodom* is an excellent example—or, at a higher plane, aspire to attainments discontinuous with any specific practical norm. Even within these nether and upper reaches, however, relation to the overall halakhic system is important both for the definition of general goals and by way of molding orientation, context, and motivation. Even while closing an interstice or reaching for the stars, one does not move in a vacuum. The legal corpus is here, to adapt Ben Jonson's remark about the ancients, more guide than commander; but it is vital nonetheless.

Finally, the halakhic connection is relevant at a third level, when we are concerned with an ethic neither as decisor of specific actions nor as determinant of a field of values but as the polestar of life in its totality. Halakhic commitment orients a Jew's whole being around his relation to God. It is not content with the realization of a number of specific goals but demands personal dedication—and not only dedication but consecration. To the achievement of this end, supralegal conduct is indispensable. Integration of the whole self within a halakhic framework becomes substantive rather than semantic insofar as it is

81

reflected within the full range of personal activity. Reciprocally, however, that conduct is itself stimulated by fundamental halakhic commitment.

Let me emphasize that in speaking of the investiture of an independent ethic with a halakhic mantle, I hold no brief for terminology per se. I would readily concede that we can, if we wish, confine the term *halakha* to *din* and find some other term to cover what lies beyond. Moreover, such limitation would probably be consonant with the use of the term *halakha* by *Hazal*. In classical usage, the term *halakha*—properly lowercase and commonly used without the definite article—generally denotes a specific rule (hence, the frequent appearance of the plural, *halakhot*) or, in broader terms, the body of knowledge comprising Torah law. It does not convey the common contemporary sense in which it is roughly the equivalent of halakhic Judaism—the *unum necessarium* of the Jew committed to tradition, in which, as a commanding presence, magisterial to the point of personification, it is regarded as prescribing a way of life; in which, as with the term *Torah* in *Hazal,* Halakha and its Giver frequently become interchangeable. Hence, we ought not be surprised if we find that *Hazal* did differentiate between *halakhot* and other normative elements. Thus, in commenting upon the verse, "If thou wilt diligently hearken to the voice of the Lord thy God, and wilt do that which is right in His eyes, and wilt give ear to His commandments, and keep all his statutes,"[70] the *Mekhilta* notes:

> "'And wilt do that which is right in His eyes'—these are wonderful *agadot* which hold every one's ear; 'and wilt give ear to His commandments'—these are orders; 'and keep all His statutes' these are *halakhot*." . . . These are the words of Rabbi Yehoshua. Rabbi Eleazar of Modi'im says . . . "'And wilt do that which is right in His eyes'—this is commercial dealing. [The verse thus] teaches [us] that whoever deals honestly and enjoys good relations with people is regarded as having realized the whole Torah. 'And wilt give ear to His commandments'—these

82

are *halakhot* 'and keep all His statutes'—these are [prohibitions concerning] forbidden sexual relations."[71]

This exposition I understand readily and, semantics apart, find fully consistent with the view I have outlined above. At most, it requires that we adjust our customary terminology somewhat and then issue with the thesis that traditional halakhic Judaism demands of the Jew both adherence to Halakha and commitment to an ethical moment that though different from Halakha is nevertheless of a piece with it and in its own way fully imperative.[72] What I reject emphatically is the position that, on the one hand, defines the function and scope of Halakha in terms of the latitude implicit in current usage and yet identifies its content with the more restricted sense of the term. The resulting equation of duty and *din* and the designation of supralegal conduct as purely optional or pietistic is a disservice to Halakha and ethics alike.

In dealing with this subject, I have, in effect, addressed myself both to those who, misconstruing the breadth of its horizons, find the halakhic ethic inadequate, and to those who smugly regard even its narrower confines as sufficient. In doing so, I hope I have presented my thinking clearly. But for those who prefer definitive answers, let me conclude by saying: Does the tradition recognize an ethic independent of Halakha? You define your terms and take your choice.

---

1. *Erubin* 100b. Soncino translates "we could have learnt," but I think "would" is more accurate. Rabbenu Hananel, it might be noted, has *lamadnu.*

2. In the passage cited from the Gemara in *Erubin,* the term has a rather narrow meaning, referring, in context, to proper conjugal gallantry. Elsewhere, however, it clearly denotes far more, sometimes civility or culture generally. The *Mahzor Vitry,* commenting on *Abot,* 3:17 (ed. Horowitz, p. 517), renders it as *nourriture,* and the Maharal of Prague spells out its latitude quite clearly: "The things that are *derekh eretz* are all ethical matters included in *Abot,* those mentioned in the Talmud, and all other ethical matters. It is that conduct which is right and fitting toward (possibly, "in the eyes of") people; and failure to pursue some of its elements is sinful and a great

83

transgression" (*Netivot Olam*, "*Netiv Derekh Eretz*," chap. 1). See also N. S. Greenspan, *Mishpat Am Haaretz* (Jerusalem, 1946), pp. 1–5; the references cited in Boaz Cohen, *Law and Tradition in Judaism* (New York, 1959), p. 183n.; and *Encyclopedia Talmudit*, Vol. 7, pp. 672–706. One might add that the flexible range of *derekh eretz* parallels those of curteisie and manners in their Middle English and Elizabethan senses.

3. *Abot*, 3:17. Cf. also ibid., 2:2, and *Tosafot Yeshanim, Yoma* 85b, s.v. *teshuva*.

4. *Vayikra Rabba*, 9:3 (*Tzav*); cf. *Tanna Debei Eliyahu Rabba*, chap. 1.

5. *Netivot Olam*, "*Netiv Derekh Eretz*," chap. 1.

6. See Saul Lieberman, "How Much Greek in Jewish Palestine?," in *Biblical and Other Studies*, ed. A. Altmann (Cambridge, Mass., 1963), pp. 128–29.

7. M. Fox, "Maimonides and Aquinas on Natural Law," *Dine' Israel* 3 (1972): 5–27. Cf. also Ralph Lerner, "Natural Law in Albo's *Book of Roots*," in *Ancients and Moderns*, ed. Joseph Cropsey (New York, 1964), pp. 132–44.

8. The statement appears in one of his *Discourses* but the exact reference eludes me at present.

9. Gen. 18:25.

10. *Gittin* 59b. This passage was cited by Maimonides in the concluding lines of *Sefer Zemanim:* "Great is peace as the whole Torah was given in order to promote peace in the world, as it was stated: 'Her ways are the ways of pleasantness and all her paths are peace'" (*MT, Hannuka*, 4:14). There may be a shift in focus, however, as Maimonides dwells upon the reason for giving the Torah while the Gemara may conceivably refer to its content and the telos to which its inner logic leads. In either case, Torah is regarded as serving the interests of peace and therefore, presumably, as axiologically ancillary to it. In the *Guide* (III: 27; and cf. III: 52), this nexus is reversed. Peace and social stability are subsumed under the welfare of the body that is merely a condition for attaining man's ultimate perfection via the soul's intellectual apprehension. There is no contradiction, however, as the passage in *Mishneh Torah* probably refers to the specific corpus of revealed Torah and the regimen prescribed by it rather than, as in other contexts, to the full range of spiritual perception.

11. See *Ha'emunot Vehadeot*, "Introduction," sec. vi; and cf. III: iii.

12. See *Hovot Halevavot*, III: i–iii.

13. This point is not explicitly developed in Maimonides' discussions of prophecy, which focus upon its nature rather than upon the need for it. However, it is implicit in the substance and tone of numerous passages concerning the Torah's revelation and dovetails with Maimonides' faith in the spiritual capacity of singular individuals, on the one hand, and his conviction about the average person's indolence, on the other.

14. See Fox, "Maimonides and Aquinas on Natural Law," pp. 15–17.

15. Alfred North Whitehead, *Modes of Thought* (New York, 1938), p. 20.

16. *Shabbat* 135b.

17. *Mishpatim, Massekhta Dinezikin,* iv (ed. Horowitz-Rabin), p. 263.

18. *Hullin* 33a; cf. *Sanhedrin* 59a.

19. *Perush Ha-Mishnayot, Hullin,* 7:6. The talmudic citation is from *Makkot* 23b.

20. See, especially, Book 2.

21. *Berakhot* 5:3 and *Megilla* 4:9.

22. See Maimonides, *Guide,* III:26, III:31, and III:48; Nahmanides' comment on Deut. 22:7; and Maharal, *Tiferet Israel,* chaps. 5–7. See also Yitzhak Heinemann, *Taamei Ha-Mitzvot Besafrut Yisrael* (Jerusalem, 1954), Vol. 1, pp. 46–128.

23. Jer. 9:23.

24. The J.P.S. translation, following A.V., has "that I am," an interpretation implicitly supported by *Ikkarim,* 3:5. However, Radak is closer to "for I am," which I am more inclined to accept. The Septuagint's *hoti* is inconclusive but the Vulgate's *quia* parallels "for." For a discussion of the verse, see Maimonides, *Guide,* III: 54.

25. The term *avera lishma* does, of course, appear in the Gemara that cites a statement by Rabbi Nahman b. Yitzhak that "an *avera lishma* is greater than a *mitzva* performed with an ulterior motive" (*Nazir* 23b and *Horayot* 10b). However, this apparent priority of telos and motivation over formal law has no prescriptive or prospective implications. At most, it means that, after the fact, we can sometimes see that a nominal violation was superior to a licit or even required act; but it gives no license for making the jump. Moreover, in the case at hand—Yael's sexual relations with Sisera—most likely there was no formal violation. Most *rishonim* assume that a woman, inasmuch as she can be regarded as passive during coitus, is not obligated to undergo martyrdom rather than engage in incest or adultery (see *Sanhedrin* 74b). This is true even when she is threatened but not assaulted, as it is the element of willful involvement that defines her sexual participation as a human action. Hence, when motivated by the need to save her people, Yael's relations with Sisera, even though she may have initially seduced him, may very well be regarded as passive and therefore no formal violation whatsoever; see *Tosafot, Yebamot* 103a, s.v. *veha* and *Yoma* 82b, s.v. *ma.* The term *avera* refers, then, to an act which is proscribed under ordinary circumstances and yet, its usual sinful character notwithstanding, here becomes superior to a *mitzva.* Likewise, Raba's remark that the verse, "In all thy ways know Him and He will direct thy paths" (Prov. 3:6), is to be understood "even with regard to a matter of *avera*" (*Berakhot* 63a), may refer to acts that are ordinarily forbidden but in certain cases have formal dispensation. See, however, Maimonides, *Shemonah Perakim,* chap. 5.

26. K. Kahana, *The Case for Jewish Civil Law in the Jewish State* (London, 1960), p. 28n (his italics).

27. *Hazon Ish: Emunah Uvitahon* (Jerusalem, 1954), p. 21. The point is

85

illustrated by a discussion of economic competition, aspects of which are very differently evaluated, depending upon their being regarded as aggressive or defensive; and this, in turn, is a function of legal right. Of course, in such a case, the moral duties include many outright *dinim*. However, the implication of the sentence stands and is clearly accepted in the following chapter, pp. 44–46. Cf., however, p. 49.

28. Many of the leaders of the *mussar* movement, who criticized what they regarded as the ethical shortcomings of their contemporary Torah community, often ascribed many of these failings to the fact that the relevant halakhot had been insufficiently developed. They therefore urged the fuller analysis and exposition of these categories as a remedy; see J. D. Epstein, *Mitzvot Ha-bayit* (New York, 1966), pp. 34–57. I am inclined to think that while such neglect could be a factor in causing the alleged failings, its importance—and the potential for resolution via fuller halakhic exposition—has been exaggerated by the *mussar* movement.

29. *Baba Mezia* 30b.

30. Lev. 19:2.

31. In his edition of Nahmanides' commentary, *Perush Ha-Ramban al Ha-Torah* (Jerusalem, 1960), II, 376n., C. B. Chavel notes that no extant source of this comment is known.

32. Rashi, Deut. 6:18, comments, "This is compromise *lifnim mishurat hadin.*" This reading—he is presumably quoting the same source as Nahmanides—narrows the scope of the remark considerably.

33. In the preceding verse, 6:17.

34. The verses cited are from Lev. 19:16, 18, 16, 14, and 32, respectively.

35. A Rabbinic ordinance that requires a seller to give first option to any prospective customer who already owns property adjacent to that to be sold; see *Baba Mezia* 108.

36. *Ta'anit* 16a.

37. *Yoma* 86a.

38. Deut. 6:18.

39. *Mekhilta, Yithro, Massekhta D'Amalek,* ii (ed. Horowitz-Rabin), p. 198. The phrase I have rendered as "their life's course" is *bet hayehem.* Rashi interprets it variously as "the study of Torah" (*Baba Kama* 100a, s.v. *bet*) and as "a trade from which to derive a livelihood" (*Baba Mezia* 30b. s.v. *zeh*).

40. *Semak,* 49.

41. *MT, Hilkhot De'ot,* 1:5.

42. See his *The Morality of Law* (New Haven, 1964), pp. 5–9; cf. also A. D. Lindsay, *The Two Moralities* (London, 1940), passim.

43. *De'ot,* 1:5.

44. Maimonides thus distinguishes here between "the right and the good" and *lifnim mishurat hadin.* Elsewhere, however, he seems to identify them.

86

See Rabbi M. Krakowski's commentary, *Avodat Hamelekh* (Vilna, 1931), *ad loc.*, and S. Rawidowicz, *Iyyunim Bemahashevet Yisrael* (Jerusalem, 1969), I, 430–31.

45. See Fuller, *The Morality of Law,* pp. 9–13.

46. *De'ot,* 1:6 and 1:7, respectively.

47. See, however, *Avodat Hamelekh, De'ot* 1:5, who expresses some uncertainty on this point.

48. See chap. 4; cf. also *Perush Ha-Mishnayot Abot* 4:4.

49. See *Nic. Eth.,* 1109b.

50. Most involve actual physical deprivation so that the passage largely anticipates *MT, De'ot,* 3:1. However, it also criticizes excessive munificence; cf. *MT, Arakhin* 8:13.

51. There is of course no question about practices such as *dina debar mezia* (i.e., "the law of the abutter") that were instituted by Hazal on the basis of the principle of "the right and the good;" see *Baba Mezia* 108. The question concerns situations that have not been singled out for rabbinic prescription.

52. *Baba Mezia* 83a. The citations are from Prov. 2:20.

53. *P.T., Baba Mezia* 6:6

54. However, Rashi, *ad loc.,* does use the term.

55. *Pesakim, Baba Mezia* 2:7.

56. This view was advanced by the author of the *Mordecai, Baba Mezra,* sec. 327, who cites his predecessors, the Ravan and the Ravya as support, but it is usually associated with the latter and cited in his name by *Hagahot Maimuniyot, Hilkhot Gezela,* 11:3. The Ravya's original text is no longer extant, however. The reference to the Ravan is presumably to *Sefer Ravan* (ed. Ehrenreich), II: 198, but that passage, while it unequivocally states that the finder, in the case in question, is fully obligated to return the lost object, says nothing about juridic coercion. Perhaps the *Mordecai* drew upon another, more explicit source. See also Z. Y. Meltzer, *"Lifnim Mishurath Hadin,"* in *Mizkeret: In Memory of Rabbi I. H. Herzog* (Jerusalem, 1962), pp. 310–15.

57. *Kiddushin* 21b.

58. *Ketubot* 103a. For an analysis of this *halakha,* see my *"Leverur kofin al midat Sodom,"* in *Hagut Ivrit Be'Amerika,* ed. M. Zohori et al. (Tel Aviv, 1972), Vol. 1, pp. 362–82.

59. *Abot* 5:10

60. *Netivot Olam, "Netiv Gemilut Hasadim,"* chap. 5.

61. See *Baba Mezia* 24b.

62. Quoted in *Mordecai, Baba Mezia,* sec. 327.

63. See *Ketzot Ha-Hoshen,* 290:3.

64. See *Tosafot, Yebamot* 100a, s.v. *ma'aser* and Maimonides, *Matnot Aniyim,* 1:8.

65. The *halakha* in question concerns criteria for assignment of priorities

among various prospective purchasers, none of whom is an abutter. In such cases, Maimonides states that while "this, too, is included within the good and the right," the priority is not enforceable, "for the Rabbis only commanded regarding this by way of *hasidut*, and it is a virtuous soul which acts thus" (*Shekhenim*, 14:5).

66. Lev. 19:2.

67. *Yebamot* 20a.

68. I know of no satisfactory English equivalent for this term. It suggests a blend of spiritual elevation and refinement with scrupulousness and pietism. Perhaps "saintliness" comes closest, though more in the Jamesian than in the popular sense, of total selflessness or other-worldiness; but that too, has too ethereal a ring.

69. *Shekhenim* 14:5. The concluding talmudic quotation is from *Avoda Zara* 34a, the verse from Cant. 1:3.

70. Exod. 15:26.

71. *Beshalah, Massekhta D'Vayissa,* i (ed. Horowitz-Rabin), pp. 157–58; see also the notes there.

72. This is pointed up by the fact that Nahmanides (Exod. 15:26) quotes Rabbi Eleazar's statement and yet, in the same passage, refers the reader to his subsequent discussions of "the right and the good."

NACHUM L. RABINOVITCH

Halakha and Other Systems of Ethics:
Attitudes and Interactions

DISCUSSIONS ON INTERACTIONS between different ethical systems are often beclouded by a habit of thought residual from earlier times when morality was identified with a particular religious basis. Thus today avowed secularists sometimes speak of *Morality,* with a capital M, having in mind some "natural morality" (as if such exists) by the standards of which all systems of religion, law or ethics are to be judged. After the sustained efforts of many thinkers, it is now widely accepted that no natural morality adequate to the needs of man and society can be unequivocally defined. Simple honesty requires that we who are Torah-loyal Jews state openly that our commitment is to the supernatural foundations of belief, in order that one may identify where these assumptions affect our conclusions. Simple prudence demands that as clear-minded investigators we acknowledge no claims of a so-called natural morality, so that we need not find ourselves confronted by spurious challenges. It is well therefore at the outset to define several terms that are essential to our analysis.

DEFINITIONS

An[1] *ethical theory* sets forth principles: (1) to systematize rules for behavior, which is then described as moral or ethical; (2) to justify these rules in the light of basic truths about man, the world, and God; (3) to promote understanding; and (4) to stimulate ethical behavior.

A *moral code* is a set of prescriptions and rules to guide behavior in specified circumstances.

Subsuming and underpinning a *moral code* is an *ethical theory*. It is conceivable that different ethical theories may correspond to the same *moral code*.

It is important to point out that any system that satisfies the definition of a *moral code* is not ipso facto worthy of approval. In fact, in terms of these definitions the term "moral" as applied to a code, does not imply a value judgment at all. The same applies to the usage of "ethical" in ethical theory. From the vantage point of some particular ethical theory with its characteristic definitions of *good* (and *evil*), some moral codes will be judged better than others, but obviously no two ethical theories need agree on such a judgment.

I

Halakha is a moral code, and the Torah makes known only a few of the most basic postulates about ultimate reality that constitute the framework of the ethical theory associated with it. This cannot be otherwise since it is impossible to formulate explicitly all the necessary assumptions about the nature of man, the character of human societies, the laws (if any) of history and nature, the relation of man to God, and the nature and attributes of God. Some of these are being progressively discovered, but all of them are certainly not known now. Moreover it is possible that adequate understanding of all of them will never be attained for it may very well be beyond the capacity of human intelligence. This leaves the field open for constructing partial and schematic conjectural ethical theories to serve as background for the given moral code that is the Halakha.

Now, no moral code can possibly be complete in the sense that it prescribes a suitable response in every conceivable circumstance. By its nature it treats of particulars or of usual and common situations. The same is true of Halakha as well, and so corresponding to different partial ethical theories, different extensions of the moral code to situations not covered will be developed.

It should be noted as well that in a historicist view, which is certainly not foreign to Torah, man and society are not static and unchangeable;[2] rather some truths about human nature, for example, must be seen as time-bound and consequently ethical theories involving such postulates as well as some aspects of the moral code dependent upon them must be seen as evolving constantly. Such an approach is certainly applicable to gaps in the halakhic code or areas for which only the most general guidance is offered.

This position is perhaps best summed up in the following passage:

> Our perfect Torah sets forth general principles for the cultivation of human virtue and for [ethical] behavior in the world, in the statement: "Holy shall you be. . . ." This means, as the Rabbis said, "Sanctify yourself in what is permitted"—that one should not be drawn after lusts. Similarly the Torah says: "You shall do that which is right and good" meaning that one should deal well and uprightly with men. It was not appropriate in all this to command details, for the commandments of the Torah are obligatory for every period and all time and in every circumstance, but the virtues of man and his conduct vary according to the time and the people. The sages of blessed memory specified some useful particulars included under these principles, some of which they made binding law and others only rules recommended before the fact, but not binding or actionable after the fact, still other rules for those who seek the way of special piety.[3]

It is clear then that in at least two respects the Halakha is open-ended, so to speak. On the one hand, individual responsibility is the bulwark of the Torah life. That is so even where the law is precisely prescribed; for although there are circumstances where the law must be imposed by outside authority, these are severely limited and ideally would be eliminated.

91

There are, moreover, important areas where, as we shall see, the individual conscience, fashioned and motivated by the life and values of *mitzvot,* is charged to decide for itself which is the right way. On the other hand, in the life of the community and the society as a whole, social, economic, technological, and other innovations and changes open up new scope for legislation to accomplish "that which is right and good."

II

The Rabbis see all of reality in terms of polarities. Thus they conceive the universe as being itself produced by the interaction of forces and serving as the arena for the creative interplay between opposed principles. *Rahamim* (love) and *Din* (justice) are the poles around which all of existence crystallizes, and the very act of Genesis, which brought being out of nonbeing, is the visible effect of the tension between *Rahamim* and *Din.* A midrashic parable illustrates this theme frequently encountered in the rabbinic literature.

A king had empty cups; said the king, "If I put hot water into them they will burst, if cold they will crack." What did the king do? He mixed hot water with cold, filled them and they stood. So said the Holy One Blessed be He, "If I create the world with the Rule of Love its sins will be great, with the Rule of Justice—the world cannot endure; I shall then create it with the Rule of Justice and the Rule of Love, and would that it endure!"[4]

In different contexts, the terminology varies. Thus *Din* is sometimes *Gevura* and *Rahamim* is called *Hesed.* Moreover the dialectics of *Din* and *Rahamim* were conceived of as of such all-embracing character that every fundamental antithesis was seen as but another manifestation of the counterpoint between Justice and Love. Under the influence of Aristotelian usage, *Gevura* and *Hesed* became identified with matter and form: *Gevura,* the principle of being—the substratum of existence, the ever present through all change, yet unchangeable—or in

92

another formulation, the passive or female element—passivity that in its constancy contains all things within itself; *Hesed,* the principle of action, or male element, forever reaching out, seemingly of no substance, yet imparting substance to all things and realization to every potential, endowing matter with meaning and significance, the power of love which in self-effacement submerges itself in its object and thus impregnates with the divine spark of life.

The Torah is the model of the world. We are told:

> The Torah is likened to two paths—one through fire and one through snow. If one turns towards this one he dies by fire; if one turns towards the other he dies by snow. What shall one do? Let him go in the middle.[5]

Thus Maimonides explains that the Torah's code of behavior represents the middle way, which if a man follows he will suffer neither burn nor frostbite.[6]

Yet, the "mean" may be a tenuous one for by its very nature, it must in many circumstances represent a compromise between the demands of love on the one hand and justice on the other. Under more trying conditions it may require a choice between alternatives all of which are guilt laden. It is evident that if love bids one act one way and justice another, even where the choice between them or a third alternative is prescribed by the Halakha, it is only on the level of behavior that the dilemma is resolved; so far as motivation is concerned there is no escape from the paradox. Yet the motives for our actions are inevitably involved in determining their ethical character. In fact, the Rabbis see motives as the characteristic determinant of virtue. Interestingly enough, Maimonides singles out as examples David and Elijah, who displayed harshness and anger, albeit in righteous causes, to show how lack of love results in loss of virtue even though in practice the exigencies of justice leave no room for choice.[7] It is not surprising therefore that the Halakha itself recognizes the suspension of the usual halakhic criteria in those instances where conflict on the motivational level is acute.

The archetype is our father Abraham. So boundless is his love for man that he rebels against accepting the divine decree against the wicked cities of Sodom and its allies. Scripture says, "Abraham approached,"[8] and Midrash comments: "R. Elazar explained thus, 'For war—I come; for conciliation—I come; for prayer—I come.' "[9] Abraham does not shrink from war, as it were, against the Almighty, and driven by love he hurls an accusation against "the Judge of all the earth."

The question reappears in various guises. In order to save lives, is every action justified? Based on talmudic remarks about Esther and Yael,[10] Rabbi Joseph Colon saw it as permissible for a woman to surrender to or even arouse the adulterous lust of bandits in order to save the lives of their captives.[11] More recently Rabbi Ezekiel Landau demurred.[12] The same question is discussed in our own time by Rabbi Yehiel Weinberg.[13] All the authorities agree that in extreme cases, there is no prescribed course of action, and the woman's own conscience must be her guide, for only she can determine what her true motives are. Not only an overwhelming challenge of love can suspend the usual norms. The same applies to the stern demands of justice. "Said R. Elazar ben Yaakov: I have heard that [the court] may inflict penalties which are not prescribed in the Torah."[14] After transcribing this ruling, Maimonides adds a warning: "All these things are according as the judge sees that this one [the accused] is culpable and the circumstances require it. In everything, his deeds must be for the sake of Heaven, and let not the dignity of men be light in his eyes."[15]

Lest one allow oneself too much freedom in taking liberties with established judicial procedure he concludes, "It is the glory of the Torah only to act in accordance with its statutes and ordinances."

III

It is only in cases of overriding urgency that the individual is given the liberty to probe his own motives and act as he sees fit regardless of the usual rules. Nonetheless even when the stakes are not nearly so high, the Rabbis recognized, at least, ex post facto, the justification for illegal deeds stemming from pure motives.

> Said Rabba bar Hanna in the name of R. Yohanan: What is it that is written: For the ways of the Lord are upright—the righteous walk in them and sinners stumble in them. . . . It is analogous to Lot and his daughters. They—whose intention was for good [mitzva]—the righteous walk in them. He—whose intention was to sin—sinners stumble in them.[16]

A general conclusion from this discussion is: "Great is a transgression for the sake of [God]." In fact the discussion turns on the point whether it is superior to a mitzva without proper intent or whether they are equal, but all are agreed that intent is no less significant than realization.[17]

The Halakha sets up a hierarchy of norms, enabling decisions to be taken in some cases of conflict. However, as we have seen, this is not a complete ordering in the sense that some pairs of conflicting values are equally weighted and consequently halakhic decision rules do not always apply. Moreover, even where a comparative scheme exists and a certain course of action is indicated, the scale is not univalent since intent and motivation can at least cancel out the priority.

This is true not only in considering actions (according to the usage of W. D. Ross)[18] as units consisting of an act together with a motive. Even with reference to acts alone, that is, behavior unrelated to intent, there are instances where the clash of commandments is unresolved and the individual is free to apply extra-halakhic desiderata to determine what is right.

There is a considerable body of halakhic opinion that the imperative "You shall not stand by the blood of your neighbour"[19] is accorded equal status with that of self-preservation, so that one is free to choose to sacrifice his own life to save another's, although it is not required by the law. The individual's own ordering of the priorities will of course imply a subjective scale

95

of values that the Halakha accepts as valid though not universally so.

IV

The permanent needs of society for a legal system that is characterized both by continuity in time and universality in scope imposes a requirement for considerable standardization and uniformity of practice in most areas. Nonetheless, every individual must see it as a challenge to himself to study the Halakha, to know it and understand it, to acquire its patterns of thought, and to be sensitized to its values and thus enable himself to make his own decisions. Thus "Mar Zutra explained in the name of Rav Hisda: Whosoever studies Scripture and Mishna, diagnoses a *terefa* for himself and engages in halakhic analysis, concerning him it is written: 'If you eat the labor of your hands, happy are you'[20]—in this world 'and it be good with you'—in the world to come."[21] The biblical reference is explained by Maharsha (ad loc.) as follows:

> "Happy is one who fears God," that is, if a case of doubtful *terefa* occurs and he fears God and is strict with himself and refrains from eating it he shall be happy in the world to come . . . but "if you eat the labour of your hands" is a higher degree. That is, one who exerts himself to resolve the doubt, finds it permitted, and then eats it, earns for himself a double reward as it is written, "*happy are you*"—*in this world,* for he eats of it, "*and it be good with you*"—*in the world to come* for he exerted himself in Torah.

The crucial point is that though no one is born with the right to make his own halakhic decisions, every one is duty bound to acquire that right by diligent study of Torah. The resolution of the Halakha as a dialectical process is not one that necessarily takes place always at a particular level of authority, and there is much room for individual judgement rather than mere obedience.

96

In this connection, the following statement of Maharal, although not a ruling, gives us an insight into what I am trying to convey:

It is more fitting and more correct that one should determine the law for himself directly on the basis of the Talmud, even though there is a danger that he will not follow the true path and not decide the law as it should be in truth. Notwithstanding, the sage has only to consider what his intellect apprehends and understands from the Talmud and if his understanding and wisdom misleads him, he is nevertheless beloved by the Lord when he decides in accordance with his mind's dictates . . . and he is superior to one who rules from a later prepared code without knowing the reasons which are the ground of the decision. Such a one walks like a blind man on the way.[22]

To my knowledge, nobody else puts it quite that sharply, nor that strongly, but it is not really an unique view that everyone ought to study the sources, analyze the various opinions, and reach his own conclusions rather than merely submit to authority. The process of halakhic decision is not meant to release us from the struggle of conscience or the toil of the intellect that must be involved in any decision if it is to be a worthwhile spiritual experience. If every decision, every act of choice, is to be laden with meaning it must be the outcome of a process in which all the forces of the soul are involved, not only the overcoming of temptation important though that is in itself.

Obviously, in many cases there are purely technical procedures for resolving legal issues and these leave little room for individual variation. That is essential for the orderly development of society. But even with all that there are still situations, such as we have noted, where the ultimate decision must be the individual's alone, taken in the privacy and loneliness of his own conscience, where the immediacy and ethical awareness of the demands of love or justice are such that only the individual himself can confront the storms within his heart and determine which demand shall prevail.

V

We turn now to the sphere of public law prescribed and administered by due authority. Because of the profound change in the status of the Jewish people that took place in our time—because of the hiatus of almost two thousand years in the development of the Halakha as applied to whole areas of national life—there is a tremendous need for new laws, and our generation is faced by an awesome challenge. The need for new law will, of course, be filled. It is being filled every day. The legislation of the Israeli Knesset already fills quite a few volumes and will continue to grow. There is, however, a real danger that unless in our time we succeed in recapturing the all-embracing character of the Halakha, of endowing with halakhic validity at least some significant parts of the legislation that today is made by the Knesset, the nature of the Jewish people as the people of the Torah will be distorted if not completely erased. What distinguished us throughout our existence was precisely the fact that we were the bearers of the Halakha, that we built what was essentially a voluntaristic society imposing on ourselves the disciplines of the Halakha as set forth and developed through the generations.

For much of our historical career in the Diaspora we had to live with a truncated Halakha. Today, most of these areas are being filled. If they are filled with non-halakhic legislation we may find ouselves not only with a truncated Halakha but with a truncated Jewish people. On the other hand, the practical necessities of our time are such that it is not conceivable to provide that legislation other than through the instrumentality of, as it has been called, *Medinat Hahok* rather than *Medinat ha-Halakha*. The need to overcome this confrontation, to resolve this paradox, is, I think, the crucial need of our time.

VI

"You shall observe and do, for it is your wisdom and your understanding in the eyes of the nations. For they will hear these ordinances and will say, 'Surely this great people is a wise nation and understanding. . . . What people is there so great that it has righteous ordinances and judgments like the whole of this Torah which I put before you today.' "[23]

That the nations can recognize the superiority of the Torah's moral code implies that its validity is unimpaired (at least to a great extent) even in the absence of some of the specifically Jewish postulates about God underlying it. Presumably for the nations other postulates suffice to validate the code. It would then have the status of a nomos in the sense described by Maimonides.

> A Law the whole end of which and the whole purpose of the chief thereof, who determined the actions required by it, are directed exclusively toward the ordering of the society and of its circumstances and the abolition in it of injustice and oppression . . . the arrangement, in whatever way this may be brought about, of the circumstances of the people in their relations with one another and provision for their obtaining in the opinion of that chief, a certain something deemed to be happiness—you must know that Law is a nomos.[24]

The Torah provides the ultimate grounds of obligation. "Holy shall you be, for holy am I, the Lord your God."[25] It gives not only understanding within the limited framework of a particular human society, rather it "desires to make man wise . . . so that he should know the whole of that which exists in its true form."[26] However, as we have seen, where the Halakha is undefined, a nomos may be admitted, and even where the Halakha is explicit, the functional value of a nomos is recognised to the extent that in practice it yields identical guidance.

The radically different and rapidly changing social and economic conditions of our time leave wide areas of life for which Halakha is undefined. Indeed, it is remarkable that in much of *dinei mamonot* (i.e., civil law) as presented in the Talmud and the codes, there is relatively little law derived from explicit

99

scriptural passages, rather much that is deduced from principles of equity that are more or less universally acknowledged. To fill the lacunae in the Halakha, to cover the vast new needs of commerce, social legislation, economic planning, international relations, and so forth, ethical directives based on halakhic principles of justice can be formulated, which might just as well be propounded as nomos. To take just one example, there is ample precedent for the practice of incorporating various commercial rules of non-Jewish provenance into the corpus of Halakha. The generally recognized norms of commerce are sanctioned by Torah law because they serve a vital purpose in regulating an important area of activity, provided only that they do not conflict with other halakhic provisions and are adjudged by Torah authorities to advance desirable ends.

From our point of view, such a code imbedded in the Halakha acquires greater significance by virtue of its becoming part of a total system. Thus to use our example from the field of commerce, many a *Din Torah* (i.e., a hearing in a rabbinic court) that takes place today in Israel (and it goes without saying, in the Diaspora) involves careful consideration of much non-Jewish legislation that is inextricably implicit in the definition of the various contracts, undertakings, and so forth. In Israel, as in other lands, new legislation in these areas is frequently promulgated. While this legislation must be taken into account by the rabbinic courts, under present conditions halakhic authorities do not contribute to framing it at all. Yet, it ought to be possible for Halakhists to take a more active part in proposing needed legislation imbued with the Torah's spirit that would be acceptable also to the nonreligious elements in Israel.

Perhaps, a more urgent subject is that of traffic laws. Israel has earned a tragic distinction for carnage on the roads. There is an imperative need for research leading to legislation on highway construction, traffic control, automobile safety standards, and related matters. This ought to be a major priority for religious Jews and this is certainly an area where joint efforts with other sections of the community could be highly successful. On a pragmatic level, the task of formulating such a code gives an opportunity for cooperation with circles who are not yet prepared to accept the authority of Torah, but for whom ethical considerations are important.

Concern with moral standards that leads to moral action is regarded by the Halakha as virtuous in its own right. For even where there is no acknowledgement of the divine sanction, contemplation and observances of the Torah's moral code is itself beneficial.

> Said R. Hiya bar Ba: "They have forsaken Me," for this I would forgive them. Have they "Kept My Torah?" For if they forsook Me and kept my Torah, the leaven in it would draw them near to Me.[27]

The state of Judaism in our time is such that although large segments of our people have little interest in God, many of these same people are deeply committed to ethical norms. Whether this devotion is a vestigial influence from the past or whether its roots are in contemporary experience is immaterial. To secure the unity of our people and to renew its loyalty to the covenant, a promising approach is through a common ethic within the framework of Torah.

Even though we find that for practical pragmatic reasons the Halakha cannot yet be given total jurisdiction for all Jews, we must strive to cooperate with them and reach agreement with them at least in partial areas where common concerns and shared conceptions of righteousness prevail. Our faith in *Netzah Israel* must be such that if we can make a little progress at a time, the day will come when the Torah will fill our lives completely.

1. On these definitions compare, Abraham Edel, *Science and the Structure of Ethics* (Chicago, 1969), pp. 7–10.

2. See, e.g., Maimonides, *Guide of the Perplexed,* III:29 and III:32.

3. *Maggid Mishneh* to *Shekhenim,* 14:3.

4. *Bereshit Rabbah*, 12.
5. P.T. *Hagigah*, 2:1.
6. Maimonides, *Shemonah Perakim*, chap. 4.
7. Ibid., chap. 7.
8. Gen. 18:23.
9. *Bereshit Rabbah*, 49.
10. *Sanhedrin*, 74b.
11. *Responsa Maharik*, 137.
12. *Noda be-Yehuda*, Tinyana, 161.
13. *Seridei Esh*, v. 3, sec. 109.
14. *Sanhedrin*, 46a; P.T. *Hagigah*, 2:2.
15. M.T., *Sanhedrin*, 24:10.
16. *Horayot*, 10b; cf., *Nazir*, 23a.
17. Cf., Abraham I. Kook, *Mishpat Kohen*, sec. 143 (end).
18. W.D. Ross, *Foundations of Ethics* (Oxford, 1939), p. 115.
19. Lev. 19:16. Of the considerable literature on the subject, see *Baba Mezia*, 62a, the controversy between Rabbi Akiba and ben-Petura; Kook, *Mishpat Kohen*, sec. 143, and sec. 144, pt. 15, 16; Malbim to Lev. 19:18; *Pithei Teshuva* to Y.D., 252:6.
20. Ps. 128:2.
21. *Hullin*, 44b.
22. Maharal, *Netivot Olam: Netiv ha-Torah*, 15.
23. Deut. 4:6.
24. Maimonides, *Guide of the Perplexed*, II:40.
25. Lev. 19:2.
26. Maimonides, *Guide of the Perplexed*, II:40.
27. P.T. *Hagigah*, 1:7.

JAKOB J. PETUCHOWSKI

The Limits of Self-Sacrifice

WE ARE LIVING IN AN AGE WHEN JEWS, as individuals and as a community, are the recipients of all kinds of demands that, in the name of a "higher goal," call for various degrees of Jewish self-abnegation and self-sacrifice. The reintroduction of the quota system in American universities, favoring the Blacks and discriminating against the Jews, is one illustration of this. Advice proffered the state of Israel by assorted New Leftists and Third Worldists on what Israel's borders should look like is another. A third, again with immediate reference to the Jewish situation in the United States, has to do with various schemes of integrating previously mainly Jewish neighborhoods. And then there is the compulsory busing of school children to make sure of racially balanced schools—with all that this implies in terms of increased violence and lower academic standards; the ever increasing rates of taxation to pay ever higher compensation to so-called welfare cases; the urging of Jews—with or without the threat of violence—to abandon their businesses in Black neighborhoods, at considerable loss to themselves; and so on and so forth.

I

Now, it is quite clear that, in all of the above instances, we are dealing with conflicts of interests—not exactly a totally unprecedented situation. There is a Jewish interest, and there are various other interests—Black, New Left, Third World, and others—that want to establish themselves at the expense of the Jews. This clash of interests could conceivably be fought out in the political arena, before the courts of justice, or—if we bear in mind both the Black militant groups and the Jewish Defense League—even in more violent forms.

What adds a certain piquancy to the present situation is the fact that there are *Jews* who have become champions of all of the causes that threaten the Jewish interest. Moreover, not all of those Jews are assimilationists or self-hating Jews, although many of them undoubtedly are. Indeed, some of the Jews who speak on behalf of the Blacks, of the New Left, and of the Third World, actually claim to be speaking in the name of Judaism! They invoke the so-called prophetic heritage of Judaism when they call upon Jews to renounce voluntarily whatever it is that stands in the way of the fulfillment of revolutionary goals. Nor can it be said that those radical voices have altogether failed to evoke sympathetic echoes within the ranks of the Establishment itself. The public postures of such organizations as the Union of American Hebrew Congregations and the American Jewish Congress, to name only two, are cases in point.

Now, we can understand that some of this yielding to the demands of the anti-Establishment forces is due to a sincere desire to prevent today's Jewish youth from falling away from Judaism altogether. If radical Jewish youth can be shown that Judaism itself is in favor of radicalism, then, so it is hoped, this youth will find ways and means of combining the espousal of radical causes with a proud affirmation of Jewish identity. Whether or not that strategem will work, is, of course, another question again. What is of immediate concern to us in the present context is whether there is indeed any legitimacy to the claim that it is Israel's prophetic heritage itself that bids the Jew to embark on a course of action leading to self-abnegation and self-sacrifice.

Although there is ample evidence to show that the ancient

Hebrew Prophets were striving for a just order of society, there is no evidence whatsoever that they laid down a concrete and detailed blueprint of how exactly such a just order of society is to come into existence, and how it is to be administered. In fact, judging by what the Prophets themselves had to say about their own impact upon their contemporaries, what is now called Prophetic Religion seems to have been pretty much confined to the Prophets and the immediate circles of their disciples. On the other hand, the fact that we today are able to speak of prophetic religion at all is due to the endeavor of the sages and the Rabbis who collected, canonized, and preserved the writings of the Prophets—those self-same sages and rabbis, that is to say, who were not only the canonizers of the prophetic writings, but also the master builders of Halakha. If, therefore, the Prophets really were the apostles of socialism and the spokesmen of political radicalism, then we would have a right to expect the Halakha to reflect this radicalism and this socialism. The question is: Does the Halakha do so?

A number of points immediately force themselves on our attention.

1. Until very modern times, the dominant mood was not one of political radicalism in those Jewish communities which, for some two thousand years, governed their affairs according to the Halakha. On the contrary, when, at the turn of the century, some Russian Jewish youths began to rebel against their parental structure of society, they rebelled not only against their fathers' economics but also against their fathers' religion.

2. Throughout our millennial literature, until the nineteenth century, we hear nothing about a prophetic religion as something other than, and distinct from, the very Torah and Halakha by which every aspect of Jewish life was regulated.

3. It is the nineteenth century that introduced the topic of prophetic religion into the discussion. At a certain stage in the evolution of Reform Judaism, when the belief in revelation was still maintained even though the binding character of the so-called ceremonial law was denied, the reformers shifted the em-

phasis from the Pentateuch to the Prophets. Ceremonies and rituals were said to be conditioned by temporal and environmental factors. But the religious and moral teachings of the Prophets had eternal validity. On the basis of this assumption, the reformers began to look upon themselves as adherents of prophetic Judaism, or prophetic religion—a hypothetical construct that to this day has not disappeared from Reform Jewish rhetoric.

4. Not to be left out of consideration are the polemical and apologetical elements in the modern Christian-Jewish dialogue. In fact, for the purpose of our present investigation, the tacit and implicit refrain of "everything-you-can-do-I-can-do-better," which marked the mutual assessments of Judaism and Christianity at the end of the last century and in the first quarter of the present century, may well be of paramount importance. Until the modern period, the Christian attacks on Judaism were primarily theological and exegetical in nature. As the Christian saw it, the Jews were "blinded" to certain biblical truths and historical events. It was the task of the Christian polemical literature to open the eyes of the Jews to those truths and events. But it did not occur to the Christian to judge Jewish teachings and practice by yardsticks extrinsic to the religious enterprise, as, for example, by the standards of aesthetics or of a nonrevealed morality. This, however, was to change radically when spokesmen of modern Protestantism, who had themselves given up such traditional Christian dogmas as the Jews always rejected (e.g., the Virgin Birth, the Incarnation, the Resurrection, and so forth), were seeking to ground their Christianity not in the literal truth of the New Testament narratives but in the putative moral and ethical superiority of Christianity over Judaism. The darker, therefore, the Jewish background of the New Testament could be painted, the brighter the light of Christianity would shine. This was basically the approach of Harnack's *Das Wesen des Christentums,* first published in 1900.

What was the Jewish reaction to this type of Christian claim?

It took various forms. Leo Baeck's *Das Wesen des Judentums,* first published in 1905, was a Jewish reply to Harnack. Baeck demonstrated that Judaism was not at all what Harnack had pictured it to have been; that, in fact, when it came to Judaism's universalism and ethical teachings, it had no need to shun any comparison with other religious systems. Similarly, Jacob Z. Lauterbach, writing on "The Ethics of the Halakah," in 1913,[1] keeps harping on the theme that, so far from marking a deterioration from the high ethical level of prophetic religion, Pharisaic-Rabbinic Judaism was, in fact, the practical implementation of prophetic idealism. The essay was written in conscious and explicit opposition to those Christian critics who would see the further development of prophetic religion in the New Testament, but who would deny any similar development in the teachings of the Rabbis. Judaism, then, is not as bad as the Christian critics claim. Judaism is not inferior to Christianity!

Not too many Jewish writers dared to assert that Jewish ethics was actually *superior* to Christian ethics. But Elijah Benamozegh (1822–1900) did, in his *Morale Juive et Morale Chrétienne* (1867).[2]

Ahad Ha'Am, too, in his famous essay, *'Al Shté Hase'ippim,*[3] accepts the distinction made—mainly by Christian writers—between Jewish and Christian ethics, as well as the notion that the former is dominated by justice, and the latter by love. But Ahad Ha'Am refuses to see in this any inferiority of the Jewish approach. On the contrary! Says Ahad Ha'Am:

Christianity seeks to turn straightforward egoism into inverted egoism; for the "altruism" of the Gospels is nothing but an inverted "egoism." It strips man of his *objective* moral worth, as it pertains to himself, and makes him the means for a subjective aim. But, whereas, "egoism" makes the "other" into a means for the advantage of the "self," "altruism" makes the "self " into a means for the advantage of the "other."

Judaism, however, removes from morality the subjective relationship, and establishes it on an *abstract objective* basis: on *absolute justice* which sees man as a substantial moral value, without distinction between the "self " and the "other.". . . .

. . . Just as I have no right to destroy the life of the "other" for the sake of the life of the "self," so I have no right to destroy the life of the "self " for the sake of the life of the "other."[4]

At this point, Ahad Ha'Am introduces into the discussion the famous *baraitha,* expounding the meaning of Lev. 25:36 ("that thy brother may live with thee"), to which we shall now address ourselves.

II

"That thy brother may live with thee." That is what Ben-Patura expounded: Two men are journeying through the desert, and one of them has a single pitcher of water. If one of them drinks it, he (alone) will get back to civilization. But if both of them drink it, both of them will die. Ben Patura taught that they should both drink and die, as it is said: *"That thy brother may live* with thee." Said Rabbi Akiba to him: "That thy brother may *live with thee."* Your own life comes before the life of your fellow-man.[5]

It is in this passage that Ahad Ha'Am sees an exemplification of Jewish ethics—contradistinction to Christianity, which calls upon the individual to sacrifice himself for others.

Within recent years, Ahad Ha'Am's claim has been repeatedly challenged by Louis Jacobs—first, in his book, *Jewish Values,*[6] then in a lecture he gave before the London Jewish Students' Association, in October 1961,[7] which, in turn, gave rise to an extended literary feud between Jacobs and the late Sir Leon Simon,[8] and, finally, in his book, *Principles of the Jewish Faith.*[9] In addition, in a private letter, dated 15 December 1971, Louis Jacobs has furnished me with additional data about recorded instances of Jewish martyrdom. And it is, in fact, the history of Jewish martyrdom that is Jacobs's principal argument against Ahad Ha'Am's thesis. Surely, there have always been Jews ready and willing to give their life for others! Therefore, according to Jacobs, when Jesus is quoted as saying "Greater love has no man than this, that a man lay down his life for his friends" (John 15:13), "he was not preaching Christianity but quoting Judaism."[10] Jacobs even expresses doubts as to whether the ultimate halakhic decision follows Rabbi Akiba rather than Ben-Patura.[11]

As against Jacobs, the late Sir Leon Simon argued that "the quotations from rabbinic literature . . . no doubt show that there were sages who held that in certain circumstances it would be a Jew's duty to sacrifice his life for another individual (there is, of course, no record of any difference of opinion as to his duty to lay down his life for the community or the nation in time of need); but they show no more than that."[12]

Jacobs countered that he never suggested that it was a *duty* for a man to give his life for his friend. "My contention is that if circumstances are such that the man with the water believes his neighbour's life to be of greater value (i.e., where he is single and his neighbour has a wife and family), Judaism would not frown upon his sacrifice . . . , but look upon it as an act of special piety."[13]

To this, Sir Leon Simon replied that "it is not only in its set doctrines or dogmas that Christianity differs from Judaism. There are also differences, not less important, of approach, of tone, of emphasis, which it does not require rabbinic learning to discover; and it is in the light of differences of that order that 'greater love etc.,' in my opinion fails most conspicuously to qualify for a place on the Jewish side of the borderline."[14]

(We may note in passing that, at this stage, in case of both Louis Jacobs and Leon Simon, the discussion has shifted from the realm of halakhic requirements to that of "special piety" and differences in "approach, tone, and emphasis.")

It was left to Raphael Loewe to write the last letter in that correspondence, in the columns of the London *Jewish Chronicle*. "Halacha," he opined, "may, indeed, often be infused with idealism, and on the whole it presupposes a relatively high degree of self-denial in those who, as Jews, acknowledge its authority over them; but its development has been governed by a common-sense appreciation of what may, and what may not, be realistically expected of the average Jewish man and woman, and this has preserved it from utopian idealism when framing its requirements, recommendations, or encouragements as to how to meet a given situation." In the light of this, Loewe observes, "it is hardly surprising if 'greater love etc.' is at home within a Christian ethical scheme but cannot so obviously be authenticated within Halacha."[15]

What emerges, then, from this whole discussion may be summarized as follows.

1. Although Louis Jacobs argues that "greater love etc." is an authentic Jewish teaching, Simon and Loewe—without actually denying that such a teaching could conceivably be accommodated within the Jewish scheme of things—do question its centrality in Judaism and the possibility of proving it halakhically.

2. Neither Simon nor Loewe, nor, in the final analysis, Jacobs himself, can find a single halakhic provision that—apart from the exceptional cases of avoiding the sins of idolatry, murder, and sexual immorality at the cost of one's life, or of laying down one's life for the sake of the Torah, the nation or the country—would make it *mandatory* for Jews to sacrifice their lives for the benefit of others.

The foregoing discussion, therefore, particularly as crystallized in Loewe's formulation of the common-sense character of the Halakha, leads us to a further investigation into what, in rabbinic literature, may be considered as halakhically binding, and what, on the other hand, may be nothing more than a form of ethical idealism, left to the pietistic inclinations of the individual.

110

III

Such a distinction obviously exists in the minds of the Rabbis themselves. Take, for example, the rather telling discussion in b. *Gittin* 90a. Rav Mesharsheya asks Rava a halakhic question: "What is the law (*mahu*) in the case where a man has made up his mind to divorce his wife, but she still lives with him and ministers to him?" Rava, instead of giving an answer based on the Pentateuch—as would be required for purposes of dealing satisfactorily with a halakhic question—replies, instead, with a verse from Proverbs: "Devise not evil against thy neighbor, seeing that he dwelleth securely with thee" (3:29). In other words, in the case under discussion, there cannot, strictly speaking, be a halakhic answer. But there can be a *moral* answer. Morality can reach higher than the Halakha can. But the Halakha, as obligatory law, represents the realm of the possible, of that which can actually be achieved by ordinary mortals.

Basically, this is the tendency of the whole tractate of *Gittin*. The Rabbis do not *like* divorce, and they claim that God does not like it either. In fact, He is said to hate it. The Rabbis quote Mal. 2:13f. (again, a *non*-Pentateuchal passage!) as their value judgment on divorce.[16] Nevertheless, ample provision is made for divorce proceedings in cases where divorce is called for in actual and concrete life situations.

(By way of contrast, we may note that the Roman Catholic Church, obliterating the distinction between ideal and reality, actually *legislated* the ideal morality, making divorce impossible for the believers—and creating much anguish and suffering as well as illicit unions. In observant Jewish circles, on the other hand, where recourse could be had to divorce when needed, divorce, until fairly recent times, was not a very common phenomenon.)

There is, then, in rabbinic Judaism, the repeatedly expressed recognition that what the law provides does not exhaust the

111

moral ideal. Those who wish to go beyond what the law requires, *lifnim mishurat hadin,* are free to do so—within the limits we shall discuss further on. But, by definition, what is *lifnim mishurat hadin* is not itself the *shurat hadin* by which the majority is expected to abide. And, certainly, the very special degree of individual piety, the *middat ḥasidut,* is just that; it is *not* the universally accepted Halakha.

Justice Moshe Silberg discusses three fundamental quasi-legal concepts that play a part in talmudic law; and he lists them in descending order, that is from the more legal to the less legal. They are: (a) the application of Deut. 6:18, "Thou shalt do what is right and good in the eyes of the Lord"; (b) *lifnim mishurat hadin;* and (c) that which displeases (or pleases) the sages, or—its equivalent—*middat ḥasidut.*[17]

It may well be, by the way, as Claude G. Montefiore has pointed out, that, when Jesus told his disciples that their righteousness would have to exceed the righteousness of the scribes and Pharisees (Matt. 5:20), he was trying to inculcate in his disciples the principle of *lifnim mishurat hadin.*[18] But it is also important to bear in mind that, in two thousand years of Christianity, there has never been a Christian state that has based its *legal system* on the "Sermon on the Mount." There *have,* however, been many *Jewish* societies that governed all of their affairs by the rules of the Halakha.

IV

In the realm of Aggada, one can find everything. Typical of the extreme lengths to which Aggada may go is the comment made by Rav Huna in the name of Rabbi Joseph, in connection with Eccles. 3:15 ("And God seeketh that which is pursued"). We may paraphrase the comment as: "God sides with the underdog." This, according to Rav Huna, applies in the case where a righteous man pursues a righteous man, in the case where a wicked man pursues a righteous man, in the case where a wicked man pursues a wicked man, and even in the case where a righteous man pursues a wicked man![19]

112

Now, this may be a comforting thought when you are the pursued man. But the fact that God sides with the underdog was very obviously not meant as a rule of life by which people were to guide their actions. Certainly, the Halakha would advise one course of action when you see the righteous pursued by the wicked; and quite a different course of action when you see the wicked pursued by the righteous!

We have chosen this extreme example to underline the obvious: that it just will not do to make a collection of choice aggadic statements, and then to adduce them as evidence that Judaism advocates this or that course of action, or supports this or that political philosophy. This is not to deny that, on occasion, an aggadic ideal may crystallize into Halakha, just as, on another occasion, a halakha may give birth to a new aggadic vision. But it is meant to assert that an aggadic vision, in and by itself, does not imply its acceptance as Halakha.

Moreover, there are definite tendencies in the realm of Halakha that actually *limit* the lengths to which a man is allowed to go in the practical pursuit of his altruistic vision.

R.Elai said: They ordained at Usha that, if a man spends liberally on charity, he must not spend more than a fifth (of his possessions), lest he himself become dependent upon his fellow-men.[20]

Let it not be argued that this was an emergency measure passed by the Synod of Usha in times of unusual upheaval! Maimonides did not regard it as such. He codified it as Halakha, noting that spending one-tenth of one's possessions on the support of the poor was "average," and less than one-tenth, "miserly." But the maximum limit, given by Maimonides, and called by him, *mitzvah min hamuvhar,* was one-fifth.[21] One wonders what a Maimonides would have said about the kind of punitive taxation, increasingly common in the modern welfare state, that aims at impoverishing the rich while enriching the poor.

But let us return to the passage in b. *Kethubhoth* 50a. After

113

Rabbi Elai's statement has been recorded, the Gemara goes on to say:

It once happened that a man wanted to spend more than a fifth; but his friend would not let him do so.
Who was it? Rabbi Yeshebab.
Others say that Rabbi Yeshebab (was the man who wanted to spend more than a fifth), and that the friend who did not let him do it was Rabbi Akiba.

If the "others who say" have preserved the correct tradition, then we would have a very striking illustration of Rabbi Akiba's consistent position. The same Rabbi Akiba who, in the *baraitha* with which we began, had argued against sharing the pitcher of water, because "your own life comes before the life of your fellow-man," is here on record as opposing Rabbi Yeshebab's overly excessive charitable impulse, which, of necessity, would make Rabbi Yeshebab himself ultimately dependent upon the charity of others! Moreover, Rabbi Akiba's position on this issue (if Akiba was the friend who prevented Rabbi Yeshebab from giving more than a fifth) would also show that the principle enunciated in the debate with ben-Patura was not to be confined to the *in extremis* situations, where life itself was at stake, but also was to determine one's economic policies.

Again, a very clear-cut case of "taking care of your own," instead of following the impulse of an excessive altruism or universalism, is provided by the interpretation that Rabbi Joseph gave to Exod. 22:24 ("If thou lend money to any of My people that is poor by thee"):

[If the choice is between] "My people" and a non-Jew, "My people" has preference; between a poor man and a rich man, the poor man has preference; between the poor members of your family and the other poor people of your town, the poor members of your own family have preference; between the poor of your own town and the poor of another town, the poor of your own town have preference.[22]

114

Thus Rabbi Joseph; and thus the codified Halakha according to Maimonides.[23]

An even more striking illustration is the following passage from the Tosefta:

> If townspeople have a well [and it is a question] whether they or strangers [have first call on it], they come first, before the strangers.
>
> [If it is a question] whether strangers or their own cattle come first, the lives of the strangers take precedence over their own cattle. Rabbi Yosé says, their own cattle takes precedence over the lives of the strangers.
>
> [If it is a question] whether their own cattle or the cattle of strangers comes first, their own cattle takes precedence over the cattle of strangers.
>
> [If it is a question] whether strangers or their own laundry comes first, the lives of the strangers take precedence over their own laundry. Rabbi Yosé says, their own laundry takes precedence over the lives of the strangers. [This, the Gemara, which quotes this passage, explains, is due to the health hazards involved in not laundering one's clothes.]
>
> [If it is a question] whether their own laundry or the laundry of strangers comes first, their own laundry takes precedence.[24]

V

The *tendenz* is becoming clear. Even the principles of *lifnim mishurat hadin* and *middat hasidut* have their halakhic limits. Those principles do not apply to all conceivable circumstances. And the limits are inspired by the consideration that Rabbi Akiba adduced in his discussion with ben-Patura: "Your own life comes before the life of your fellow-man!" This consideration applies not only to the situation where life itself is at stake. It even applies to such relatively "minor" matters of economics like limiting the support one gives to the poor or the priorities in the distribution of one's charity. Nor does it apply only to the individual. It also protects the self-interest of the community.

115

There are, of course, exceptions, as in the various instances enumerated by Louis Jacobs. But they are *exceptions,* and they apply to unusual circumstances. Martyrdom is *kiddush hashem;* but plain suicide is a sin.

Anyone who advocates self-sacrifice, or the voluntary sacrificing of legitimate Jewish (individual or corporate) interests, as a philosophy and policy for Jewish life today, had better make quite sure beforehand that the self-sacrifice he is advocating (for *others,* and not just for himself!) truly represents a *kiddush hashem,* and not simply the kind of suicide that is bereft of meaning and significance. Admittedly, there may be occasions when the line between them is hard to discern. It probably never was easy to draw that line. But this much can be said: that, in the past, the Jewish people have always manifested a healthy instinct for survival. Its consciousness of a mission to mankind has never involved any self-abnegating readiness for its own disappearance.

Veḥai aḥikha 'immakh, our brothers, our fellowmen are to live *with us.* For that to be possible, we ourselves must be around. And, therefore, "our own life comes before the life of our fellowmen."

We may have to remind ourselves of this again today.

POSTSCRIPT

A number of points that emerged from the discussion of this paper at the session on 12 July 1972 may help to clarify some of the major thrusts intended by this presentation.

1. It was, in part, the purpose of this paper to demonstrate—in the face of a great deal of contemporary rhetoric—what prophetic religion, as understood by halakhic Judaism, is *not.* We did not intend to imply that the Jew whose political orientation is to the left of ours could not be a good Jew. Nor did we wish to convey the impression that an individual Jew, *qua* individual, could not demonstrate a superior selflessness by giving up his *individual* (!) rights and self-interest. (Although there do seem to be some halakhic limitations to the distance that one is

allowed to go here.) What primarily matters to us within the present context is simply that such individual acts of supererogation are just that, and cannot be made the norm for the behavior of a whole Jewish community. To the extent, therefore, to which Halakha is normative, the Halakha cannot be adduced to justify—let alone to demand—the abrogation of Jewish self-interest.

2. Dr. Uriel Simon, therefore, in his contribution to the discussion, was quite right in insisting that there is a canon of prophetic literature that exists quite independently, that is, without the interpretations that the rabbinic sages have placed upon the texts. But what has guided Jewish life for the last two thousand years is not what the individual Jew has found in the written text, but, rather, what the Halakha has legislated on the basis of *its* understanding of that text. The prophetic canon, therefore, in its pristine and rabbinically unencumbered purity may—and should—continue to serve as a source of inspiration; and it may—and should—constitute a yardstick for man's aspirations. But, again, those aspirations are not, as such, a matter of legislation, of Halakha. That is not to say that halakhic legislation has not been informed by an awareness of prophetic idealism. It certainly has! Indeed, that is precisely why, in our paper, we have argued that the only kind of prophetic religion we Jews have known historically was the prophetic religion embodied in the halakhic tradition. But just because of that relationship between prophetic religion and Halakha, it is, at best, a matter of superior piety (*middat ḥasidut*) if an individual Jew wants to go beyond the halakhic requirements in his political and economic life. It cannot be mandatory (Halakha) for the totality of Jews.

3. We can thus agree with Rabbi Walter Wurzburger's assertion that the Halakha does not oppose the various programs that go into the making of the modern welfare state. Certainly, the Halakha does not oppose them. But—and this is the main point we have tried to make—the Halakha does not *demand* them, either; and the Halakha does set limits for those who are willing to espouse them.

1. Reprinted in Jacob Z. Lauterbach, *Rabbinic Essays* (Cincinnati, 1951), pp. 259-96.

2. Translated into English, and published as *Jewish and Christian Ethics* (San Francisco, 1873).

3. *Kol Kitvé Ahad Ha'Am,* 5th ed. (Tel-Aviv, 1956), pp. 370-77.

4. Ibid., p. 373.

5. *Sifra, Behar, parashah* 5:3 (ed. Weiss), p. 109c; and note variants in b. *Baba Metzi'a* 62a.

6. Louis Jacobs, *Jewish Values* (London, 1960), pp. 125ff.

7. Cf. *The Jewish Chronicle* (London), 27 October 1961, p. 11.

8. *The Jewish Chronicle,* 3 November 1961, p. 56; 24 November 1961, p. 29; 1 December 1961, p. 24; 8 December 1961, p. 22.

9. Louis Jacobs, *Principles of the Jewish Faith* (New York, 1964), p. 27.

10. *Jewish Values,* p. 128; *Jewish Chronicle,* 27 October 1961, p. 11.

11. *Jewish Values,* pp. 132f. But see, *contra* Jacobs, the invocation by the *Tosafot* (ad b. *Nedarim* 80b, s.v. *ma'yan*) of Akiba's position in order to account for the ruling in the case of the priorities in the use to be made of the water in a well belonging to townspeople. The case itself will be discussed below.

12. *Jewish Chronicle,* 24 November 1961, p. 29.

13. *Jewish Chronicle,* 1 December 1961, p. 24.

14. *Jewish Chronicle,* 8 December 1961, p. 22.

15. *Jewish Chronicle,* 15 December 1961, p. 20.

16. B. *Gittin* 90b.

17. Moshe Silberg, *Kakh Darko shel Talmud* (Jerusalem, 1961), pp. 97-133.

18. Claude G. Montefiore, *Rabbinic Literature and Gospel Teachings,* 2d ed. (New York, 1970), pp. 191f.

19. *Leviticus Rabbah* 27:5.

20. B. *Kethubhoth* 50a.

21. *Maimonides, Yad, Hilkhoth Mathnoth 'Aniyyim* 7:5.

22. B. *Baba Metzi'a* 71a. I am indebted to Professor David Halivni for drawing my attention to the tannaitic source of this passage: *Mekhilta, Neziqin,* chap. 19 (ed. Horovitz-Rabin), p. 315.

23. *Maimonides, Yad, Hilkhoth Mathnoth 'Aniyyim,* 7:13.

24. *Tosefta Baba Metzi'a* 11:33-36 (ed. Zuckermandel), p. 397. The passage is quoted in p. *Nedarim,* chap. 11 (ed. Krotoshin), p. 42c, and in b. *Nedarim* 80b. I am grateful to Dr. Nachum L. Rabinovitch for pointing out, in the course of the discussion on this paper, that there was such a passage as this—all the more so because Dr. Rabinovitch does not associate himself with the present-day sociopolitical implications that I derive from those sources.

Part Three

THE PHILOSOPHICAL BASIS

EMMANUEL LEVINAS

Ideology and Idealism

CONTEMPORARY THOUGHT IS the thought of the nations among whom we live, even in Israel, which I do not view as a new ghetto or as a country separated from the world like those that in France are called "underdeveloped." Contemporary thought is the thought of a human society that is undergoing global industrial development, a fact that should not be treated lightly. Contemporary thought stands at a very great distance from the world of the Halakha and from many problems that have been under consideration at the meeting of the Institute for Judaism and Contemporary Thought.

I

NOTE: The present text of this essay is based on a combination of the Hebrew version, the shorter French version, and the longer French version. The shorter French version was presented to the Societé de Philosophie of Fribourg, Switzerland, in June 1972. The Hebrew version, under the title, "Ethics as Transcendence and Contemporary Thought," was presented at the Summer Institute on Judaism and Contemporary Thought at Nir Etzion, Israel, in July 1972. The paper was also presented at a public conference under the auspices of the Katholieke Theologische Hogeschool of Amsterdam, in November 1972.

The translation was done by Arthur Lesley with the assistance of Sanford Ames, both members of the faculty of the Ohio State University. The editor wishes to acknowledge the devotion and skill of the translators, who managed the almost impossible task of rendering into English the highly specialized and intricate language of Professor Levinas.

Contemporary thought does not know Joseph, or at least pretends not to know. Is there a bridge between the ethics of the Jewish people and contemporary thought, or between this thought and Jewish ethics? Do they have a common language? This question must be answered, but to do so we must begin from another point. We must speak, first of all, not of the relation between ethics and Halakha, but rather of the passage from the nonethical in general to the ethical, for this is truly the necessity of our time. This question must be answered on behalf of that Jewish youth which has forgotten the Holocaust, and which sees in the rejection of all morality an end to violence, an end to repression by all forms of authority. We must answer a youth that sees in the particularism of Judaism, in the world of the commandments and of true Jewish distinctiveness, only support for an anachronism, for a world that is passing away. For us, who live in the Diaspora that extends even to Israel, there is a special problem of Judaism. The problem of Judaism is the problem of opening a way to Judaism that will show it to those who being blinded are now outside. I speak of those who, unlike the wicked men of Sodom, are knocking at the gate and seeking to enter; and even those who are not yet seeking entrance.

The assimilation of these young people who stand outside and do not hear us as we deliberate within the framework of Halakha (would that we were truly considering Halakha!), this form of assimilation in our time has a new motive that distinguishes it from that which was common a hundred years ago. Our young people today no longer assimilate for the sake of an easier life in the contemporary world. They take on the burden of participating in the building of a new world, a world that is difficult to build and to sustain.

So we turn to our topic, which seems to be metaphysics. Is this laudable or shameful? But all metaphysics in Europe is now both laudable and shameful. We are deep into the end of metaphysics, and at the end of metaphysics we are all occupied with it.

II

Ideology and Morality

Ideology pretends to be science, while the very admission of its concept leaves morality suspect. The least suspicion of ideology delivers to morality the most severe blow it has ever sustained. This suspicion probably signals the end of traditional ethics, and, in any case, overthrows the theory of duty and of value.

Morality understood as an ensemble of rules of conduct based upon the universality of a set of maxims, or upon a hierarchical system of values, contains its own rational justification within itself. It has its own kind of evidence and is apprehended in an intentional act analogous to knowing. Like the categorical imperative, axiology belongs to Logos. The relativity of morality in relation to history, its variation and variants according to social and economic structures, do not basically compromise this rationality. We may correctly interpret historical situations and social conditions as determining the subjective conditions under which we have accession to the moral Logos; they may also determine the time necessary for this accession. These are variable conditions of insight that does not fall full-blown from heaven, and that knows periods of obscurity. The relativism to which the experience of these conditions might seem to invite is mitigated in proportion as historical evolution is understood as the manifestation of Reason itself, as a progressive rationalization of the subject toward the absolute of a reason becoming free act or efficacious, practical reason.

In modern thought, at least in Western Europe, the morality that was understood as an actualization of rational understanding received a nearly fatal blow from the concept of ideology. The concept of ideology, which was Hegelian in origin, and which is used in the Marxist critique of bourgeois humanism, received much of its persuasive force from Nietzsche and Freud. This is the novelty of this concept: that the appearance of rationality could be more insinuating and more resistant than a paralogism, and that its powers of mystification could be so hidden that the art of logic would not be adequate for demystification, that proceeding from an unconscious intention, the mystification mystifies the mystifiers!

It is, however, permissible to think that the strange notion of a *suspect reason* did not arise in a mode of philosophical discourse that simply allowed itself to lapse into suspicions instead of furnishing proofs.[1] The notion of a suspect reason forced itself upon us in the "spreading desert," in the increasing spiritual misery of the industrial era. It is a notion that finds its meaning in agonized groaning, or in a cry denouncing a scandal to which Reason—that Reason which is capable of considering as ordered a world in which the poor man is sold for a pair of sandals[2]—would remain insensitive if there were not this cry.[3] A prophetic cry, scarcely discourse; a voice that cries out in the wilderness; the rebellion of Marx and some Marxists, beyond Marxist science! A meaning that is rent as a cry, which is not stifled by the system that absorbs it, where it does not cease to echo a voice other than that which bears coherent discourse. It is not always true that not-to-philosophize is still to philosophize. The forcefulness of the break with ethics does not evidence a mere slackening of reason, but rather a questioning of the validity of *philosophizing,* which cannot lapse again into philosophy. But what a strange reversal! On account of its historical relativity, on account of its normative aspects that are called repressive, ethics becomes the first victim of the struggle against ideology that it inspired. It loses its status as reason for the precarious condition of Ruse. It passes for an unconscious effort, but one susceptible of becoming conscious and, from then on, courageous or cowardly, in order to fool others, those faithful to it, or those who preach it. Its rationality, henceforth merely apparent, is a stratagem in the war of class against class, or a refuge for the frustrated, a bundle of illusions dominated by the class interests or by the needs of compensation.

Ideology and Disinterestedness

That ideology—like Reason in the transcendental dialectic of Kant—could be a *necessary* source of illusions is probably a still more recent view. If one were to believe Althusser, ideology always expresses the fashion in which consciousness experiences its dependence on the objective or material conditions that determine it, conditions that scientific reason grasps in their objectivity. One necessarily wonders if that does not, at the same time, teach us about a certain eccentricity of consciousness with regard to the order controlled by science and to which science, to be sure, belongs, a dislocation of the subject, a yawning gap, "play" (*un "jeu"*) between it and being.

If illusion is the modality of this play, it does not render illusory this play, this gap, this exile, or this ontological "homelessness" of consciousness. Could this gap be simply the effect of the incompleteness of science, which, as it completed itself would gnaw away to the quick of the subject, the ultimate vocation of which would be only service of the truth and which, with science perfected, would lose its reason for being? But then this indefinite postponement of the perfection of science would itself signify the separation of the subject from being. Science would then have put ideology back in its place, and deprived it of the pretension of being a truthful kind of knowledge and of directing effective action. Meanwhile, this gap between the subject and being appears again in the possibility that the subject will forget the knowledge that would have returned it to the rank of a psychological factor to be modified by praxis, like any other factor of the real. The achievement of the perfection of science would not, however, have prevented this ideology, henceforth inoffensive, from continuing to assure the permanence of a subjective life that lives upon its own demystified illusions. In such a life, one commits follies under the nose of science, one eats and distracts oneself, one has ambitions and esthetic tastes, one weeps and is indignant, all the while forgetting the certainty of death and all the physics, psychology, and sociology that, behind life's back, govern this life. The separation of the subject

125

and reality, which is affirmed by ideology, would thus tend either to this completion of science that is always postponed, or to this forgetfulness of science that is always possible.

But does this separation come from the subject? Does it come from a becoming that is filled with concern for its *being* and for its persevering in being? Does it come from an interiority cloaked in the fixity of character, from a singularity reveling in its exception, solicitous of its own happiness—or its own health, having its private doubts, even in the heart of the universality of truth? Is it the subject himself who will have hollowed out an empty space for ideology between himself and being? Does not this empty space come from a previous break with the illusions and the ruses that filled it, from an interruption of essence, from a nonplace, from a utopia, from a pure interval of the *epoche*[4] opened by *disinterestedness*? Science would not yet have had either consoling dreams to interrupt, nor megalomania to restore to reason; it would only have found the necessary distance for its impartiality and objectivity. Ideology would thus have been the symptom or sign of a dismissal of charges by which the objectivity of science would refrain from taking sides. How can one decide between the terms of the alternative? Perhaps another moment of the modern spirit and a more complete analysis of disinterestedness will suggest the direction of the option to choose.

Science Interrupted

Modern epistemology pays little attention to this unconditioned condition, this necessity for extracting oneself from being in order to situate oneself, as subject, upon an absolute, or utopian, ground, on terrain that makes disinterestedness possible. Epistemology even distrusts this disinterestedness. In its eyes every step away from reality favors ideology. The conditions for rationality are all henceforth on the side of knowledge itself and of the technical activity that results from it. A kind of neo-scientism and neo-positivism dominates Western thought. It extends to the disciplines that have man for their object of study; it extends to ideologies themselves, dismantling their

126

mechanisms and disengaging their structures. The mathematical formalization practiced by structuralism constitutes the objectivity of the new method, which is consistent to the extreme. Never, in the new science of man, will value serve as a basis for intelligibility. It is precisely in this new science that the great Lie would be concealed: impulse or instinct, a mechanical phenomenon objectively discernible in man gives, by its spontaneity, the illusion of being the subject and, by its extent, the appearance of a goal; the end is made to pass for a value, and the impulse, henceforth decked out as practical reason, is guided by a value promoted to the rank of a universal principle. What a drama! We would do well to recall Spinoza, the great demolisher of ideologies (though still ignorant of their name), and of knowledge of the first kind: it is the desirable that is valuable, not the valuable that arouses desires [Cf. Spinoza, *Ethics*, II, Prop. 40, Scholium II where he introduces that which he calls "knowledge of the first kind, opinion, or imagination." He goes on in Prop. 41 to assert that, "knowledge of the first kind is the only source of falsity." Ed.].

In the ambiguity of desire, which still allows itself to be understood, either as provoked by the value of its goal or as founding value by the movement that animates it, only the second term of the alternative is maintained. That is where the death of God began. It ended in our time in the subordination of axiology to desires, understood as impulses that arrange themselves according to certain formulas in the "desiring machines" that men become. The new theory of knowledge no longer grants any transcendental role to human subjectivity. The subject's activity of knowing is interpreted as a roundabout way by which the various structures to which reality is reducible show themselves and are made into a balanced system. What was formerly called the effort of a creative intelligence would thus be only an objective event in the intelligible itself and, in a certain respect, a set of purely logical connections. According to structuralism, and contrary to Kantian teaching, true reason has no interests. Thus, theoretical reason is absolutely supreme.

127

Contemporary thought thus moves in a being without human traces, where subjectivity has lost its place in the middle of a mental landscape that one may compare to that which presented itself to the first astronauts who set foot on the moon, where the earth itself appeared as a dehumanized star. Enchanting sights, never before seen! Deja vu—now, on to the next trip! Discoveries from which pounds of stones composed of the same chemical elements as our terrestrial minerals are carried away. Perhaps they will answer questions that, until then seemed insoluble to the specialists; perhaps they will enlarge the horizons of particular problems. They will not erase the imaginary line that, of course, is no longer the meeting of heaven and earth, but that marks the boundary of the same. In the infinity of the cosmos presented to the travels of the cosmonaut or space-walker, man finds himself shut in without being able to set foot outside.

Has science produced the beyond-being disclosing the whole of being? Has it given itself the place (or the nonplace) necessary for its own birth, for the maintenance of its objective spirit? The question is open. The superhuman adventure of the astronauts, to treat it as a parable, will certainly at some particular moment surpass all the knowledge that made it possible. This occurred when the ancient biblical verses were recited by Armstrong and Collins. Perhaps this *ideological* recitation expressed only the silliness of petit-bourgeois Americans, who were unworthy of their own courage, and also the infinite resources of rhetoric. This is rhetoric in the platonic sense, which according to *Gorgias* flatters the listeners and which "is to the judicial art what cooking is to medicine" (465c); a rhetoric felt in all the fullness of its ideological essence, as "an image of a kind of political art" (463d). Such is rhetoric according to the *Phaedrus,* a force of linguistic illusion, independent of any flattery and of any interest: "not only in connection with judicial debates, nor in connection with all those of the popular assembly . . . but . . . in connection with any use of speech . . . one will in the same way make anything resemble anything else" (261d–e). Such is the rhetoric that applies, not to speech that seeks to win a case or a position, but rhetoric that eats away the very substance of speech, precisely insofar as it "functions in the absence of all truth." Is this not already the possibility of signification that is reducible to a game of signs detached from meanings? From now on, we face an ideology more desolate than all ideology, one that no science could rehabilitate without running the risk of being bogged down in the very unproductive game that it sought to break up. This threatening ideology hides in the core of the Logos itself. Plato is confident that he can escape it by means of good rhetoric, but he soon hears within discourse the simian imitation of discourse.

In the parable of interstellar travel, however, there is also the silliness attributed to Gagarin; his statement that he did not find God in heaven. To take this seriously, we may hear in it a very important assertion: the new condition of existence in the weightlessness of a space "without place" is still experienced by the first man sent there as a *here*, as the *same*, without genuine *otherness*. The marvels of technology do not open up the beyond where science, their mother, was born. In spite of all these movements, there is no outside here! What immanence! What a wretched infinite! Hegel expresses it with remarkable precision: "something becomes an Other, but this Other is itself a Something, therefore it likewise becomes an Other, and soon *ad infinitum*. This infinity is the specious or negative, infinity, insofar as it is nothing but the suppression of the finite which, however, is reborn again, and is, consequently, never completely suppressed."[5]

The evil infinity originates in a thought incompletely thought out, a thought only of the intellect. But thought from beyond the intellect is necessary for the understanding itself. Does not a break with Essence become apparent in the objectively modern mind?

The Other Man

What, then is ("objectively" manifest in modern times) this movement and this life, neither illusory ideology nor yet science, by which being appears as a dislocation, in the guise of subjectivity or of the humanity of the subject? Does not the visible face of this *ontologic interruption,* this epoche, coincide with the movement "for a better society?" The modern world is even more shaken by this—shaken to the very depths of its religious sensibilities—than by the denunciation of ideologies, although, this movement, like Harpagon crying, "Stop, thief!" is quick to suspect itself of ideology. To demand justice for the other man, is this not to return to morality? Indisputably, to the very core of morality. But the invincible concern for the other man in his destitution and in his lack of resources, in his nakedness, in his station or lack of station, as proletarian, this concern escapes the doubtful finality of ideologies. The seeking out of the other man, however, distant, is already a relationship with this other man, a relation in all its directness, which is already proximity. How tautological it is to speak of "drawing nigh to the neighbor" (*l'approche du prochaine*)! What occurs in this case is something other than the complacency with ideas that suit the particularism and interests of a group. In that relationship with another man (who, in the nakedness of his face, as a proletarian, has no homeland) there emerges a transcendence, an exit from being, and, thus, impartiality itself, by which both science in its objectivity and humanity, as the "I," become possible. Like the demand for scientific rigor, like the opposition to ideology, rebellion against an unjust society expresses the spirit of our age.[6] That spirit is expressed by rebellion against an unjust society. Even if in its injustice it is stable, ruled by law, submissive to a power and forming an order, a state, a city, a country, or a professional organization; a rebellion for another society, but a rebellion that begins where the other society is satisfied to leave off; a rebellion against injustice that begins once order begins; a new tonality, a tonality of youth, within the old Western progressism. As if it were a matter of a system of justice that accused itself of being senile and decrepit as soon as there were institutions to protect it; as if, in spite of all recourse to doctrine and to political, social, and economic sciences, in spite of all references to reason and to techniques of revolution, man had sought within revolution to the extent that it is disorder or permanent revolution, a breaking of frameworks, an obliteration of ranks, liberating man, like death, entirely, from everything and from the whole; as if the other man were sought—or approached—in an otherness where no administration could ever reach him; as if through justice a dimension opened up in the other man, that bureaucracy, even if it were of revolutionary origin, would block because of the very universality of the dimension, and by the admission in this new dimension, of the singularity of others that the notion of universality implies; as if in the guise of a relation with others denuded of all essence—with an *other,* thus irreducible to the individual of a species, and to an individual of humankind—the beyond of essence would open up an idealism of disinterestedness, in the strongest sense of the term, in the sense of a suspension of essence. The economic deprivation of the proletarian—to be sure, his condition as one who is exploited—constitutes this absolute stripping of the other as other, the de-formation to *formlessness,* beyond the simple changing of form. Is this idealism suspect of being ideological? We see here, however, a movement, so little ideological, so unlike the repose in an acquired situation, so unlike self-satisfaction, that it is the putting into question of the self, positing oneself from the start as "de-posed," as for the other. Such a placing in question signifies not a fall into nothingness but a responsibility for the other, a responsibility that is not assumed as a power but responsibility to which I am exposed from the start, like a hostage; responsibility that signifies, in the end, to the very foundation of my position in myself, my substitution for others. To transcend being through disinterestedness! Such a transcendence comes *under the species* of an approach to the neighbor without hesitation, even substitution for him!

131

Western thought does not learn of idealism behind ideology only from the century's youth movements. Plato sets forth a *beyond* of institutional justice, like that of the dead judging the dead (*Gorgias* 523e), as if the justice of the living could not pass beyond the clothing of men, that is, could not penetrate the attributes that in others, offer themselves to knowing, to knowledge, as if that justice could not pass beyond the qualities that mask men; as if the justice of the living judging the living could not strip the judges of their nature, which they always have in common with those qualities that hide the judges; as if justice could not, consequently, come near people who were not people of rank and, in the proximity to others, reach out towards the absolutely other. In the myth of the *Gorgias*, Zeus, with extreme precision, accuses the "last judgment," which he intends to reform in the spirit worthy of a god, of remaining a tribunal where "fully dressed" men are judged by men equally fully dressed, by judges who "have placed in front of their own souls a veil made of their eyes and ears and their whole bodies." A veil made entirely of eyes and ears! Essential point: dressed up, others lack unity.

In the social community, the community of clothed beings, the privileges of rank obstruct justice. The intuitive faculties, in which the whole body participates, are exactly what obstructs the view and separates like a screen the plasticity of the perceived, obscures the otherness of the other, the otherness precisely because of which the other is not an object under our control but a neighbor.

We must note that for Plato a relation may be possible between the one and the other, though they are "dead to the world,"[7] and lack, as a result, a shared order; that a relation might be possible without a common ground, that is to say, a relationship in difference; that the difference signifies a nonindifference; that this nonindifference might be developed by Plato as ultimate justice, and here, with all the approximations of myth, there is expressed in the *essence* of being an eccentricity, a dis-inter-*estedness*. It comes under the species of

132

relation with others, under the species of the humanity of man; beyond essence, dis-inter-estedness; but as just judgment, not at all a nothingness. Ethics is not superimposed on essence as a second layer where an ideological gaze would hide, incapable of looking the real in the face. The commandment of the absolute, as Castelli states in a different context, is not "in the system of a possible ideology" and, with regard to the rationality of knowledge, it "constitutes a disorder." The signification—each for the other—ethics, and the breaking of essence are the end of the illusions of its appearance. Plato speaks of a judgment bearing finally on merit. Would this merit be some real attribute underneath the apparent qualities, some preexisting attribute, which judgment could not do without, introducing in turn others by way of concepts and lacking any way of escape? Or, going from oneself to others, as if each of us were dead, the last judgment, is this not the manner in which a being puts himself in the place of another, contrary to any perseverance in being, to all *conatus essendi,* to all knowledge that receives from others only concepts?[8] And what can be the meaning of the movement to put oneself in another's place, if not literally drawing nigh to the neighbor (*l'approche du prochain*)?

The Other as the Other Man

One may be surprised by the radicalism of an affirmation in which the breaking of the essence of being, irreducible to ideology, has meaning as responsibility for the other man approached in the nakedness of his visage, in his noncondition of proletarian, always "losing his place," where the beyond of being has meaning as my disinterestedness, that of a dead man who expects nothing from a dead man. It is not difficult to see that the *for* in the "for-the-other" of my responsibility for the other is not the *for* of finality; not difficult to see that the *for-the-other* of the one who is exposed to others without defense or covering, in an incessant disquiet of not being open enough, in the anxiety of being "encapsulated in oneself," is an opening of

133

the self, a disquiet to the point of denucleation. We shall not take up this theme again; it has frequently been developed elsewhere. This absolute "otherness" of the "beyond the being" . (set forth by Plato and Plotinus), against the irrupturable identity of the Same, whose ontological stubbornness is incarnate, or comes to a head in Ego, would be produced nowhere if not in the substitution for another.

Nothing, in fact, is absolutely other in the Being served by knowing, in which variety turns into monotony. Is that not the thought of Prov. 14:13: "Even in laughter the heart acheth; and the end of mirth is heaviness." The contemporary world, scientific, technical, and sensual, is seen to be without issue, that is to say, without God, not because everything is permitted and is possible by means of technology, but because everything is the same. The unknown immediately becomes familiar, the new, habitual. Nothing is new under the sun. The crisis described in Ecclesiastes is not of sin, but of boredom. Everything is absorbed, sunk, buried in sameness. In the enchantment of places, the hyperbole of metaphysical concepts, the artifice of art, the exaltation of ceremony, the magic of rites—everywhere one suspects and denounces theatricality, transcendence that is purely rhetorical, games. "Vanity of vanities": the echo of our own voices, taken as answer to the few prayers that still remain with us; everywhere landing back on our own feet, as after the ecstasy of some drug. Except for others, whom, with all this boredom, one cannot drop.

The otherness of the absolutely other is not just some quiddity. Insofar as it is a quiddity, it exists on a plane it has in common with the quiddities that it cuts across. The notions of old and new, understood as qualities, are not adequate for the notion of the absolutely other. Absolute *difference* cannot itself delineate the plane common to those that are different. The other, absolutely other, is the Other (*L'autre, absolument autre, c'est Autrui*). The Other is not a particular case, a species of otherness, but the original exception to order. It is not because the Other is novelty that it "gives room" for a relation of transcendence. It is because the responsibility for the Other is transcendence that there can be something new under the sun.

My responsibility for the other man, the paradoxical, contradictory responsibility for a foreign liberty—extending, according to the Talmud (*Sotah* 37b), even to responsibility for his responsibility—does not originate in a vow to respect the universality of a principle, nor in a moral imperative. It is the exceptional relation in which the Same can be concerned with the Other, without the Other's being assimilated to the Same, the relation in which one can recognize the inspiration, in the strict sense of the term, to bestow spirit upon man. What does it matter? At the heart of the rhetoric of all our enthusiasms, in the responsibility for others, comes a meaning from which no eloquence, not even poetry, can distract, a rupture of the Same without resumption by the Same of its sameness without aging, novelty, transcendence. All in all, it can be expressed in ethical terms. The crisis of meaning, which is evident in the dissemination of verbal signs that the signified no longer dominates (for it would only be illusion and ideological deception), is opposed by the meaning that is prior to the "sayings," which spurns words and is unimpeachable in the nudity of its visage, which is felt in the proletarian destitution of another and in the offense he suffers. This is what the talmudic sages (who already knew a world in which language had corroded the meanings it was supposed to bear) probably had in mind when they spoke of a world in which prayers cannot penetrate to heaven, because all the heavenly gates are closed except those through which the tears of the sufferers may pass.[9]

That the Other as other is not an intelligible form bound to other forms in the process of an intentional "unveiling," but is, rather, a visage, proletarian nakedness, destitution; that the Other is others; that the departure from the self is the approach to the neighbor; that transcendence is proximity, that proximity is responsibility for the Other, substitution for the Other, expiation for the Other; condition—noncondition—of serving as hostage; that responsibility, as response, is the prior speaking;

135

that transcendence is communication, implying, beyond a simple exchange of signs, the "gift," "the open house"—these are some ethical terms through which transcendence has meaning, in the guise of humanity, or of ecstasy as disinterestedness. Idealism confronts Science and Ideology.

In the discussion that followed the presentation of this paper by Professor Levinas a number of questions were raised. What follows is Professor Levinas's response, translated from Hebrew.

1. In my opinion, the problem of God is related to the problem of the Other. Divinity is not met as a great Other, as "the absolute Thou" of Buber. It has within itself a sign of the Other, but the meaning of this sign is complete and requires philosophical analysis. One must be very careful here! The passage from the Other to divinity is a second step, and one must be careful to avoid stumbling by taking too large a step.

2. The philosophic status of the meaning of the word, "God," as best understood by the religious, by believers, has never been clarified properly, so that it is very difficult to establish any identity of what the believer understands with what the philosopher defines. I am not sure that one has the right to speak of "divinity," rather than saying always, "God." I am not sure that it is possible to distinguish between the property and the name. When God is spoken of as a being that is the Supreme Being, a superlative is mentioned whose meaning does not have its source in Being, and is surely dependent on what Plato understood as "beyond Being." "Beyond Being"—is this the Sinaitic revelation? I heard in this discussion the arguments of those who have the merit and the good fortune to stand at Mount Sinai. No philosopher (qua philosopher) has ever stood there. I shall not respond to the complaints of those people who do not understand why I need the ultimate Other to approach God. For them there are no problems at all, as is well known.

3. I shall respond to the serious and fundamental question of Professor Petuchowski who asks why I pass from ethics to di-

136

vinity. Is morality possible without God? I answer with a question: is divinity possible without relation to a human Other? Is such a thing possible in Judaism? Consider Jeremiah, Chapter 22, or Isa. 58:7: "to bring to your house the poor who are outcast." The direct encounter with God, *this* is a Christian concept. As Jews, we are always a threesome: I and you and the Third who is in our midst. And only as a Third does He reveal Himself.

4. Is my discourse deficient in concern with concrete reality? Does all this metaphysics of mine have the ability to solve actual ethical problems? I have no ambition to be a preacher. I am neither a preacher nor the son of a preacher, and it is not my purpose to moralize or to improve the conduct of our generation. It is likely, in any case, that sermons have no power to raise the level of morals. I have been speaking about that which stands behind practical morality; about the extraordinary relation between a man and his neighbor, a relation that continues to exist even when it is severely damaged. Of course we have the power to relate outselves to the other as to an object, to oppress and exploit him; nevertheless the relation to the other, as a relation of responsibility, cannot be totally suppressed, even when it takes the form of politics or warfare. Here it is impossible to free myself by saying, "It's not my concern." There is no choice, for it is always and inescapably my concern. This is a unique "no choice," one that is not slavery.

Finally, I have never said that we must be satisfied with "It doesn't concern me." Indeed, if there were only two of us in the world, I and one other, there would be no problem. The other would be completely my responsibility. But in the real world there are many others. When others enter, each of them external to myself, problems arise. Who is closest to me? Who is the Other? Perhaps something has already occurred between them. We must investigate carefully. Legal justice is required. There is need for a state.

But it is very important to know whether the state, society, law, and power are required because man is a beast to his neighbor (*homo homini lupus*) or because I am responsible for

137

my fellow. It is very important to know whether the political order defines man's responsibility or merely restricts his bestiality. It is very important, even if the conclusion is that all of us exist for the sake of the state, the society, the law.

1. The following lines are an attempt to respond to the stringent critique that Claude Bruaire makes of the idea of suspicion.

2. Cf. Amos 2:6.

3. It is just in this way that Plato's denunciation of rhetoric presupposes the moral scandal of Socrates' condemnation.

4. We owe to a remark of Professor Filiasi Carcano the connection with the Husserlian step from the transcendental reduction that evokes the term, "epoche." The exception to being that we call disinterestedness will have (as will be seen further on) an ethical meaning. Ethics would thus be the possibility of a movement as radical as transcendental reduction.

5. *The Logic of Hegel* from the *Encyclopedia of the Philosophical Sciences,* trans. William Wallace (London, 1904), secs. 93, 94, p. 174. We have adjusted the Wallace translation slightly to conform to the French version which Levinas used [Ed.].

6. It expresses the spirit of the age or, perhaps, already caricatures it. This strange destiny of revelation in a caricature deserves separate consideration. But the caricature is itself a revelation from which a meaning must be extracted; a meaning that requires correction, but which cannot be ignored or disregarded with impunity.

7. In talmudic literature, the burial of a human corpse, to which no one nearby is attending, is called "mercy of truth" (*hesed shel emet*). Even the high priest, if he should find the corpse as he is on his way to the Temple to celebrate Yom Kippur must not hold back from burying this dead man out of concern that he will become impure and unclean and thus prevented from performing the sacred rites of the Holy Day. This is a symbol of mercy that is given absolutely without expectation of reward, mercy that one does to another "as if he were dead," and not a law for the dead, for which the Gospel had a harsh phrase.

8. This is how we read, with forceful emphasis, the talmudic saying: "Do not judge your neighbor until you have stood in his place" (*M. Abot* 2:4).

9. *Berakhoth,* 32b, *Baba Metzia,* 59b. The two passages should be read conjointly.

ABNER WEISS

Ethics as Transcendence

And the Contemporary World:

A Response to Emmanuel Levinas

THE TASK OF A RESPONDENT to a paper of this nature is twofold: He must make the contents as intelligible as possible to those who are not familiar with the writer's conceptual foundations, and he must offer a critique of his leading ideas as a basis for further discussion.

A brief introductory survey of the main features of Emmanuel Levinas's thought will facilitate the subsequent analytical summary of his present paper. For the sake of clarity, this conceptual background will be presented under four headings: totality; infinity; the dynamics of transcendence; and encounter as ethics.[1]

I

Totality

Levinas applies the term *totality* to the totalizing tendency of the human Reason.[2] Western philosophy, he contends, since the Greek period, is dominated by the concept of totalization,[3] the concept of unity. The perspective of plurality is only a starting point, for, since unity is discovered in plurality, in the final analysis, plurality becomes accidental.[4] The absorption of the plural in the unitary, moreover, is not confined to metaphysics. Man's social existence, too, reflects the totalizing tendency of the Reason. Man is seen as part of a totality; his individuality is obscured. He is the bearer of a function. When one asks what someone *is*, one is not asking an ontological question. One is merely enquiring into his *position*, which situates him in the social totality. This social position is constituted by his *function*.[5] Inasmuch as the person disappears behind the *persona*, totalization, in this sense, implies individual anonymity.

Levinas highlights this tendency in his discussion of war,[6] which he sees as the outstanding expression of political reality. Man is obliged to assume a role in which his own identity is eclipsed. He is made to dress and to act in accordance with his function, in a manner that differs from that in which he dresses and acts in civilian life. He is subordinated to a fundamental, total objective purpose. The same situation obtains in peace that follows war. In almost the whole realm of his public existence, political, economic, and so on, his individual personality is effaced by his situation within one or other totalizing objective purpose.

Infinity

In a fine analysis of Levinas's concept of infinity, Remy C. Kwant dwells on Levinas's indebtedness to Rene Descartes.[7] In the experience of doubt, Descartes acknowledges his own finitude. But he could not know himself as finite if he had no idea of infinity. Thus, he must have an idea of infinity. But infinity cannot possibly inhere in him, since he is finite. It must be external to him. It must transcend him. Accordingly, he has an idea that is at once his own, and that is, at the same time, radically other, radically transcendent. This idea teaches him his own finiteness.

Interestingly, Kwant infers that, according to Levinas, an encounter with the infinite is implied in Descartes's thought. Levinas applies this notion to authentic encounter with another person.[8] When man becomes self-transcending, when he transcends the enclosedness of his individual ego, submerged as it is in the closedness of the totality, he is in the sphere of the infinite.[9] This encounter with the infinite, in turn, restores his

140

own individuality, which was effaced through totalization.[10] Totalization is thus broken through by man's contact with the infinite, and this contact occurs within his encounter with another person.[11]

The Dynamics of Self-transcendence

Everyone partakes of the totalization of Reason; every man totalizes his world. In our totalization we are inclined to assume other persons, but by so doing we make them part of our world. We reduce them to roles in our individual universe. We do not really recognize them as radically other persons. How, then, can we meet other persons in authentic encounter?

The other, as part of my individual universe has meaning for me. This is not exceptional, since inanimate objects also have meaning for me. But *they* cannot protest the meaning I attach to them. When I view the other as a *person,* however, I become aware that the human person can refuse to be reduced to the meaning I attach to him. He appears as a self-determining meaning.[12]

Active and passive meaning are thus distinguished. We are not *addressed* by the other in the sphere of totalization. When we truly encounter him, however, the other person is the source of self-interpreting meaning.[13]

Our openness to the radically other, as self-interpreting meaning, is articulated by Levinas as contact with the *visage signifiant.*[14] When I accept the other person as the *visage signifiant*—as constituting meaning—I break with my totalizing reason, I break with the system, the closed schema, and I am in the realm of the infinite.[15]

Encounter as Ethics

For Levinas, ethics is authentic encounter.[16] The other can only present himself—not impose himself. Because I am free, he presents me with the choice of acknowledging him or of ignoring him. Levinas speaks of the "naked visage" of the other,[17] evoking the biblical image of the widow and orphan,[18]

141

whose need places an obligation upon me.[19] The other is "needy," however, in a wider sense also. He requires my acknowledgment of his presence as a person, stripped of the clothes of his context, free, indeed, of all contexts that situate him in the realm of totalization.[20]

My choice of acknowledging the other as a person is an ethical decision. Levinas terms this acknowledgement "justice."[21] Acknowledgement, as justice, however, is not an isolated ethical act but the only possible access to ethical living. He who does not acknowledge the other is not *bad,* for *that* evaluation would place him in a context of ethical judgment. Remaining in his self-enclosed sphere of totalization, he is amoral.[22]

Generally, then, Levinas conceives of justice in its biblical sense as a synthesizing cornerstone of all moral behavior.[23] Specifically, justice is *cet abord de face, dans le discours*— "this access to the face in discourse."[24] Justice consists in my allowing the naked visage of the other person who addresses me to become open to me. I judge the other person as making an appeal on me. But he is also *my* judge, in the sense that he judges the self-enclosedness of my individual world if I send him away.[25]

The immediate practical effect of justice is hospitality. As long as I am sunk in my own individuality in the world, as in "the element" of my existence, I can live in my isolation without guilt. Authentic encounter, however, makes this impossible. The other *is* a call on me to share my world with him.[26] His appearance is a claim. I am responsible for him.[27] I have to account to him for my existence. My life becomes apologetic.[28]

II

These general features of Prof. Levinas's thought recur in his paper in the present volume.[29] In his survey of the contemporary world, Levinas is struck by the widespread revolt, which, he declares, "sums up the essence of our age."[30] He analyses the causes of the revolt, and its significance. Accordingly, the first

142

part of the paper deals with those factors that occasion the revolt,[31] and the second with its aim and purpose.[32] The revolt, he
suggests, is occasioned by the effects of the totalizing tendency
of the human Reason. Of these, the dehumanization of the
person is of primary concern to Levinas. The aim and purpose
of the revolt is the rehumanization of the person, which is at-
tainable by his transcending the *totalité* in authentic encounter.
This intersubjectivity, as has been indicated,[33] is articulated by
Levinas as "justice."

Levinas begins his analysis with a discussion of the totalizing
tendency of the Reason in the sphere of morality. His survey is
necessarily brief, but is replete with allusions to the writings of
other thinkers. He alludes to Husserl's notion of the apriority of
moral knowledge, which—it will be recalled—originates in the
practical function of the Reason.[34] He then alludes to the Kantian distinction between *pure ethics* (the metaphysic of
morals), and *applied ethics* (moral anthropology). The concern
of pure ethics is the principles of morality and the nature of
moral obligation as such. Applied ethics, on the other hand, is
the study of the subjective conditions, favorable or unfavorable,
for carrying out these a priori principles.[35] Levinas concludes
this section of the paper by accounting for the Hegelian notion
of human history as the self-revelation of spirit as a mitigation
of the relativism that subjective conditions seemed to invite.[36]

He then proceeds to account for the eclipse of the acceptance
of apriority of morality as a function of Reason. The development of ideology, which he traces, discloses the purely
functional nature of morality. Reason is transformed into rationalization.

It is noteworthy that, in terms of Levinas's conceptual foundations, it is irrelevant whether morality is Reason or mere rationalization. Both reflect totalization. Marxism, for example,
simply interprets man in terms of its initial economic categories, and Freudianism functionalizes him in another way. The
point made by Levinas in his analysis of the contemporary
situation is, however, that ideology has replaced purely rational

143

morality. But ideology has, he claims, itself been discredited. Hence there can be no acceptable ideological solution to the problem of man in the contemporary world.

The disenchantment with the possibility of honest rationality in the sphere of morality, in turn, accounts for a new expression of the totalizing tendency of Reason. The impulse to rationality is transferred to the fields of scientific and technical activity— including the human sciences. It is reflected in French structuralism, a method whose primary intention is to permit the investigator to go beyond a pure description of what he sees in the direction of the rational quality underlying the phenomena—physical or social—with which he is concerned.[37] The ultimate effect of the structural analysis of man is his dehumanization. His activity "is interpreted as a passage by which the diverse structures to which reality is reduced align themselves in system and display themselves. . . . [It is] nothing but an objective event of the intelligible itself . . . a purely logical concatenation."[38]

The totalizing effect of the structuralization of all that is experienced by man, the result of the discovery of the similar in the diverse, is the obliteration of otherness from all experience. Even the "beyond" of space is the "same." Levinas invokes Hegel's notion of evil infinity to explain man's imprisonment within the infinite enchainment of structures. In the hope of escaping one's finitude, one moves dialectically from something to its antithesis—only to find a new synthesis, another something. And so on, endlessly. The attempt to escape is futile. It is nothing more than an activity neurosis. To leap out of this paradoxically endless finity would seem to require an act of faith. *That* alternative, however, has been discredited, reflecting, as it does, an "ideological state of the soul." The dilemma is perpetuated. Only honest Reason is credited, but because it totalizes, it perpetuates the imprisonment.

From totalization in general, Levinas proceeds to its specific social dimension, the structured, ordered society, in which man is described in functional terms.[39] Man's revolt against totaliza-

144

tion, which renders him anonymous within ordered structures, is motivated by his search for himself beyond order—or, as Levinas puts it, in disorder. Man's search for his humanity, through his liberation from order, is expressed as his demand for justice, in the sense in which Levinas understands the term. The self-enclosed ego belongs to the realm of totalization. Unless one encounters another, one can achieve nothing more than "pretended transcendence." One simply ages.[40] Only authentic encounter with a radically external source of meaning enables one to break through the "same" and to meet the other. Accordingly, only by opening oneself to the visage of the other, stripped of all his contexts and definitions, can one transcend the boredom of the human condition.[41] "It is not because the other is novelty that he makes room for a relationship of transcendence—it is because the responsibility for the Other is transcendence, that there can be anything new under the sun."[42]

Through justice, then, with its concomitants of responsibility and hospitality,[43] man is rehumanized, freed from his enchainment in the "evil infinity" of the "same."

III

The theme of intersubjectivity that is central to Levinas's thought, both in *Totalite et Infini* and in the paper now under discussion, locates him, more or less,[44] within the personalistic tendency of contemporary existentialism. He shares, with other personalists, a sense of the concrete, and with them he cannot accept the individual person, either as the empirical ego or as a moment of subjectivity of a transcendental ego. With them, he rejects functionalism, because it makes a man appear to himself and to others as an agglomeration of functions, and with them he asserts that man is more than embodied social function and more than a biological urge. Like other personalists he distinguishes the ego (*le moi*) or self-enclosed consciousness, the individual—man considered simply as part of the anonymous "one" (*l'on*)—from the person. Like them, too, he seeks the

145

person behind the persona through transcendence, articulated as openness to the other; and, with them, he affirms that openness implies being available, as a person, to another person through that commitment which stems from accepting responsibility for the other.[45]

To this extent, the criticisms that have been directed at the writings of the personalists, apply, in large measure, to the thought of Levinas as well.

The fundamental difficulty of this position, is that, although it is true that the person is part of *l'on,* he does not generally feel that his preoccupations as a member of society are a burden to him, and he does not resent these preoccupations as pressures from the outside, "because each individual is, from the start integrated into society and orientated to society."[46] It is natural, therefore, that he be absorbed in the discharge of his social functions, and that the world, as the field in which they are discharged, should be given meaning in terms of these functions.[47]

It would follow that the call for justice which underlies the widespread revolt, which, according to Levinas, is the outstanding characteristic of the contemporary world, may stem more from man's concern for the society in which he feels he should be integrated than from his unconscious desire to transcend it. It may well be the case—inverting Levinas's formulation—that the revolt proceeds from the pathos rather than from a human ethos. It is by no means clear that those who foment revolution in the name of justice accept the thesis that all ideology is suspect, and that the experience of disillusionment with ideologies in the past has caused the revolutionaries to despair of finding *any* ideological solution to the problems of society. The testimony of David Sidorsky of Columbia University, in his reaction to Levinas's paper,[48] suggests the contrary. The call for justice *is,* he states, an ideological demand, motivated, in the case of the student revolt at Columbia, in all events by the students' view of society and of the position of the individual in society. Moreover, if Levinas were correct in his assumption that the value of an idea is repudiated by the

experience of the failure of those who have been its protagonists, the notion of transcendence, as it has been formulated in modern existentialism, should also be repudiated. The
personal failings of such of its exponents as Sartre should make
this abundantly clear. If, on the other hand, Levinas will
contend that this argument cannot apply to transcendence as he
understands it, because the meaning with which he invests the
term is different, he must grant that those who are disenchanted
with the past failure of ideology can, likewise, formulate new
ideologies using the same old terminologies. Their demands for
justice and a just society therefore may still be ideological.

Levinas's conception of justice, moreover, raises a serious
moral problem. How, for example, do I relate to a thief or
murderer? Only if I strip him of all social contexts can I encounter him authentically. If justice, as "transcendence is communication, implying, beyond a simple exchange of signs, the
'gift' and the 'open hearth,' "[49] how can I hand him over to the
authorities? I must surely accept him as he is and for what he is.
My encounter with him, if I am not to totalize him into my objective world, must not curtail his liberty.

This problem, indeed, raises a fundamental difficulty inherent
in Levinas's approach: What are the practical applications of
ethics as transcendence in the contemporary world? Even if we
accept authentic encounter as the source of moral obligation,
what is the basis of decision-making in specific situations? Levinas does not discuss the role of the intellect in the analysis of
these situations, nor does he suggest norms that facilitate moral
judgments. His problem is complex. Any objective moral law
that is independent of specific encounter bespeaks apriority and
totalization. On the other hand, in his reply to the debate, Levinas concedes the requirement of such a law, because his approach is valid only when there are two persons. The presence
of a third, that is to say, the reality of society, must necessarily
alter one's whole approach. Accordingly, Levinas does not deny
the macroworld, for to do so would invite chaos. But he does
not elucidate the passage of the microcosmic relationship be-

147

tween two persons to the macrocosmic relationship between the individual and a multitude of persons in a social context. How does the work of justice proceed from its kernel—as Kwant puts it[50]—in the encounter between two persons?

Unfortunately, Levinas does not provide us with a system, nor with practical guidelines, for ethics in the contemporary world. He is, first and foremost, a visionary. He situates himself within his vision and invites one to share it. He presents a kind of philosophical message rather than a fully developed moral philosophy. The phrases *ha-edut sheli* (my testimony) and *al zeh raziti le-havi edut* (I wished to bear witness to this), employed when he delivered his paper in Hebrew, are significant.

In the introductory remarks with which Levinas prefaced the presentation of his paper at the conference, he defined the problem of Judaism and contemporary thought. Contemporary thought is the thought of the gentiles—even in Israel. Can a bridge be found linking Jews to contemporary thought? Jewish youth, he claimed, finds Jewish ethics oppressive and rejects the distinctions that the Halakha imposes. It resents being separated from mankind in general. Can an opening into Judaism be found, he asks, for those Jewish youth, particularly in the Diaspora, who seek it—perhaps even for those who do not do so—but who have assimilated, not as an easy way out, but as an expression of their commitment to the difficult challenge of building a better world?

Levinas's vision of ethics as transcendence is his attempt at building the bridge and providing the opening. Does he, in fact, succeed? Stated differently, is his vision of ethics—certainly, as has been indicated, part of the contemporary world view—also a Jewish vision?

A Jewish ethic—in its accepted sense in all events—is also a religious ethic. Although Levinas explained his omission of a discussion of God in his reply to the debate, one would have welcomed the inclusion of the religious implications of his thought. The increasing interest of young people in God, and the religious orientation of many contemporary existentialists, moreover, would not only have warranted its inclusion but would also have provided a sounder bridge between Judaism and contemporary thought.

Furthermore, the centrality of *l'on* in Judaism is undeniable. Judaism *does* categorize people into classes within society, and does, for example, define our obligations, to a king, a priest, a levite, a slave, the *anonymous* poor and the *anonymous* stranger—witness the commandments relating to the gleanings of the field and its corners, the preference for charity given *anonymously*, and prayers uttered in the plural. There are, indeed, in Judaism fixed ways of reacting to events, of thinking and of feeling, as, for example, in the response to death.

Nor is the Jewish concept of justice exhausted in intersubjectivity. It, too, is situated in *l'on*, and is determined by fixed norms. The case of ben-Petura is a striking example of the conflict between the Jewish normative ethic and the demands of justice defined as intersubjectivity. It is the more striking since only two persons are involved. There is no third to complicate the issue. Notwithstanding, the view of Akiva is that *hayekha kodmin*—one's own interests supersede that of the other.[51] In the absence of a clear case like that of ben-Petura one might solve Levina's dilemma by suggesting that there is, indeed, an independent moral law, but that it can be *appropriated* only in real encounter with the other, and that it can only be applied *authentically* when one moves in the sphere of the transcendent. The case of ben-Petura, however, makes this solution quite impossible.

IV

It was suggested in our discussions that the possibility of the application of Levinas's thought to the teaching of Jewish ethics in schools, yeshivot, and universities be considered, and I turn briefly to this question. Although the reality of life in an organized and structured society cannot be ignored in any system of education, and although students must be taught a practical ethic in order to cope with the multitude of functional relationships that characterise contemporary society, Levinas's contribution is significant. Man requires society to satisfy his private needs, and moral norms to define and determine his societal relationships. The problem, however, that Levinas correctly intuits is the increasing dehumanization of society, and the increasing degeneration of ethics into a sterile and soulless moral behaviorism, which constricts, oppresses, and alienates the young. Clearly, the goal of moral education should be achievement of a "society of persons." Even if it is not clear how Levinas's concept of justice can be applied to macrocosmic societal relationships, it *does* suggest the *spirit* for encounter within the societal macrocosm. It may well be the case that our relationships with many individuals must be purely functional, but as long as we truly encounter as many people as possible, we shall indeed discover the humanity of other persons and in so doing recover our own humanity.

The desirability of this emphasis in Jewish moral education cannot be sufficiently stressed. The Judaic ethical tradition is based upon the uniqueness and infinite value of the individual, human being created, as he is, in the divine image. Repeated emphasis upon this fundamental ethical principle can alone prevent the degeneration of normative morality into ethical behaviorism.

The notion of man as a being created in the divine image is *implicit* in Levinas's conception of ethics as transcendence, and is, after all—the specific difficulties notwithstanding—the bridge between Judaism and contemporary thought that he sets out to build.

1. Based upon Emmanuel Levinas, *Totalite et Infini* (The Hague: Martinus Nijoff, 1961) and a series of lectures on Levinas's thought delivered by Professor Remy C. Kwant of Utrecht, when he was visiting professor in the Department of Philosophy of the University of Natal, South Africa, in August 1965. Levinas's later articles, published in various journals, were not available to me at the time of the conference. I am informed that these arti-

cles will be republished as a complete volume, and that a new major work is soon to appear.

2. Levinas's approach is different from that of Jean Paul Sartre, who discusses the same tendency in his *Criticism of Dialectic Reason.* Levinas discusses his own approach in *Totalite et Infini,* p. xvi ff.

3. See, e.g., ibid., p. x.

4. Ibid., p. 196.

5. Ibid., p. 152.

6. Ibid., pp. ix ff. and 197 ff.

7. See note 1, above. Kwant probably refers to *Totalite et Infini,* p. 18ff. See also, ibid., pp. 185–87.

8. See, e.g., ibid., p. 154.

9. Ibid., p. 167.

10. Ibid., p. 185–86. Cf., ibid., p. 153.

11. Ibid., pp. 178, 271.

12. Ibid., pp. 272–73.

13. See, ibid., p. 191.

14. *Inter alia,* see ibid., p. 152.

15. Ibid., pp. 168–71. Cf., ibid., p. 191.

16. Ibid., p. 172 ff.

17. Ibid., pp. 173, 174, 188, passim.

18. Ibid., pp. 174, 188, 190, 229.

19. Ibid., pp. 153, 178, 184, 188, 194, 282.

20. Cf., ibid., pp. 152–53.

21. See, *inter alia,* ibid., pp. 188–90.

22. Kwant makes this point with force. See note 1, above.

23. Levinas, *Totalite et Infini,* pp. 188–89.

24. Ibid., p. 43.

25. Ibid., p. 190.

26. Ibid., pp. 47, 282.

27. Ibid., pp. 153, 178, 184, 188, 194, *inter alia.*

28. See especially, ibid., p. 229.

29. Levinas's presentation of this paper in Hebrew at the 1972 conference clarified a number of points in, and made a number of important interpretive additions to, the English draft paper, itself a translation from the original French version.

30. Emmanual Levinas, "Ethics as Transcendence and the Contemporary World," a paper delivered at the sessions of the Summer Institute on Judaism and Contemporary Thought (Israel, 6–12 July 1972), p. 4. Quotations throughout are from the English and Hebrew versions of this paper by Le-

vinas that were available in 1972. They may differ in some respects from the final French version and its translation that appears in this volume.

31. Ibid., pp. 1–3.

32. Ibid., pp. 4–7.

33. See, above, p. 142.

34. Note Levinas's comment on the primacy of the practical Reason in his Hebrew addition to the end of "Ethics as Transcendence."

35. Immanuel Kant, *Groundwork of the Metaphysic of Morals,* trans. with an introduction by H. J. Paton (London, 1950), Preface, p. 389.

36. Cf. Hegel, *Werke* (Stuttgart, 1927–39), p. xi and pp. 34–36; *Philosophy of History,* trans. by J. Sibree (London, 1861), pp. 9–10.

37. See Michael Lane, *Structuralism: A Reader* (London: Jonathan Cape, 1970).

38. Levinas, "Ethics as Transcendence," p. 2.

39. See above, pp. 139–40.

40. The allusion is probably to Heidegger's "sorg," rather than to Sartre's notion of transcendence of the past.

41. Cf. *Totalite et Infini,* pp. 152–53.

42. Levinas, "Ethics as Transcendence," p. 6.

43. Ibid., pp. 6–7.

44. He claims to have been influenced primarily by Franz Rosenzweig; cf., *Totalite et Infini,* p. xvi, and admits to the influence of Buber, among others. His thought, however, is to some extent also reminiscent of Gabriel Marcel.

45. Cf. Gabriel Marcel, *Homo Viator* (Chicago, 1951), p. 26ff. Marcel's second reflection, through which a person attains "Being served by knowing"—to use Levinas's phrase—which Levinas views as a reassertion of totalization, and the Christian orientation of his thought, sets them apart.

46. See Frederick Copleston, *Contemporary Philosophy* (Westminster, Maryland: The Newman Press, 1965), p. 205.

47. Ibid.

48. Based on his oral comments as reported in the transcript of the discussions and as reflected in my notes.

49. The Hebrew is even more striking: *Lev patuah u'vayit patuah.*

50. See above, note 1.

51. *Sifra* (ed. Weiss), *Behar* vi, p. 109c, *Baba Mezia,* 62a. Cf. the discussions of this case in the papers by Ernst Simon and Jakob J. Petuchowski in this volume.

152

DAVID SIDORSKY

The Autonomy of Moral Objectivity

THE THESIS THAT THERE ARE DISTINCT and competing religious and secular justifications for moral attitudes and doctrines is a familiar one. This thesis has been asserted often in works of philosophy and religion. It is found in many literary and psychological studies, and has been held as common sense at various times and places in Western society.

The reasons for the thesis seem straightforward and even self-evident. Since religious belief and practice are important aspects of a person, it seems that they would characterize moral attitudes and moral justification sufficiently to differentiate religious from secular ethics. Further, a religious morality is usually derived from a divine source, either through revelation or tradition. Secular ethicists, on the other hand, have sought to deny this derivation through any of its modes, and to systematically replace it by an appeal to Nature or to Reason or to History. It is a point of departure for much modern intellectual history to sketch that history as one dominated by a conflict between these competing foundations of moral belief that have been afforded by religious tradition and secular thought.

THE APPEAL TO NATURE, REASON, OR HISTORY

The broad outlines of that history are easily traced. In the seventeenth century, the morality of naturalism had been developed in a manner that explicitly challenged religious ethical justification. Hobbes and Machiavelli had concluded that the new nation state could not be religious, that the modern "prince" could not be a Christian prince. Rather, the political order could only be understood and its morality could only be examined by reference to a "materialist" view of human nature and a structure of secular motives. Even in the founding of the principles of international law, for example, Grotius had sought an alternative to the religious and hierarchical conception of social order prominent in medieval views. Laws among nations were to be derived from laws of Nature that hold among diverse religions and nation states. Most completely, Spinoza developed self-consciously, in the *Ethics*, a counter morality of naturalism centered around a faith in the existence of a unified order of Nature. The acceptance of that determined natural order as well as the cultivation of the direction of its latent dynamism provide a locus for individual moral growth. Other ethicists of the seventeenth century illustrate this convergence upon moral justification by an appeal to Nature, whether the route of that appeal be natural rights, or natural law, the natural order of things, human nature, or God as Nature.

Concomitantly, human reason was identified as the unique instrument for determining and apprehending moral virtue. In contrast to the "good heart" or the "fear of the Lord," it is by the invocation of Reason that the philosophers of the Enlightenment sought to undermine and to transvalue the inherited moral beliefs of the eighteenth century. In its most sophisticated theoretical formulation, that of Immanuel Kant, human rationality, committed only to the conception of man as an autonomous moral agent and to the minimal consistency that rationality imposes, is able to derive the operative moral norms required for the moral life. In the political context, Reason is capable of discerning the General Will or public interest independent of the conflicting institutional or personal interests and of the idiosyncracies of personal sentiment or religious tradi-

154

tions. There is accordingly a rational standard for public policy. Further, in the multiplicity of historical and social conflicts, Reason can chart the direction of institutional reconstruction and reform. Such confidence in Reason is not limited to Condorcet or to the philosophes of the French Revolution and the Enlightenment. The British utilitarians, who recognize pain and pleasure to be the nonrational sovereigns of human action, still maintain that Reason is competent to calculate individual and social utilities and hence to adjudicate all moral issues. The range of diverse formulations of confidence in Reason is broad but the convergence on the replacement of a traditional appeal to supernatural source by faith in rationality is dominant.

The difficulties raised for ethical justification by the appeal solely to Nature and to Reason were recognized even in the very early stages of their adoption and use. Probably the most familiar statement of the difficulties is Hume's argument that Reason is always only the slave of the passions. Further, Hume had suggested in a celebrated but controversially interpreted passage that judgments of what ought to be could not be derived from judgments of what is the case in Nature or from a set of rational relationships among ideas.

It was in partial response to these lines of critical argument as well as by the development of the categories of Evolution and of History that dominated so much of nineteenth century social thought that a shift in moral justification took place. If the order of natural processes could not provide moral guidance, then perhaps the order or the dialectic of historical and social process would. If objective Reason examining social institutions is morally neutral or passionally inadequate for moral direction then possibly rationality embedded in the developing or concrete consciousness of nation, race, or class can discern or dictate the trends of social progress. Consequently, the processes of survival or of evolution, of development or of history are put forward as criteria of moral worth. This standard is used by philosophers as diverse as Spencer and Comte, from

155

both the Right and the Left. It can even be found in the religious thought of the period in surprising formulations. In some of these formulations, Judaism, for example, was justified as a religion of History, not of Nature, "verified" through historical survival and achievement. Its institutional survival, on one view, is connected with its capacity for incremental historical development.

The most characteristic and complete appeal to the deification of History as moral agent was of course, Marxism, which became a major secular religion and subsequently a state orthodoxy. Oversimplifications are inevitable in compressed historical review yet such compression does permit the assertion of the significantly obvious. In contrast to patterns of traditional and institutional religious justification in ethics, there have emerged secular religions with distinctive ethos and morality: an ethics of the order of Nature; an ethics of the derivations of Reason; and an ethics of the dialectics of History. Further, these secular religions systematically asserted the intellectual propositions of traditional religious systems of belief. For example, they identified man's place within Nature or Reason or History; they interpreted the moral imperatives derived from Nature or Reason, or History; and they affirmed that individual freedom or dignity or salvation would be found in acting on behalf of the ideals of Nature, or Reason, or History. As a corollary to these intellectual claims, a number of institutional criticisms and institutional proposals were advanced, including rationalist reconstruction of the Church among theorists of the French Revolution and historicist revolution of bourgeois society among Marxists. In one sense of the term "religious" a postreligious ethic would require a purgation of the elements of faith in these secular moral visions. Alternatively, a scientific or rational criticism of the assumptions of naturalist, historicist, or rationalist visionary ethics is in order. In an oblique but destructive manner, that examination took place in ethical theory of the twentieth century.

THE CRITIQUES OF ETHICAL NATURALISM,
COGNITIVISM, AND HISTORICISM

The dominant ethical theorists of the twentieth century have provided an analysis of the nature of moral concepts and of the function of moral judgment that has excluded any of the characteristically modern moralities that derived their moral standards by reference to Nature, Reason, or History. This remarkable fact of major significance for contemporary ethical beliefs has been overlooked in the forum of public morality, in part, because normative ethical judgments have proceeded independently of metaethical theory. Yet the tensions to which this fact has given rise have been pervasive. The history of this analysis of ethical concepts and judgments in twentieth-century ethical theory is familiar to the technical philosopher but merits a review in this particular context. There have been four distinctive aspects of that history.

It is a phenomenon of literary and art history that G. E. Moore's *Principia Ethica* dominated the mores of Bloomsbury at the turn of the century, as witnesses as diverse as Bertrand Russell, J. M. Keynes, Leonard Woolf, and D. H. Lawrence have testified. It is also true that Moore's work became for much of contemporary philosophy the logical bar to any acceptance of ethical naturalism.

Moore accomplished this with an extraordinarily simple approach, which I shall simply restate in compressed fashion. "Good" was generally conceded to be the characteristic adjective or predicate for asserting moral value in the vocabulary of moral terms. Moore argued that "good" was "indefinable." This conclusion could readily be demonstrated by examining any proposed definition of good. The demonstration was straightforward.

Assume, as naturalist utilitarians seem to, that good means "the maximization of pleasure over pain"; or as historicist Marxists seem to, that good means something like "the realization of the next or socialist stage in social evolution." Then the

157

Moorean critic would ask whether the maximization of pleasure over pain, whether in some particular instance or as a general rule, was good, or whether the realization of socialism, was good. Even for the utilitarian or for the Marxist the question was not a closed question equivalent to the trivial tautology of whether the good was good. The question was an open question, and the openness showed that there was a difference in meaning between the term good and its proposed definition. Consequently, any effort to define good in the language of natural or historical process commits a "naturalistic fallacy." To the extent to which naturalists proposed such definitions of their fundamental moral terms, and from Spinoza through Bentham and Marx they have seemed to, they committed the fallacy. However sympathetic on normative or humanitarian or political grounds various schools of contemporary philosophy were to utilitarianism or evolutionism or Marxism, for many of them the defense of these positions was fundamentally fallacious in the light of Moore's argument that naturalism was tainted by the "naturalistic fallacy."

Moore himself proposed that good be understood as an objective nonnatural quality that could be "intuited" by those appropriately sensitive to the manifestation of goodness in human affairs. This position, however, was in conflict with the strong noncognitivist tendency of twentieth-century ethical theory.

Although Moore's positive intuitionist thesis was rejected, his critical views contra ethical naturalism found a surprising reinforcement in the effort to set the boundaries of moral knowledge that stemmed from the scientific philosophy of the Vienna Circle and among the later logical positivists. For the positivists, truth can be realized only in logic, in mathematics, and in the empirical sciences. Their views culminated in a remarkable vision, rigorously developed, of the mansions of human knowledge. In stark simplicity the mansions of knowledge can be demarcated.

First, logical and mathematical statements are true by virtue of their consistency with the rules of language. If they are con-

158

sistent, then they are true; if they are contradictory, then they are false.

Second, empirical statements are true or probably true if they are confirmed by sense evidence. They are false or probably false if they are refuted by sense evidence. They are neither true nor false if there can be no theoretical confirmation of their truth claim by sense evidence.

So, April is the fourth month of the year is true by virtue of the rules of the English language, and April is the rainiest month of the year is true by virtue of meteorological confirmation. "April is the cruelest month of the year" is neither true nor false, no matter how expressive, emotive, or moving the line may be. Similarly, the claim that it is warm in this room, may be true or false, but the imperative to "Open the window!" is neither. Bar-Ilan University in truth may have an efficient computer, but the subsequent "Hurrah for Bar-Ilan" is not a cognitive statement.

These results in themselves seem sensible and are not disturbing. The inference that all characteristic moral claims should be classified as noncognitive was disturbing. It meant that a philosophical generation in Europe that took the lead in anti-Fascism found itself with a particular thesis regarding the nature of morality in which it could not say that "Thou shalt not kill!" is true or that "Nazism is good" is false. And to the extent to which moral cognitivism is implicit in the faith in reason in moral judgment, there was a severe impingement upon confidence in moral rationality.

The conjunction of Moore's nonnaturalism with the noncognitivism of logical positivism stimulated a significant number of detailed analyses of the nature of moral concepts and of the character of moral disagreement throughout the 1930s and 1940s. Moore's original claim that "good" was not reducible to "natural qualities" was reinforced but the reason for this claim was changed. In the analysis of moral language, it was argued, that "good," like "ought" or "right" were prescriptive or imperatival or emotive terms that functioned to

159

command, praise, order, exhort, persuade, or goad. This accounted for their nondefinability or, more correctly, their irreducibility to terms that functioned to describe or inform. Accordingly, good was neither a natural nor a nonnatural quality. The naturalist fallacy actually had revealed a "descriptivist fallacy." Significantly, the gulf between the facts or reasons that were adduced to support any moral ought, and the assertion of the moral claim itself, was widened on this account. And the appeal to rational intuition of nonnatural goodness objectively present in things, which was Moore's own position, was then construed as too ambitious a conception of moral rationality. If Moore's argument pointed to the nondescriptive character of moral judgment, then the assertion of moral imperatives had more in common with the expression of emotive attitudes than with the intuition of moral qualities.

The most sophisticated presentations of the position worked out paradigm cases of ethical or moral disagreement. If two partisans disagreed morally, say a Marxist with a liberal democrat, or a Fascist with an egalitarian, then they might pursue moral dialogue, as the rationalist dream of Reason had hoped or believed, only to the extent to which their moral attitudes were reflections of factual disagreement. Ultimately, however, the dialogue would break down, since each partisan would express conflicting emotive attitudes. There was then, for the champions of scientific rationality, no procedure to verify or to derive emotive attitudes, that is, moral propositions.

By the outbreak of World War II, ethical theorists, including those who condemned Nazism and fought against it, had reconciled themselves to the painful truth that their moral claims represented expressions of attitude that could not be justified by appeal to Nature, to Reason, or to History.

It is a cultural fact of some significance that this tension between a metaethical subjectivism or noncognitivism and traditional assertiveness in normative moral judgment and action was also found in European existentialism, although derived in a different way and formulated in a different idiom. The positivist and emotivist position reflect more than the methodological inhibition and scientific imperialism that empiricism imposes on moral speculation. For just as ethical emotivism had determined that there was a gulf between the empirically descriptive and the emotive moral attitude, so the existentialist argued that there could be no bridge between the reasons that justify or motivate moral action and the affirmation of moral commitment.

The ethos of the existentialist position is antirational. If a mathematician *must* conclude from the premises of his system that a particular theorem holds, then he has surrendered his moral autonomy to assert or to deny the theorem. If a scientist *must* derive his conclusions on the basis of the evidence by virtue of his method, then he has abdicated moral freedom with respect to those conclusions. Moral autonomy presupposes this view, and moral freedom requires that ethical commitment not be derivable from systemically held premises but that each moral decision constitute an act of authentic commitment.

Although it has usually been recognized that an ethical decision cannot be coerced, on this view, apparently, an ethical decision can never be motivated, either by the character of the agent or by the consistent commitment to the rules of moral behavior, or by the reasons and grounds of the decision. It may be that this view reflects some of the unusual preoccupations with moral commitment and action under the conditions of terror during the first phases of the Nazi occupation of France. For Sartre, at that time, moral autonomy might involve the freedom of a person to decide to act, even when the rational evidence suggested the fruitlessness or absurdity or counterproductivity or irrationality of the action.

Critics of Sartre have maintained that in Sartre's interpretation of the conditions of moral freedom, only the morally arbitrary can be free. Sartre's own repudiation of any existentialist ethics in his conversion to revisionist Marxism gives partial confirmation to this criticism. In the present context, however, whatever the verdict on the adequacy of

161

existentialist ethical theory, it becomes clear that here too there was a denial of the characteristically modern secular appeal to Nature, Reason, or History for ethical justification.

I have not sought to trace the vicissitudes of the particular values that were championed and celebrated by naturalists, rationalists, empiricists, or evolutionists in the twentieth-century philosophical thought. The justification of those values through appeals to processes in Nature, to apprehensions of rational clarity, or to development of social process, however, had been systematically subverted and repudiated in the major tendencies of twentieth-century ethical theory.

THE RECONSTITUTION OF THE OBJECTIVITY OF MORAL JUDGMENT

Since the end of World War II, analytical ethical theory has been involved in a major effort to restore ethical naturalism and to reconstitute a significant measure of moral rationality. In part, this effort stemmed from the breakdown of the coherent structure of logical positivism through internal self-criticism. In part, this effort derived from the implications of the Wittgensteinian and Austinian analyses of language that replaced the positivist interpretation of the nature of language. These redrew the previously restricted limits of moral knowledge. In part, as Iris Murdoch has recently pointed out, this effort reflected the philosophical frustration and sense of inadequacy in asserting that ethical conflict of enormous moment must be construed on the paradigm of "Hurrah Oxford" versus "Hurrah Cambridge!"

The most obvious move in the restoration of ethical naturalism and moral rationality was to stress the degree to which moral attitudes were reducible to questions of fact. If a person morally approves of Castroism because he believes that in fact it will raise the standard of living of the Cuban people, and it fails to do so, then his moral approval is open to revision in the way in which any empirical hypothesis is subject to revision in the light of new evidence. It is a commonplace that persons resist revising their moral attitudes when faced with new evidence. The point is that such resistance has also been characteristic of the empirical sciences where scientists do not lightly abandon developed theories on the basis of experimental evidence. Accordingly, this line of argument involved narrowing the gulf between the "is" and the "ought" both from the analysis of the character of descriptive theories and from the analysis of moral disagreement.

If we consider the case where the moral debate breaks down, as for example when the supporter of Castroism refuses to accept the negative evidence on the performance of the Cuban economy, we need not conclude that the situation reflects conflict of ultimate moral attitudes. Alternatively, he may accept these facts but realize that his support was conditioned by other facts that can be cited in defense of Castroism. And the debate would continue. At some point we may have to conclude commonsensically that one party has refused to acknowledge relevant facts.

It is true that ethical naturalists and rationalists were unable to demonstrate convincingly that all or most fundamental moral disagreement could be understood as factual disagreement that is resolvable by scientific and rational methods of inquiry. But it is also true that ethical emotivists and noncognitivists were unable to produce cases of complete factual agreement that were riven only by difference in emotive attitude. To a marked degree, the conclusion is that agreement as to facts results in convergence of attitudes.

In sum, moral inquiry was interpreted again, as John Dewey and an earlier generation of ethical naturalists had argued, much more closely to the model of the resolution of dispute in rational contexts.

A second major theme in the postwar effort to reassert moral rationality derived from the detailed analysis of moral language and moral concepts. Language analysis examined the commitments presupposed by the use of terms like "justice,"

163

"equality," "ought," and in doing so restored much of their traditional moral function in linguistic guise. I shall briefly review only one illustration, although that is a remarkable phenomenon: the revival of the doctrine of natural rights as a linguistic theory of universal human rights.

In the positivist analysis, since natural rights were not statements of empirical fact and since they were not statements of logical truth, they were noncognitive claims that were neither true nor false; they represented the expression of emotive attitudes in favor of human equality. The logical analysis of the language of moral rights, however, shows that the special function and linguistic use of rights-claims relates to justification of interference with another person's freedom. Hence the argument is developed that in a culture that recognizes any claims of rights or makes any use of the language of rights, it is committed logically to a prior recognition of a human right to freedom. This must be so since it would be self-contradictory to recognize that particular grounds must be advanced to justify interference with another person's freedom in specific contexts, and then to deny that *any* ground is ever required to justify interference. Yet the meaning of universal human right to freedom is precisely and simply that a ground must be given to justify interference with another person's freedom.

Consider a society, even a Nazi society, that recognizes the *right* of the S.S. man, say, to extra pay for overtime work. This recognition presupposes that a ground is given for interference, since otherwise he would have no *right* to the pay. The society cannot then consistently deny that in interfering with another person, no ground need be given. Of course, the leaders of a society may introduce criteria that justify interference claiming that a particular group is parasitical or represents to threat to governmental security. These criteria are then open to critical examination. The point is that the introduction of such arguments concedes that such grounds must be supplied and that in their absence everyone would have the right of freedom. The

164

leaders may of course act inconsistently or arbitrarily, but this is beside the point. Moral rationality has never required the extreme view that Reason compels assent.

Regardless of the degree of efficacy or persuasion of the particular argument here advanced for universal human right to freedom, the point is that such arguments are advanced by ethicists operating from the linguistic analysis of moral concepts. In the spirit reminiscent of Kant, the formal interpretation of rational use of moral language is sufficient to commit a person on behalf of particular values of normative ethics.

Finally, even for those moralists who insist that moral claims must be construed as imperative or attitudinal, the scope afforded to moral rationality has been broadened. Imperatives in everyday affairs, it is conceded, like the command to "Open the window!", hinge upon a structure of reasons. Even attitudinal preferences are supported by grounds. If challenged as to why he uttered a hurrah for this entity rather than for another, or on this occasion rather than on another, the rooter supplies grounds and does not simply retreat to the arbitrary. It is a matter of public knowledge that judgments of taste, from wine tasting to cooking to literary criticism, admit of standards, sometimes of extreme rigor and precision. So the view that moral judgments are not factual need not exclude the development of moral criticism or the assertion of objective standards, or even a high degree of convergence among connoisseurs or judges.

On this view, moral rationality does not depend upon the ability to assimilate ethical claims to empirical hypotheses that are confirmable by scientific methods. Rather it depends upon the fact that moral assertions are supported by a structure of reasons. Even when persons disagree as to what constitutes good or sufficient reasons, such disagreement cannot be arbitrary. It is bound by logical coherence, by growth of sensitivity to data and to quality of perception, and by appeal to relevant information.

165

The crux of moral rationality for the moral absolutist has traditionally resided in the fact that when faced with moral disagreement, say, that Suttee was justified or head-hunting should be permitted, he could respond that his opponent was "blind" or "deluded" or "mistaken" or "underdeveloped" or "wrong." Even while retaining some aspects of noncognitivism, the contemporary analytical ethicist is once again capable of a rational condemnation of morally conflicting attitudes.

It has been the perennial situation of philosophy to subvert and then to restore ultimate claims about the nature of things, or the character of human values, or the possibilities of human understanding. The philosophical contribution lies in the significance of that process for understanding and in the degree to which the precritical position and the postcritical position differ.

Modern philosophical ethics, as we have seen, confronted the traditions of religious ethics with secular faith in Nature, Reason, and History. It then systematically subverted this faith. It is now bent on restoring it, but the manner of the restoration differs significantly from the claims that were subverted. Ethical naturalism is restored, but without any of the major ideological claims of the Age of Reason. It involves fundamentally the recognition of the limits imposed upon moral claims by the consistent use of moral concepts and by ordinary canons of human rationality. Moral historicism or any sweeping vision of a Hegelian or Marxist variety is rejected. Such claims could at best commit us to the recognition of the relevance of historical understanding to moral decision.

The revived limited claims of Nature and Reason are not trivial. For proof of their significance we need only reexamine the situation created by their denial. Their reformulation in contemporary linguistic idiom, however, poses in fresh perspective the question of the difference between secular and religious ethics.

The relevant point here is that the conjoint doctrines of ethical relativism, of arbitrariness in the meaning of moral concepts, and of moral discourse as irrational or nonrational have often been viewed as the common enemy of both religious and secular ethics. The major achievement of secular analytic ethical theory has been the reconstitution of a measure of ethical objectivity, the denial of arbitrariness in moral concepts, and the interpretation of models of rationality for moral discourse. It would seem, then, that except for existential or irrational religious ethics, much of religious ethical theory especially in the casuistic tradition could be consistent with analytical ethical theory. Even more than some contemporary secular philosophical movements, casuistic religious ethicists have been concerned with fidelity to fact or with sensitivity to moral concepts and to the constraints of rationality. This is probably so because casuistic religious ethicists have been bound by rational constraints in the important practical contexts of interpreting the religious revelation or tradition or covenant for the concrete historical and social circumstances of its application.

The tentative conclusion then of this survey is not that there is a reconciliation between secular and religious ethics. It has perhaps always been true that, to the extent that secularists have not been pursuing particular ideological moral visions of one kind or another that go beyond the limits of their own methodological commitments, and to the extent that religionists have not been concerned with the theological foundations of their morality but with its implications in specific situations, there has always been a tacit convergence.

The recognition that in concrete ethical situations there may be convergence between religious and secular ethicists should not be extended to an ethical theory of moral ecumenicism. The force of this analysis has been counter to the domination of contemporary moral perception by secular faiths that have projected liberating visions of technological progress, or of liberal democracy, or of socialist transformation. Its formulation reflects the disillusionment and shock that has come to partisans of those moral visions, particularly in the twentieth

167

century. Yet this adversary stance should not lead to any misconstrual of the implications of philosophical ethical theory toward religious ethics. It does not endorse the claims of the religious ethicist, in particular the negative claim that denies the competency of secular ethical analysis, rationalist or naturalist, to provide guidance on moral issues. Further, since the arguments here surveyed restrict metaphysical rationalism or historicism in deriving support for its moral claims it would be equally critical of any transcendental religious or theological justification for moral judgment. The failure of modern ideologies—democracy, liberalism, socialism, science, when these were interpreted as secular religions that would transform the human condition and the conceptual framework of traditional morality—is a significant fact for the religious moralist. It is not, however, a vindication of any religious position in politics or morals.

INSTITUTIONAL RESPONSIBILITY OR ULTIMATE COMMITMENT

For many students of morals, the crucial evidence for or against the significance of the distinction between religious and secular ethics is not to be sought in the examination of different patterns of justification of ethical principles or theories but rather in the generating of different normative attitudes and policies that are adopted or supported by religious individuals or groups in contrast to secular persons and societies. The preliminary question then becomes whether it is possible in fact to identify any demarcation between secular and religious views on major and practical issues of normative ethics.

Certainly, there are concrete instances closely bound to the history of institutions, whether religious or secular, where such differences can be demonstrated. The position of a Roman Catholic or Orthodox Jewish spokesman on abortion or on obscenity will differ significantly from that of a Civil Liberties Union lawyer or an official representative of the Social Democratic party. The critical question is whether in areas not directly linked to particular institutional commitments, the presence of religious belief generates a different set of normative ethical views than those held by secularists. There is apparently no empirical evidence to confirm this hypothesis, in part because the variables that correlate with normative views on questions of social policy do not function in isolation. The differences between the Roman Catholic, the Protestant, or the Orthodox Jew and a "radical chic" or "secular socialist" may often be related to differences of class or social position rather than to different religious beliefs.

In this complex empirical area I should like to explore one tentative kind of differentiation, even though this probe will only highlight the difficulty involved in trying to differentiate secular from religious attitudes.

My point of departure is the famous distinction Max Weber drew between an ethics of institutional responsibility and an ethics of ultimate commitment. The distinction is readily illustrated. A parent or a husband, a soldier or a diplomat, an employee or a trustee, assert or accept by virtue of their station, role, or function a set of institutional goals and responsibilities. In an important sense, their morality is assessed in terms of the adequacy with which they perform their functions or achieve institutional goals. Even more familiar, there seem to be a set of generally recognized moral ideals like peace, social justice, freedom, and so on. In another important sense, a person's morality is assessed by reference to his participation or contribution to the achievement of these ideals.

This distinction, between institutional responsibility and ultimate commitment, does not set up competing moralities. Hopefully, a person in responsibly carrying out his institutional goals may be furthering moral ideals. Again, the realizing of any abstract ideal involves commitments to institutions. In many significant instances, the distinction can be identified as pointing to the difference between short-term institutional goals and more long-range goals or it may differentiate between a narrow conception of institutional goals and a more inclusive or broader set of goals. So a parent may not only be held accountable for his child's education but it may also be construed as part of his parental responsibility to assert civic concern about the school system in which his child will function.

It is extremely simple to parody either of these patterns of morality. The figure of the Mafia chauffeur who does an honest day's work for a day's pay and brings his pay check faithfully home to wife and family, like the stereotype of the "good German" represents an extreme of institutional responsibility unenlightened by any vision of moral purpose. The equally familiar figure is that of the moral universalist who is the champion of all causes while neglecting elementary human decencies and considerations in his immediate environment.

The distinction appears in varieties of moral systems. It overlaps significantly and interestingly with an analysis of the dichotomy between the morality of priest and prophet or even between that of rabbinic Judaism and Pauline Christianity.

This distinction has been acutely drawn in the analysis of moral schism that has seemed to characterize American society in the past decade. The critics of American institutions have often seemed to propose the quasi-utopian values of ultimate morality as an appropriate criterion for judgment. The defenders of those institutions have appealed in justification to the ways in which those institutions—the Army, the State Department, or the business corporation—have fulfilled their traditional responsibilities and legitimate expectations, if not those of an ultimate morality. That split in perception of the moral criteria of judgment is reflected in varieties of political and social attitudes on a cluster of questions that range from attitudes to censorship of movies to an evaluation of the nature of totalitarianism. The relevant question for explanation in this context is whether this line of demarcation also draws a distinction between secular and religious ethics.

The answer to that question seems to be that the moral division is itself reflected within the religious community. Or-

170

thodox Jews or traditionalist Roman Catholics and conservative Protestant groups may find themselves sharing moral attitudes on issues as diverse as Viet Nam, crime in the streets, or university governance whereas Reform Jews, liberal Protestants, the younger Jesuits seem to be on the opposing side of these questions. Even if this sociological observation is true, then it is not religious belief or commitment to religious values but the manner in which belief or commitment is interpreted that is crucial for moral perception. That interpretation seems to depend upon aspects of contemporary society other than religion. Critics of the radical or liberal view often have suggested that it depends upon social alienation or upon insulation from the consequences of the failure of political or military institutions or upon an interesting psychological need among radicals or liberals to transcend ethnicity. Critics of the conservative view have argued in turn that the conservative attitude stems from parochialism or bigotry or from the lower middle-class status of its protagonists. The suggestion seems to be that the crucial distinction is an ideological one, between liberal and conservative attitudes in society. Yet terms like liberalism and conservatism are themselves ambiguous.

There is a possible interpretation of the difference between Liberals and Conservatives that depends upon the location of the burden of proof in social change. On that interpretation, Liberals place the burden of proof upon the existing institution or historical practice when these are confronted with programs for reform or innovation. In contrast, Conservatives place the burden of proof upon proposals for change, since the existing institution or practice has the prima facie merit of existence. Many of the traditional arguments for liberalism and conservatism can be best understood as efforts to justify this location of the burden of proof. The reverence for history, sensitivity to organic connections among institutions, the tacit value of tradition in itself, are among the reasons Conservatives offer for probing proposed changes. The horror of current situations, their contrast with forms of equality or patterns of rationality, allow the Liberal to place greater weight upon programs of reform as opposed to institutional practices.

To these well-known patterns of argument, the experience of the recent past has added, particularly in psychological terms, the imagination of historical disaster. On one account, while Weimar may have reformed Imperial Germany, it led to Nazism; while Kerensky may have overthrown the Tsar, he was succeeded by Stalinism. The horrors of the Nazi and the Stalinist dictatorships even when not explicitly conceded by ideologists have had a pervasive influence in social imagination. There is certainly a lesson in the phenomenon of the father of the Soviet hydrogen bomb advocating minimal human rights of all men based on shared human nature, as a revolutionary program. It is instructive to read the works of the greatest novelists that the Soviet Union has produced, Solzhenitzyn and Pasternak, who express their moral faith by the use of the symbolism of the Orthodox Russian church. The lesson seems to be one of the fragility of moral values and the reality of potential disaster through movements of social idealism. Yet that lesson has been learned or forgotten by both religious and secular groups, with a monopoly of error to neither.

Any effort to identify religious morality with conservatism and secular ethics with liberalism, however, in the last analysis, does a disservice to religion, secularism, conservatism, and liberalism. We are left with the disturbing conclusion that no matter how important religious belief seems to be for moral attitude, it is extremely difficult to document any decisive way in which religious thought correlates with a normative ethical position. Although the historical evidence would seem to strongly suggest that a society that is post-Christian or post-Judaic will develop a different set of values than those that characterize Jewish or Christian societies, in the complex historical transition to modernity religious groups have identified with new values in many diverse ways. Accordingly the demarcation that might have been expected between religious mo-

rality and secular morality is blurred by the cumulative persuasive redefinition of moral concepts and attitudes. It is easy to
cite striking examples. Abortion, which had been condemned by
both traditional Christianity and Judaism, for example, has now
been defended on a variety of *religious* grounds while it has been
criticized in terms of the natural right to life. The construction
then of any model of distinctive and competing religious or
secular ethical positions accordingly becomes a distortion of a
complicated social reality. Both the diversity of moral attitudes
and the convergence achievable by moral objectivity do not
seem to be directly illuminated by the presence or absence of religious belief.

Religious faith or secular ideology may set out from different
starting points in their perception of the moral situation and in
their assertion of values. Yet partisans of any ethical theory
when they exercise human rationality and moral responsibility
investigate the relevant facts of the situation as experienced by
all involved persons and must examine the consequences of
competing courses of action. That inquiry must recognize ante-
cedently different priorities of value achievement. There is no
guarantee that the inquiry must result in moral convergence.
Yet the overlooked fact in discussion of competing foundations
for value judgments is that of how convergence does take place
despite antecedent and initial conflict of moral attitude. If this
analysis is correct, this convergence can take place because
moral evaluation, like empirical evaluation, requires and permits the objective investigation of the morally relevant facts.
That objective investigation has the potential to become autonomous from any secular or religious presuppositions and attitudes that were initially brought to the investigation.

MARVIN FOX

On the Rational Commandments in

Saadia's Philosophy: A Reexamination

IT IS A COMMONPLACE IN THE HISTORY of Jewish
thought that Saadia first introduced the notion of rational commandments. Whatever interpretation we may put on those
talmudic passages, which seem to support the claim that some
commandments are rooted in reason, it is clear that Saadia is
the first major Jewish writer to refer to certain commandments
specifically as *sikhliyyot*. In this paper I want to raise the questions, What does Saadia mean by the term "rational," and on
what basis does he rest his claim that some commandments are
rational? I intend to show that there is no philosophically acceptable sense in which Saadia can be said to have shown that
there are rational commandments. Commentators on Saadia
have gone the extremes. There are those who hold, like Guttmann, that Saadia is arguing that "reason is capable of reaching
through its own powers the content of divine truth. This holds
equally for the theoretical as well as for the moral contents of
revelation. Both fundamental metaphysical truth and the moral
demands of revelation are evident to our unaided reason."[1] This
would equate the rational in Saadia's usage with logical
necessity. Other writers, taking a more restricted and cautious
view of the matter, construe Saadia's position as one in which

This paper, which was presented in a preliminary form at the Institute for
Judaism and Contemporary Thought, 1972, was read in this final form at the
Sixth World Congress of Jewish Studies, Jerusalem, 1973.

rationality is understood in purely utilitarian terms, that is, that the rational commandments are reasonable in the sense that they can be seen to serve useful purposes. Although both these positions can find some support in the text of the *Sefer Emunot veDeot,* neither addresses itself sufficiently to the bewildering complex of problems that careful study of the texts forces us to confront.

When we pay close attention to the variety of ways in which Saadia uses the various terms for "reason" and "rationality" in his book, we see that no simple explanation of these terms will suffice. In fact, it may not be possible at all to emerge with a completely satisfactory explanation, precisely because Saadia appears to say a variety of things that are not internally consistent. The strategy of interpretation that tries to understand Saadia in terms of his relationship to the Mutazilite background of his thought is useful and illuminating, but insufficient. In the last analysis, whatever the origins of his doctrines and whatever purposes they may have been intended to serve, we must still try to see and understand them in their own context. Saadia's readers are not required by him to know the entire intellectual history of the concepts and arguments that he develops. They are only required to be able to follow the course of an argument, and it is this that is so inordinately difficult in the case of the topic before us.

Early in his book Saadia adopts certain standard views concerning logical necessity. In his discussion of the procedure by which one attains rational certainty he leads us through various stages of progressive clarification until we come to the point where we must examine the statement we want to prove. At this point he informs us that statements are of three types, necessary, impossible, and possible. His example of a necessary statement is, "The fire is hot," and his example of an impossible statement is, "The fire is cold." He is either affirming here that "hot" is contained in "fire" analytically and in this sense the statement is logically necessary, or he may be making a logico-metaphysical claim to the effect that the essence of fire is heat.

175

In either case, we have a standard and rigorous version of rational certainty. (It is needless to add that we do not want to subject a tenth-century philosopher to criticisms concerning analyticity or essentiality that are familiar to contemporary philosophers. At least, this is not our purpose here.) The rational is understood here as that the contrary of which is contradictory, and for this reason is held to be necessarily true. He goes on to make clear that if we are talking not about a single statement but about a conclusion drawn from premises, he also understands and endorses fully the classical treatment of the deductive syllogism.[2]

If Saadia had maintained consistently this standard sense of "rationally necessary," he could not have said most of what he did about the rational commandments. For it is fully evident that not a single one of them is rational by this standard.

The problems we have to face emerge first in the epistemological discussion early in the book. Affirming that there are three sources of knowledge, Saadia identifies as the second source that which we know immediately through reason. His example is that we know immediately that we should approve of truth and disapprove of falsehood.[3] Yet, there is no analysis that one can produce of the statement, "Truth is good and falsehood bad," that can show it to be necessarily true, given Saadia's own definition of necessary truth. Despite the fact that in a later discussion he equates this principle with the law of contradiction so far as its certainty is concerned,[4] he offers us no ground for this equation. There is nothing internally contradictory about the assertion that truth is bad and falsehood good, or that truth merits disapproval and falsehood approval. It is true that some of our preferences or prejudices may be offended by such a suggestion, but that in no way has the effect of making the original statement a necessary truth. Whoever doubts this need only confront Nietzsche's shattering question in which he asks why truth rather than falsehood, and goes on to show how often we do, in fact, approve of falsehood and disapprove of truth.[5] In all this there is no element of rational necessity.

Once we turn to Saadia's discussion of the commandments the difficulties increase dramatically. For we find that he offers us a variety of cases in which he asserts that something is required by reason, but none of them is a case that on examination meets the standards of rational necessity he himself has set. To begin, we are told that the explanation for the fact that God did not bestow "upon His creatures complete bliss and perfect happiness without giving them commandments and prohibitions" is that "according to the judgment of reason the person who achieves some good by means of the effort that he has expended for its attainment obtains double the advantage gained by him who achieves this good without any effort but merely as a result of the kindness shown him by God."[6] In fact, reason recognizes no equality between these two. What can Saadia mean by the "judgment of reason" in this instance? It is clearly not a case of rational necessity by his own criterion. At best, there may be here some appeal to the evidence of common experience, though even this is by no means immediately evident. We have here a case in which Saadia labels as a rational judgment that which cannot qualify as such by any known standard, unless he uses the term "rational" very loosely to mean something like "reasonable" in the sense of "based on widespread experience."

Some support is given to this interpretation of rationality by certain other instances where Saadia uses the term. He holds that it is a conclusion of reason that while an isolated individual might be fooled by a false prophet, this could never happen to a large community.[7] In the explanation that follows it is evident that Saadia treats as a rational judgment that which is no more than a generalization from experience. As such it is subject to error and, if sound, is no more than probable, which is quite different from being rationally necessary. Another instance of a similar sort is the case in which he explains that reason ap-

177

proves extreme forms of punishment like the death penalty, on the ground that just as we amputate a limb in order to save a life we should destroy one life in order to save a whole community from corruption.[8] Here again we have a case not of rational necessity but rather of an appeal to experience through an argument by analogy. Now analogical argument is the basic form of all probability claims, but it certainly cannot lead to conclusions that a rational man must affirm as necessarily true. These are only a few instances of this loose usage of rational that occurs with some frequency in Saadia's discussions.

Central to our interest are those cases in which Saadia treats reason as the ground of a significant number of commandments, and insists that we can know immediately and intuitively that these commandments are binding. Among them are his affirmations that reason requires that we compensate our benefactors by reciprocal acts of beneficence or by gratitude, that wise men should not permit themselves to be insulted or treated disrespectfully, and that men generally should not be permitted to injure each other.[9] In his initial discussion of these rules of behavior he gives no further explanation of them, beyond the claim that they are required by reason. His only justification for this claim is his view that approval of the required acts and disapproval of the forbidden acts are implanted in our mind (or reason).[10] It is immediately apparent, however, that they are not implanted in the sense of being logically necessary or required by a correct metaphysical understanding of the essences of things, since their contraries are not self-contradictory. What is left then appears to be a claim like that of the natural law theorists that we are endowed in our very nature with certain modes of response, with what was called in later times a moral sense, and that we respond automatically with approval of the commanded and disapproval of the prohibited. This is not the place to take up the arguments against theories of natural moral intuition. It is sufficient, for our purposes, if we note that such claims are called into serious question, if not totally refuted, by the common fact that many people do not have this

178

supposed natural moral sense. Saadia himself, in a later discussion, states quite explicitly that good and evil must not be allowed to rest on acceptance or rejection by men. This would make them completely contingent, which he regards as absurd, and for this very reason he holds that they must derive from divine commandment.[11] It is evident from this that Saadia cannot consistently maintain his view that God has implanted a natural moral sense in us, since he fully recognizes the vagaries of human response to moral situations, and he seems to know also that this is inconsistent with the immediate rational certainty that he expects every man to possess.

Up to this point every instance in which I have used the term reason is one in which Saadia uses the Arabic term *akl*, or *sekhel* in Hebrew. At a key point in the discussion of the rational commandments he shifts his terminology from *akl* to *hikmah* or Hebrew *hokhmah*, which is usually translated as wisdom. In introducing the term, Saadia explicitly makes it synonymous with reason when he refers to "Wisdom, which is identical with reason,"[12] and he seems to make no significant distinction between the two terms.[13] In his further discussion of the rational commandments, he now attributes them to wisdom, and explicitly identifies the rationality of the commandments with their personal or social utility. It may be granted that wisdom dictates that we should take account of the practical consequences of our acts and should choose those consequences that reasonable men would find desirable because they serve widely approved purposes. What is crucially important for the present analysis, however, is to see that these purposes or ends are not themselves rationally necessary. He argues, for example, that wisdom prohibits murder since otherwise men would destroy themselves. Or again, that wisdom prohibits unrestrained fornication since otherwise we would become like animals. No man would know his own father and so could not pay honor to him or inherit his property. We may grant that if one has as his end honoring his father, or maximizing his inheritance, or preserving the human race, then one is bound to adopt the recommended rules of behavior. However, what we have here is only a hypothetical imperative, whose necessity is simply rooted in the rule of reason that one who chooses an end is bound by reason to choose the means that are requisite for its realization. There is no necessity whatsoever in these ends, and hence they do not bind us categorically. A utilitarian view of rational morality is no stronger or more binding than the ends that it recommends. Whoever finds these ends attractive will be constrained to choose these commandments as means, but no man *qua* rational must necessarily find these ends binding on him.

The significance of the shift to *hikmah* and its identification with *akl* emerges more forcefully when Saadia turns somewhat later to a direct discussion of the nature of this faculty. He asks what it is that distinguishes man from all other creatures, and answers that it is his *hikmah,* his wisdom. One cannot fail to see in this discussion an echo of the standard treatment of this question in Greek philosophy, where the usual answer is that man is a rational animal. Saadia is following in that tradition and treats wisdom as the evidence of rationality. It is therefore remarkable and instructive to see just exactly what Saadia includes in the notion of wisdom, for it turns out to be basically *techne,* a capacity for doing and making, a kind of practical intelligence. Wisdom, he says, is the power that endows us with memory, the ability to predict future occurrences, to domesticate animals, build water pumps, construct houses, make clothes, cook food, lead armies, conduct governments, and do astronomical measurements.[14] Especially noteworthy is the omission of all theoretical reason from this list. There is no reference to our ability to do logic, mathematics, physics, or metaphysics. Instead reason, which is wisdom, which is in turn the power that makes us certain of the binding force of the commandments, is understood by Saadia as nothing more than a capacity to do and make, to choose ends and to fashion the means for their realization. This is a far cry, indeed, from that intellectual power through which we apprehend the rationally necessary. Insofar as it is the ground of supposedly rational commandments, it depends on the wholly unfounded assumption that all men, at least all reasonable men, necessarily recognize as desirable those ends which Saadia has set forth. To deny their desirability is neither a logical contradiction nor a metaphysical error.

The emphasis on the usefulness of the commandments is extended to the revealed commandments as well. Although they appear for the most part to be without rational justification, Saadia holds that they are rational just to the extent that they have useful consequences. In his discussion of these *mitzvot* we can see how arbitrary is the conception of usefulness that Saadia invokes, and how little it is connected with anything like rational necessity. He holds, for example, that the benefit of the laws prohibiting sexual relations with one's immediate relatives is that "since the relationship with them is necessarily intimate, the license to marry them would encourage dissoluteness on their part."[15] Moreover, if a man could marry his own sister, homely girls would end up as old maids because every potential suitor would say that they are so ugly that not even their own brothers would marry them. In another case, he says that the benefit of the laws of cleanness and uncleanness is that it makes a man feel very humble about his own body. It is sufficiently clear that these instances of the useful are in no way such as to compel the assent of a rational man. There is no evidence that these are cases of behavior that is required or justified by reason.

It is no wonder, then, that despite all of his repeated efforts to show us that the commandments are grounded in reason, Saadia regularly invokes divine authority as well. He does not seem able to rely only on reason as a source of commandments, and this, not only for the familiar reason that we still need revelation to set out for us the details of procedure with respect to the various rational commandments. Precisely because he cannot supply a truly rational ground for the *mitzvot,* he shifts his ground and affirms that to justify them we must appeal to

181

divine revelation and authority. He expresses his amazement at those people "who, being slaves, yet believe that they have no master, and who are confident that any object the existence of which they deny must be non-existent and whatever they declare to be in existence is so."[16] Now this is exactly the state of those who claim to know what is rationally necessary, and what is rationally impossible. They affirm as an article of rational certainty that what reason requires must be the case in reality, and that what reason finds impossible cannot be the case in reality. Yet, Saadia, who calls on reason over and over, is saying that not our apprehension but what a higher power dictates is what determines the state of affairs in the world. This is why he goes on in that same passage to assert that "it is sheer folly on the part of people to imagine that their refusal to acknowledge the sovereignty of the Lord exempts them from His commandments and prohibitions." It would appear that not independent human reason but rather divine commandment is decisive and binding.

In his introduction to the discussion of the commandments, Saadia again stresses the primacy of the divine source. God has taught us through his prophets, he says, the ways in which we are to serve Him, and these consist in the laws that he has revealed to us. The certainty of these laws derives from the fact that they are transmitted by prophets who prove their authenticity by performing miracles.[17] Only after we have received the revelation can we establish that it has some rational foundation, which is to say that the laws serve some useful purpose. It may not be without significance that in making this point Saadia does not say initially that it is by way of *akl* or *sekhel* that we come to know that these laws are necessary. Instead, he uses the term *nazar*, which carries the sense of a more general kind of overview of the phenomena. This is why Altmann is correct in translating the passage as follows: "Later we found that speculation confirms the necessity of the law for us."[18] At this point Saadia seems to be saying clearly that we are ultimately dependent on divine revelation for all the commandments, and that only after the fact of being commanded can we use our general intellectual capacity to discover some elements of usefulness in the commandments, but not strict rational necessity. In the latter case, we would certainly be free of any need for divine revelation.

The same kind of appeal to the authority of revelation is made when he describes man as distinguished by his wisdom. Man is superior to all other creatures on earth. He alone has free choice and the capacity to obey God or defy Him. God gave us his law and "miracles and marvels were wrought by the prophets, wherefore we accepted it as binding."[19] Even in this prologue to the identification of man as a rational creature, the commandments are represented as deriving their force from divine authority. Furthermore, Saadia holds that man is the foundation of the world, the center around which all creation revolves, and therefore "it is only right that man should be subject to commandments and prohibitions."[20] How else can we be certain that he will fulfill his responsibility to all creation? What makes man truly superior to all creatures is the fact that God has "made him the bearer of His commandments and prohibitions, as Scripture says: And unto man He said: Behold the fear of the Lord, that is wisdom."[21] Apparently, man's true distinction is not in anything that he achieves by way of independent reason, but only in the fact that he is subject to divine commandment. The highest practicality, which wisdom teaches, is not independent rational moral knowledge, but "fear of the Lord."

Although this appeal to the authority of revelation is strong, we cannot overlook an equally strong pull in the opposite direction. We must pay attention to a passage that ranks as Saadia's most forceful invocation of the primacy of reason in the knowledge of good and evil. In a defense of the permanence of the Mosaic law and of the superiority of Mosaic prophecy, Saadia adopts a position that seems to contradict and reject any appeal to authority. He asserts that we accept the teachings of Moses not because of any signs or miracles but because we

183

discerned that what he taught us was right or lawful. The signs and miracles only served to strengthen his authority. If, however, a presumed prophet should come to us with the most impressive collection of marvels and miracles, but commands us what we know to be wrong, then we must reject him categorically. If he tells us that God commands us to commit adultery, or any similar violation of the law, then we know that he is utterly unworthy of any attention on our part, because "what he called upon us to do is not sanctioned either by reason [akl] or tradition."[22] So strongly does Saadia maintain this position that he goes on to make the remarkable statement that no matter how impressive the miracles of such a man, "our reply to him should be the same as that of all of us would be to anyone who would show us miracles and marvels for the purpose of making us give up such rational convictions as that the truth is good and lying reprehensible and the like. He was therefore compelled to take refuge in the theory that the disapproval of lying and the approval of truth were not prompted by reason but were the result of the commandments and prohibitions of Scripture, and the same was true for the rejection of murder, adultery, and stealing. When he had come to that, however, I felt that I needed no longer concern myself with him and that I had my fill of discussion with him."[23]

Consider how uncompromising this statement is. The message of prophecy is verified only by reason and the rational recognition that what the prophet teaches is binding. So confident is Saadia here of this rational power that he will have it stand against all forces, even those that appear to be unquestionably miraculous in character. Whoever questions that reason teaches us, independently of all scriptural authority, that lying, adultery, murder, and stealing are wicked, has placed himself beyond the pale of rational men. He is unworthy of our attention and we cannot hope to carry on any discussion with him. Unhappily, despite the vehemence of his tone, Saadia never shows us how we can know that reason forbids these acts. If the answer is in utilitarian terms, then it is subject to all the criticisms that were made above. If the answer is in terms of rational necessity, then he has the impossible task of demonstrating that a statement like, "Murder, adultery, lying and stealing are good," involves us in an internal contradiction. If the answer is in terms of the claim that we have a moral sense that teaches us immediately that these actions are evil, then he must face the equally difficult task of accounting for all those people who have no such awareness at all. Saadia was surely familiar with the tannaitic midrash which teaches that God offered the Torah to various nations of the world and each of them rejected it because they could not accept the moral restrictions that it contains. They could not give up murder, adultery, or theft because they found it rooted in their nature to engage in these practices.[24] How, then, could he possibly argue that all men know by nature that these modes of behavior are evil? Yet, even though there appears to be no ground for his forceful conviction, there is no question that the conviction is expressed in this passage. I can only explain the extreme position, in spite of its obvious weakness, as stemming from the polemical character of the passage. He is seeking here to defend the prophecy of Moses and the Law of Moses against claims that there have been new revelations, those of Christianity and Islam. If we allow signs and miracles to serve as authentication of claims to prophecy, then Judaism is in danger of being superseded by new religions. To prevent this he goes to the extreme of making a supposed rational claim the judge of Scripture and thus eliminating all the claims that base themselves on miracles alone. The technique may be effective. Unfortunately, the argument is unsound.

It is now clear what little weight we should place on the claim that Saadia shows that there are rational commandments. He has certainly not shown that there are commandments that are in any strict sense rationally necessary. At best, he has shown that many commandments have consequences that men might reasonably be expected to consider useful. This is an extremely weak sense of rational, one that does not merit that designation

185

at all. His further claim that we have an innate moral sense is refuted both by tradition and by experience. For this very reason, he himself is forced regularly to invoke scriptural authority as the ground of the commandments and finally to give it priority over any claims that the commandments can be known by unaided reason. The limits and limitations of his position are most clearly exposed when we consider the thorough inadequacy of the extreme position he takes when he seeks to defend Judaism against other faiths by making its law rest on reason alone. We can now see that the facile statements about rational commandments in Saadia's philosophy that occur frequently in the literature, derive from a reading that pays attention to the terms Saadia used rather than to the argument on which his statements are based. Calling a statement rationally necessary does not suffice to make it so.

1. Julius Guttmann, *Philosophies of Judaism,* (New York, 1964), p. 64. For general discussions of the topic see the four most recent papers on the subject, which also contain references to the earlier literature. They are: Alexander Altmann, "Halukat ha-Mitzvot LeRaSaG," in *RaSaG: Kobetz Torani-Mada'i,* ed. J. L. Fishman (Jerusalem, 1943); Alexander Altmann, "Saadya's Conception of the Law," *Bulletin of the John Rylands Library* 28 (1944); Joab Elstein, "Torat ha-Mitzvot beMishnat Rab Saadya," *Tarbiz* 38 (1969); Haggai ben-Shammai, "Halukat ha-Mitzvot uMusag ha-Hokhmah beMishnat RaSaG," *Tarbiz* 41 (1972).

2. Saadia Gaon, *The Book of Beliefs and Opinions,* trans. Samuel Rosenblatt, (New Haven, 1948), pp. 11–12. All references are to this translation, unless otherwise noted.

3. Ibid., p. 16; cf., pp. 60, 131.

4. Ibid., p. 131.

5. Friederich Nietzsche, *Beyond Good and Evil,* trans. Walter Kaufmann, (New York, 1966), pp. 9–12.

6. Saadia Gaon, *Beliefs and Opinions,* pp. 137–38.

7. Ibid., p. 157.

8. Ibid., p. 185.

9. Ibid., p. 139.

10. Ibid., p. 140.

11. Ibid., p. 193.

12. Ibid., p. 140.

13. For a general discussion of this theme see, Alexander Altmann, "Halukat ha-Mitzvot le-RaSaG," in *Rab Saadia Gaon*, ed. J. L. Fishman, (Jerusalem, 1943).

14. Saadia Gaon, *Beliefs and Opinions*, pp. 181–82.

15. Ibid., p. 144.

16. Ibid., p. 15.

17. Ibid., p. 138.

18. Saadia Gaon, *Book of Doctrines and Beliefs*, in *Three Jewish Philosophers*, ed. and trans. Alexander Altmann, (New York. 1972), p. 95. Contrast this careful version with the looser reading of Rosenblatt, "Afterwards we discovered the rational basis for the necessity of their prescription" (p. 138).

19. Saadia Gaon, *Beliefs and Opinions*, p. 181.

20. Ibid., p. 182.

21. Ibid., p. 183.

22. Ibid., p. 164.

23. Ibid.

24. *Sifre Debarim* (ed. Horowitz-Finkelstein), sec. 343, pp. 395–97. Cf. also, *Mekilta* (ed. Lauterbach), *BaHodesh*, pp. 234–35.

Part Four

THE CONTEMPORARY SITUATION

MEIR PA'IL

The Dynamics of Power:

Morality in Armed Conflict

After the Six Day War

THE MORAL ASPECT IS of great importance in any
military phenomenon. After all, the military profession involves
work with human beings, both within our own army and on the
other side of the line, within and against enemy forces. Such
moral considerations encompass an immense landscape of
ethics that is difficult to cover in a single article or lecture.

This paper proposes to deal with one aspect of the question
only: our approach to the enemy; under the conditions of the
State of Israel, this means the Arab enemy.

It is very difficult to explain whence the unique phenomenon
of the I.D.F. (Israel Defense Force) originated, but there can be
no doubt that it is rooted in the long tradition of thirty-five
hundred years of Jewish history, as well as in the serious study
of the best in military tradition. However, in order not to avoid
praising the I.D.F., it is in place to state that we—the Zionist
movement—have managed to build, within three or four
generations, the best military force in the Middle East. There
are no prospects that any military force in the Middle East will
become capable of overpowering the Israeli military establishment in the foreseeable future. The I.D.F. is the best military institution to be established in the Middle East; it developed interesting and original values of professional military doctrine,
of organization and leadership, and also moral and human
values.

The supreme value of adherence to the mission is one example of a universal value, accepted in all the armies in the world; the basic value of the military arm's subordination to the democratic, political, and civilian authority is part of the Jewish tradition, as well as a lesson learned from modern European civilization; the value of a popular mass army includes elements of ancient Jewish tradition, as well as the application of modern methods developed since the French Revolution.

There are also original values: the supreme concern to reduce to the absolute minimum the loss of human life; the value of sacrifice for the sake of one's comrade (which in the Palmakh was given the name "brotherhood of warriors"); that important original I.D.F. value that requires leadership to be based on human relations, on persuasion, on an understanding of the justice of the cause, above and beyond mere military discipline; the original value of promoting initiative and independent thought, in order to develop an ever rejuvenated military doctrine.

The very process of the I.D.F.'s emergence from the Haganah underground organization is a unique element of Zionist historic creativity; undoubtedly, this is a subject worthy of the attention of historians. Until now, at least, the I.D.F. has been an original phenomenon—no less original than the kibbutz, which probably is one of the most important social contributions made by the Zionist movement to humanity.

Indeed, the importance of the I.D.F. and its specific gravity in Israel is so great, and it constitutes so interesting a phenomenon, that I can only be proud of having been among its officers and founders.

This article, as stated above, proposes to discuss only one of the spheres in which the I.D.F. is active: attitudes toward the Arab enemy. This does not cover the entire subject of morality in our military life but constitutes a primary yardstick for our army's morality.

When the book *The Seventh Day*[1] was published in 1967, I had the opportunity of addressing a large gathering at Kibbutz Ein Hahoresh, which assembled to mark the book's appearance. On that occasion I expressed some concern about a possible decline in the soldiers' moral standards, because of technological development.[2]

Soon the simple soldier will activate his weaponry by means of telescopic sights, radar, lasers, and television. No longer will he encounter human beings in front of him, nor see the blood he spills. The modern soldier already is capable of causing destruction without having to look with his own eyes at the result of his action—without having to sense the extent of the havoc he causes. This greatly reduces the pangs of conscience that stem from a moral humanity.

In that same lecture I developed four theses, as to why the moral ideal of the "purity of arms" must be maintained.

WE NEGATE THE PRINCIPLE OF AN EYE FOR AN EYE,
IN ITS VULGAR SENSE

Even if our Arab enemies still are at a historical stage in their development where "an eye for an eye" is an inherent part of their culture, and they have little concern for "purity of arms", this still does not justify our acting the way they do. We don't operate the way they do in almost any other field—not in scientific research, not in economic development, not in the way we work, not in farm development, not in our political and social systems, and not even in our military doctrine and methods. Consequently, there is no reason whatsoever for us to begin learning from them their primitive criteria of murder and crude retribution. If we have transgressed in such matters, from time to time, we must have the courage of being ashamed of it. We must free ourselves of such acts, rather than sanctify them.

MAINTAINING THE PURITY OF OUR ARMS
DOES NOT REDUCE OUR COMBAT CAPACITY

During my lecture I demonstrated—with examples taken from the I.D.F.'s actual experience—that maintaining purity of arms does not detract from any unit's fighting ability, from the

193

soldiers' courage, or from the units' accomplishments. The I.D.F.'s experience proves clearly that one can fight well while completely observing the principle of purity of arms and while maintaining a moral attitude toward the Arab enemy.

PURITY OF ARMS IS A POLITICAL TOOL

This argument is even more important than the two previous ones: it states that, under the specific conditions of the State of Israel and the Zionist movement in the Middle East and throughout the world, the maintenance of this principle is an implement for the furthering of our national movement's political interests. In spite of all our military superiority over our Arab enemies, we will not be able to destroy them and to take over the whole Middle East and the Arab states. In the final analysis at some time in the future, there is the possibility that our struggles will result in a political system of mutual respect and coexistence with our present enemies. Because of this we will do well to make sure that as little suffering as possible be caused to innocent people. The political damage to our cause from the Dir Yassin affair can serve as one example of the political importance of the purity of arms.

OVERALL NATIONAL MORALITY

This is the most important point of all; it asserts that the maintenance of purity of arms is one of the most important ways in which the decency of the nation, as a whole, can be preserved. Many colonial armies, even those of democratic countries such as Great Britain, France, Holland and the United States, have committed immoral acts overseas. Such were usually the work of mercenary, professional, or volunteer elements in these armies. Although most of these volunteer mercenaries came from the mother country, obviously only a tiny proportion of that country's citizens dirtied their hands with such inhuman deeds.

In connection with the Nazi holocaust and German excesses

194

during the occupation in World War II, we accused the Germans that all that was the work of their popular mass army and not that of a small group of mercenaries. In other words, almost all strata of the German people participated in such activity and consequently the morality of the entire German nation was sullied.

The I.D.F. is an outstanding example of a popular, or a citizens', army of a twentieth-century democratic country. Consequently anyone who argues that strict adherence to moral standards is not necessary in an army such as ours automatically denies the need for moral behavior on the part of all the country's citizens; the I.D.F., after all, consists of all the country's men of ages 18 to 55, and all its women 18 to 25.

Whoever takes the precept of "pure arms" lightly in effect adopts a concept of general reeducation for all of us, from the very beginning. This would involve the serious internal danger of an Israel that could develop gradually into something resembling a Middle Eastern Prussia. Such an image would certainly be far removed from the political vision and social aspirations of the Zionist movement.

The above four theses, all of which posit the principle of purity of arms, possess constant validity—at least under the concrete conditions of the State of Israel. However, historical circumstances do change, creating new conditions and bringing with them new ideas, necessitating the repeated reexamination of this problem both for purposes of purely academic study, as well as of educational and practical policy.

In the course of almost one hundred years of Zionist history, the attitude of the Jews engaged in warfare against Arab opponents developed in a most interesting manner. One may sum it up as an escalation of the dimension of hate. During the Hashomer period, before World War I, the attitude was one of near affection. The Jewish fighting man then considered his Arab opponent as a likable robber, a kind of diminutive *gazlan,* a nice little thief. The Jewish combatant organizations then proposed to demonstrate to the Arabs that Jewish settlements

195

knew how to defend themselves, that Jews were not to be pa-
tronized and that their lives and property were not without pro-
tection. The dominant idea was to protect oneself decisively, but
politely, always doing one's best to avoid bloodshed and thus to
reduce, as much as possible, the distance between the two peoples. This approach was expressed in its simplest terms by Av-
raham Shapira, who although never formally a member of
Hashomer, did represent that period. In his old age he explained: "I never killed anybody, nor was I killed."

After World War I, during the early 1920s, the conflict between Jews and Arabs assumed a more and more national
character. However, even at that time the Jews tended to
abstain from anything that would intensify the military aspects
of this conflict, striving to moderate political tension. For more
than fifteen years the political leadership imposed the need for
moderation on the people engaged in defense, forcing them to
build fortifications, to defend settlements from behind the
fence, leaving the initiative to the Arabs in the riots of 1920,
1921, 1929 and 1936, repelling attacks in the hope that the
conflict would not spread, but rather be contained. Under these
circumstances the principle of Havlaga ("self-restraint") was
developed; this was a political idea, designed to reduce
bloodshed. However, with all its moderation, "self-restraint"
was still more violent than the ideas that had prevailed at the
time of Hashomer, when the Arab opponent had been
considered a likeable character, without any national and
political aspirations.

The process of "coming forth from behind the fences" took
place during the 1936–39 "disorders"; this meant a transition to
aggresive nonstatic activity outside the Jewish settlements
themselves—a vital necessity, from the military point of view, in
response to the escalation of Arab armed action. At that time
the emergence of the reprisal type of action began to develop—
though aimed against those directly responsible, Arab commanders and fighters. We began to engage in mobile activity at
night, as well as during the day, to forestall Arab activity in the

area, in order to achieve control of the countryside lying between the Jewish settlements, and in order to force the Arab bands to remain in their own houses and villages, afraid to come out and to take military action. In the course of this stage we developed the concept of ambush, of attack, of mobile harrassing action on foot and from vehicles, at night and during the day. This change in the style of activity automatically resulted in the significant intensification of hate toward the Arab enemy. This change actually was an objective result of the intensification of the Jewish-Arab national conflict; at that time some people in our midst first began to enunciate the slogan that "the Arab problem must be viewed through gun sights."

At that time certain parts of the Zionist movement—especially at its extreme right wing—began to develop the idea of vulgar revenge. There were cases of grenades thrown into Arab market places, and shooting at Arab buses without concern for the fact that most of those hurt were innocent civilians. The proponents of the idea of retribution argued that it was a response in line with the cultural norms of the Middle East. The idea was completely rejected by the political leadership of the Zionist movement, who were also decisive in determining the policy of the Haganah. It retained the ideal of purity of arms, adopting a slogan first raised by Yitzhak Sadeh. Sadeh was the first proponent of taking the military mobile initiative, but it was also he who preached: "Love the rifle, but hate war."

The War of Independence (1947–49), was the climax of the life-and-death struggle between the Arab and Jewish national movements. If ever there was a danger of complete destruction and the eradication of the Zionist idea, it was in 1948. In spite of the military victory, the feelings of terror and of hate among Jews—results of the objective circumstances—were extremely severe. Quite possibly these emotions were only intensified on the backdrop of the holocaust of World War II. To this very day, in the 1970s, we still carry these feelings along with us, and it is very difficult to overcome them under the ongoing circumstances that prevail in the Arab-Jewish conflict.

With our victory in the Six Day War (June 1967) the Jewish-Arab conflict entered into a new stage. All aspects of the Jewish and the Arab national movements were affected. In order to continue the discussion of the moral dimension of warfare we shall examine only one of these aspects: a task new to the I.D.F. since the Six Day War—that of an army of occupation.

Since June 1967 we exercise political sovereignty over most of the Palestinians. For a prolonged period of time, sizable numbers of the I.D.F. and of the Israeli police have operated an occupation government over the occupied areas and that over people who do not wish to see in us either liberators or legitimate rulers. This reality encapsulates the continued growth of hatred and alienation. That which is upon the surface can be estimated to a degree, but that below it, the latent hostility, cannot.

From the purely military point of view the problem is by no means severe. We have had fantastic successes in our war against the Palestinian guerilla movement. There is no certainty, however, that our success in bringing about a political and ideological rapprochement between the Jewish and Arab national movements has been nearly as great. Because of this, it is likely that enmity will break out in varying degrees of intensity in the future. In other words, these circumstances of occupation create the objective conditions for growing ideological and political enmity between Jews and Arabs; this reality already results in significant changes in the emotional and the moral approach of the Jewish soldier to the Arab, and this will continue in the future. On this point more shall be said below.

Meanwhile, let us clarify the extent of our military prowess, in relation to the Palestinian nation. It must be emphasized that Israel has nothing to worry about militarily at any time in the foreseeable future, even if there should be serious outbreaks of violence on the part of the Palestinian public and the Palestinian guerilla movements. Even if the Palestinians under Israel's control in Judea, Samaria, Gaza, and elsewhere manage to develop such intensive guerilla activity that Arab rule crystallizes in their areas and the Israelis lose their hold upon them—even then the war here will not develop along the lines of Vietnam, but in a different manner altogether. If this guerilla activity reaches very serious dimensions, there will be no alternative but to mobilize most of the I.D.F., and to clean up the area in a thorough manner, with the help of helicopters, armor, infantry, with support from the air force, the engineers, and the artillery. The result of such an action—it would not take long—would be disaster for the Palestinians, along lines similar to what was done in Biafra by the Nigerian army. Israel, of course, will continue to exist, but the Palestinian people will no longer constitute a communtiy, in the political sense of the term, within this country. This is the immense difference between Israel and Vietnam. This is the ultimate perspective of Palestinian guerilla warfare, if it does reach powerful dimensions, and if the outside world does not interfere with Israel's free use of its military force. This would be a tragic conclusion to the occupation; its losers would be mainly the Palestinians, while the most important strategic and political advantage would be Israel's.

What would be the moral cost of such a gain? It would seem that the people's army of Israel that would be forced to participate in such a filthy war would emerge with different values from those which characterized it at its beginning. Some of the Israelis would return from this conflict with hearts broken by the injustice that stems from their military strength, but most of our soldiers are likely to silence their conscience through the adoption of a nationalistic ideology of Jewish mastery over this country and the complete denial of any right and status to the Palestinian national community. This would bring about the adoption of a racist attitude toward the Arabs, one that considers them as inferiors; or perhaps even of a theory that the Palestinians, damn them, must solve their national problem among their fellow Arabs outside this country. However, it is very questionable just how happy a people we would be after such a future war; most certainly we would not be a more humane, more just people, especially since our war with the other Arab countries would not yet be concluded even after that "victory."

Of course, we have not yet reached the possible nadir of the Palestinian nation's tragedy. However, the growth of Arab-Jewish enmity during the last three generations and Israel's increasing military strength can lead to such a disaster at some time in the future. Even if we do console ourselves that the major cause of the conflict lies in Arab, rather than Jewish, enmity—even if we accept the explanation that the escalation of mutual hostility was an inexorable objective process that nobody could have prevented—even then it is our responsibility to consider the extent of hatred at present and its prognosis, this in light of the problem's moral aspects on our, the Jewish, side. In the final analysis it is this moral element that will affect the quality of Israel's society; consequently, we must take it into consideration even in making day-to-day decisions at this time.

The fact is that a stalwart State of Israel does not in and of itself constitute the solution for all the problems of the Jewish people and the Zionist movement. Also, force and strength have a dialectic dynamics of their own that at times require us to reflect on questions of morality.

Should we want to learn something about the network of relations that develop out of the day-to-day reality of military occupation, we must study the actual circumstances of what happens at the camps of the Israeli forces in the field, among the soldiers themselves. Below we shall quote several sections from Yigal Lev's book, *War Likes Young Men* (Bitan Publishers, 1972),[3] which deals with the I.D.F.'s tasks as an occupying army. The author himself is a combat officer, with the rank of major; his book is based on "facts and situations borrowed from reality, although no character in the book can be identified with any real person."

Here are four sections from this book.

200

MURDER OUT OF SHAME

Things already were quiet in our sector, that day. Uri, the battallion intelligence officer, informed us that there were two corpses in the nearby village, and that we should see to it that the inhabitants bury them.

We rushed over there. They lay in the familiar posture of corpses, as if cut down in the midst of flight. One held some food in his hand, and the other two boxes of rifle ammunition. And they were no more than children.

I asked Uri what had happened. He hesitated a moment, but then the story came out in a rush.

"A colonel visited here, one of the staff officers. He wanted to tour the lines, so I took him in my jeep and we went. Suddenly, near the bunker, I saw them . . . nu, these two here, coming out with something in their hands. When they noticed us they began to run away. So he said to me: 'Hit 'em'. There was a machine gun in the jeep and . . . "

I looked at Uri, unable to believe what I had heard. "You . . . you . . . ," I stammered, "you shot these kids and all they did was run away . . . ."

"But I had an order," he said as if to defend himself.

"An order? What kind of an order, Uri?" I screamed at him. "An order to do what? . . . ."

"He said to hit 'em."

I felt everything around me growing hazy.

"But why, Uri? What the hell for?"

"He was my superior and he said . . . ."

"Don't lie. Why did you do it?"

"I was ashamed . . ." he said, as if spitting out the very essence of his secret. Then he was quiet.

"What were you ashamed of?"

"That second, just before I pulled the trigger, I thought there's still a war on, and what will people say afterwards? Uri is chicken; he can't even shoot. He's an intelligence officer; he has to stand on a stack of moral tracts and stretch so he'll see what war is really like. By the time he gets down out of his ivory tower, the war'll be over. He wants others to do the dirty work for him. I was ashamed . . . I thought people'll laugh at me . . . but . . . ."

201

I knew that Uri and what he had done were rare exceptions, not the rule. However, it was a question of human lives, and a question of Uri, who had grown up in a kibbutz yet killed because he was ashamed that somebody would say he is not a man. What cried forth from Uri's silence, cried forth from what he had done, was the fear of what somebody might say.[4]

FUNDAMENTAL ENMITY

Our jeep moves through the small town's silent streets. The market place is colorful and excites the imagination. An oriental market, with fruit loading down all the stands. There are strings of dry onions and garlic, mountains of apples, pears, grapes; sandals are hung by their straps, gently moving in the wind. There are chickens, stacks of earthenware jars, a noisy crowd in lively motion.

Eyes look at us with curiosity, suspicion and fear. Strange eyes—when did you ever see their likes? Then, in those far-off days just after the Six Day War, when the mass of refugees fled just ahead of our armored columns. Except that then these eyes were opaque, dead, not even afraid. Now there is something new in them, poisonous and bitter. I understood—these eyes will follow us from now on. These eyes one finds it difficult to turn one's back on: they might turn into a knife.

Doctor Livni is silent. Do I look like him also, shaken and nauseous, but stubborn of chin? Everything in me wants to say something, but he sits as frozen to his seat.

Yossi's face is more open. He is at the wheel and I can see his expression in the mirror: he is disgusted, but some sort of hardness has come into the corners of his mouth. He spit out contemptuously:

"Look at all this filth. If you don't jam the Uzi barrel to their backs they'll stick you with a knife quicker than you can say Jack Robinson. And that sickening sheikh—he probably has a whole store of explosives in his basement for the terrorists. 'Of course I'll cooperate with you'—he imitated the voice of the sheikh who had escorted us to our jeep. In his mother's grave he'll cooperate. What a miserable people these are. Smooth and slimy, like an eel. Wherever you grab it, it slips out of your hands and just leaves you with a feeling of disgust."

202

Livni remained silent. I wanted him to answer; perhaps what Yossi said would shake him out of his frozen tranquility, but he didn't say anything. It seemed to me that he was biting his lips.

"Doctor, watch out!" Yossi called. He stepped on the gas and the jeep suddenly moved like a rocket, pushing through the crowded market street. For a long moment I failed to understand; only after we had gone some distance I heard the explosion.

We stopped in a screech and turned the jeep around, to go back to the market. As if by magic, our two halftracks on patrol arrived at the same time.

Amidst all the noise and screaming and crying I understood what had happened: somebody had thrown a grenade at the jeep. The chances of hitting a moving vehicle with a grenade are poor. When we accelerated, the grenade rolled under one of the stands, where it exploded and caused a bloodbath: legs torn off, a stream of blood, desperate cries. Twelve people were wounded, all of them local residents. Four of them later died of their wounds, including a little girl and a woman.

In the midst of all that awful noise of cars blowing their horns, the groaning wounded and anxious mothers looking for their lost children, I thought: God almighty, what kind of people are these who throw grenades in the midst of a crowded market place—in the midst of their own families? And all they had was a slight hope that the grenade would hit some Israelis?

The people at the stands undoubtedly had seen who had thrown the grenade; for nobody can move through the market without their eyes examining him to determine what he wants to buy and how much he has to spend. They saw death rolling and never warned anybody. Do they really value human life so cheaply?

A strange people. Four dead, eight wounded—most of them women and children, all of them Arabs, fellow townspeople. Can anyone imagine a Jew doing anything like that among his own people?

I wanted to ask the doctor what he thought, but I saw that he was busy with the wounded. He staunched bleeding, cleaned wounds, had them taken to the town's small hospital. Everything he did was done quietly, with a kind of unshakable authority.

203

We imposed curfew. Our special unit went into action. Its men met with whomever they were supposed to meet, had short conversations with anonymous people whose faces remained hidden and quickly went to a house on the outskirts of town. It was a fancy house, two stories. The son of the owner of this house had thrown the grenade, and now, of course, he had run away. Did the father know what his son had been up to? There could be no doubt about it.

The father wore the long robe, embroidered with silver threads, on his head the traditional black headdress, an eagle beak for a nose, his voice mellifluous, accustomed to command. He owns much land in the town, is the sheikh's brother. However, his sense of superiority melted away as the jeeps pulled up all around his house. He met us with whimpers and broke into tears when we informed him that his house would be blown up within twenty-four hours, that he had to get out. He sprawled on the broad stairway of the house and wept. His robe no longer betokened majesty.

We were told that Sheikh Yasser el Husseini wanted to see us. We waited for him in our headquarters, in the town's school building. He came in proudly, with all his accustomed ceremonial and form.

He expressed no sorrow about his town's dead, about the people who had been wounded, about the curfew we had imposed. He came to request us not to destroy his brother's house. He did not petition for life, only for property.

What value is there in the death of a little girl, of some women and two peddlers, of lost arms and legs? These are of no importance. What is human life after all? A woman can have ten babies, so what does one child matter? The house, however, has been standing for a long time. It represents the family's status; it symbolizes the greatness of all the relatives. The family continues.

The sheikh stood there in the classroom which now served as our office, and attempted to explain the logic of his request: "Life and death are in the hands of Allah. What is human life? Like a burning candle: one puff of air, and it goes out. What is the value of a life? Allah in his mercy has created so many people and every one of them lives and then dies. What's the point of shedding tears over them?"

204

I wanted to ask him if his own life came under the same heading, but he continued to speak, as if intoxicated by his own words: "Man is the cheapest animal of all. One makes him in a moment of pleasure, without investing anything in him. He isn't like grapevines that have to be cultivated, fertilized, plowed, irrigated, harvested. A human being grows up just like that. Before you know it he's old enough to support himself."

Dr. Livni and I sat there, as if in shock. We were being taught new concepts in the value of human life. Our teachers had told us that "to save a single life is equivalent to saving the whole world," and here was the sheikh, trying to prove the opposite.

"In terms of our concepts," he said, "when there is a goal it becomes the most important thing, and the lives of people around are worth nothing. Isn't it the same with you? Don't you sacrifice lives to conquer some hill-top which in the final analysis isn't worth anything?"

"War is war," I replied, "but to throw a hand grenade at an army jeep in the midst of your own people?"

"The man who threw the grenade does not think the injured people and those who were killed are worth anything. The only value was to achieve the goal—to hit the jeep."

"But these people are your brothers. They believe in your religion. They even are your relatives."

"Because of that they also understand that they have become the victims of a great cause."

It was strange conversation, in a vacuum. It was clear to us that there would be no common language with the sheikh who had come to ask that property be saved, not human lives.[5]

THE CHASE

When we closed in from all sides on the opening of the caves where the marauders had hidden, we saw her.

There she sat calmly, as if there were nothing strange about men, with sunburned faces, dripping sweat and armed with automatic rifles, climbing up the steep mountainside at dawn. She neither smiled, not did she run away. All she did was smooth her skirt, the way a bashful woman will when men look at her.

We could have killed her, just to be sure, because she stood on top of the bare hill, next to the cave opening. We could have

205

killed her, just to be sure, the way cowards do—kill everything, so nothing can hurt you.

But we never thought of that. It is hard to imagine that anyone among us even thought of that.

To kill a woman?

And we learned that, also—the most terrible lesson there is. It isn't the chase, the fleeing enemy who looks for a place to hide, the attack, the bullets that tear the living flesh—it is something deeper than all that, deeper than even a bullet can penetrate. Something inside was killed. The education we got was murdered—that education about the decency of warriors, about the laws of combat. You can't play at chivalrous knights any more, when three armed men hide behind the skirts of a woman.

Now everything is permissible. All the rules died, together with Eli and Haimke.

These two men went up to her. Without that instinct of caution that had become almost second nature they went up to that woman chewing her piece of pita in front of the cave, to ask if she had seen the fleeing marauders. No, she shook her head, she had seen nothing. Haimke offered her a drink of water. He took his canteen off his belt, opened it for her and she, with a lazy motion lackadasical almost, moved away from the cave which her skirts had hidden. And then, before we grasped what our eyes had seen and our ears heard, Eli and Haimke were down and three terrorists in camouflage uniforms tried breaking away from the cave. Everything happened so slowly, like a movie in slow motion. Yossi was the first to shoot, and then all of us fired in the madness of our shame. They fell, the three of them . . . .

They died as cowards—men hiding behind the skirts of a woman and trusting our damned weakness: that Jewish soldiers never hurt a woman.

They were fully aware of our weakness and exploited it—that damned hesitation that keeps us from playing to the hilt. That is the hesitation that says you must remain a human being, always decent, always defeating the enemy while endangering yourself to the utmost. As if in facing danger you made up for manslaughter; as if baring your own flesh to enemy bullets purified your war. This is the decency of battle.[6]

206

SEARCH

We went out on a search mission. Our information took us to a house on the outskirts of the city, occupied by several families. Instructions were clear: hurt nobody; don't shoot except in self-defense, and even then, don't hurt women and children.

We knocked at a door. A pale woman opened. Her hair was wrapped in a piece of cloth—something between handkerchief and towel. She wore a faded robe and dragged her feet.

"No, nobody home," she said through the crack in the door. We went into the apartment, broke into one of the rooms. I saw how uncontrolled Yossi was when we searched the place. He turned furniture over. The gleam in his eye terrified me. Yossi had completely changed. Before I could do anything to control him, the door to the next room flew open and a burst of gunfire swept us. Moshe, one of our men, was wounded, and then a grenade was thrown into the room. With incredible speed, Yossi threw the grenade out the window. Everything happened too quickly, confusedly. First Yossi the wild man, destructive, and then Yossi who jumped at the grenade and coolly threw it outside, where it exploded with a loud bang. We sprayed the rooms with automatic fire. You pull the trigger madly, switch magazines only after your uzi has stopped jerking in your hands.

When the tempest settled, there were two dead terrorists. A third, wounded, hid under one of the beds. The smell of gun powder, of lime and fallen plaster was everywhere. The woman sat bunched up screaming in a corner, her fear and despair filling the room.

Reinforcements arrived from our unit. By then there was no need for them. The medics took the dead and wounded to the helicopter pad. Together with Yossi and the others I went back to our headquarters, in the school building.

What kind of a man is this Yossi? Is there some kind of link between his wildness during the search and his naiveté? Now, riding with me in the jeep, he was relaxed, as if drained of all the energy that had burned in him before. He sat there with his head hanging forward, his body lurching with every bump in the road. A tired little boy, a child who has finished playing and now yields to every movement of the vehicle. When we arrived, I woke him

207

up. "Wake up, Yossi. You did a good job; now you can go to
sleep."

He smiled, and that moment he really looked like a little boy,
well-satisfied with himself: "What a wreck we made of that
place! Gee whizz!"[7]

If we want to examine to what extent Yigal Lev's descriptions
in his book are authentic, let us add some of the reports by soldiers on their conduct during certain curfew and search operations. In Israel these have been called "exceptional"—in other
words, conduct more severe than the standards for such action
now accepted in the I.D.F. In most instances the general public
learned of such occurrences through reports from soldiers on
regular or reserve service who had participated in these actions,
or from civilians who happened to be present. Only a small
number of such occurrences, however, came to the public's attention from Arab sources leaking information to the press. On
the other hand, in almost no instance did the army authorities
themselves publicize such exceptional conduct. But in most
cases the I.D.F. took disciplinary action quietly against persons
guilty of such misbehavior and also made attempts to draw conclusions, in order to reduce the extent of exceptional conduct in
the future.

At any rate, such things did happen and still are happening.
By the very nature of our position in the administered areas, exceptional conduct will again happen in the future.

Let us look at what soldiers tell of a four-day curfew, imposed early in 1971 on a refugee camp in the Gaza Strip, after
inhabitants of that camp repeatedly committed many acts of
terror.

One of the officers reported that men in his unit beat Arabs.
He did not know if that included women, but he saw children
beaten with his own eyes. Adult men had been beaten severely.

One of the noncoms reported seeing a woman walking down
the street, shortly before the curfew began. He called her, but
she ran away. In her hand was a bundle wrapped in a piece of

cloth. His patrol ran after her and caught her. Then they beat her and prodded her along the way to her house with their night sticks. Finally they literally kicked her through her own door.

One of the soldiers reported seeing with his own eyes how one patrol separated an elderly man from his family, told all of them that he would be executed (a lie, of course) and then shot off a gun in the air, no more than eight inches from him.

One noncom told of entering a house, in which there was not even a single man. To frighten the women they told her that they would take her child away if she didn't tell where her husband was. She refused to talk, so then the men took the child outside, pretending to take him away. When the child began to cry they took him back to his mother, of course.

One of the officers reported that our people caused damage to houses in the course of their search. They tore up floor tiles, broke holes through walls and tore doors from their hinges.

Whenever information is received of any such acts, the I.D.F. conducts an extensive investigation. Usually this ends with officers of all ranks and soldiers being brought to trial. Beginning with the spring of 1971, every unit going on duty in the administered areas received special educational training on the right way of dealing with local residents. However, in spite of all the efforts by both the civilian and the military authorities to reinforce the purity of arms, cases of exceptional conduct have also occurred after the above events.

Such exceptions are the inevitable result of circumstances in which the two national movements—Jewish and Arab—find themselves. The point of contact most sensitive to the appearance of hate—on the part of both Jews and Arabs—lies in the relationships developing between Israel's armed forces and the Arab citizens of the occupied areas.

This objective reality necessarily results in serious conflicts of conscience on the part of the soldiers and all the others engaged in the day-to-day work of occupation. Each man has to deal with this inside himself. Some of this quandary is emphasized in the following excerpt from the book by Yigal Lev.

209

MODERN JEWISH ETHICS

"What happened to us, Dr. Livni?"
"We do violence to nature, and it takes its revenge."
"Do violence to what?"
"To human nature."
"Conquerors have always garrisoned the towns and cities they conquered. There always have been armies that ruled areas after their victory. As far as I can remember, it only did them good."
"But not Jews."
"We're not normal, like all other mortal human beings?"
"As far as mortality is concerned, yes. But as far as life is concerned, we Jews have something that finds it hard to get along with domination—domination through force. That's why it eats Yossi, and Yankele, and Itzik—actually, every one of us here."[8]

This conflict of conscience cannot possibly be a transient phenomenon; it takes time—a different length of time for each individual soldier. During this time the human being that is in each soldier searches for a way out of this dilemma—a psychological mechanism that will enable him to do his job, efficiently and at peace with himself.

The above analysis leads to the conclusion that the maintenance of purity of arms in the units stationed in the occupied areas completely accords with the political and moral interests of the Jewish political community in Israel. However, this approach contains within it a serious psychological drawback since it fans the doubting and the questioning moral spark of each soldier's conscience. The men never stop "eating themselves." A short newspaper article[9] reflects this process; Gal Avinoam had been a squad leader who fell in December 1970 in the course of a search he conducted in the Gaza Strip.

Aharon: . . . The Gaza Strip is a tremendous complex of all things—women and children and old people, and men who support the terrorists, and some who oppose them. There are people who want to kill you, and some who only want a little peace and quiet. And you have to find the solution to all the contradictions. You know that the terrorists send little kids to

210

throw grenades. You know those grenades can kill, and you ask yourself the tragic question whether Israeli soldiers can kill a little child. Am I capable of doing a thing like that? That's the supreme test of all your human values, of all you've absorbed, of all you believe in.

Gal personified all the good in humanity to a complete, almost to a shocking, extent: "Don't hurt the innocent! Don't shoot at anybody who just happens to be around! Always look only for the guilty!" And being what he was, he never left us alone. He drove us all crazy. Day and night he talked about it: "We didn't come here to break them; we've already defeated them. We're here to try and build a new life together with the Arabs. They're no enemies of ours; only the terrorists are enemies. This population—they are ours. We'll have to live with them all our lives. Don't humiliate them. Don't make them hate you. I know, this is plowing in depth, an investment for the long run. But we have to start along this way, in spite of all the disappointments along it. Our people have charged us with the beginning of this work. This is a tremendous responsibility; don't spoil it. By God, don't ruin this chance!"

And he behaved according to his own value system. he believed every word he said. Once he reprimanded a squad leader; he insisted on a detailed search, but without breaking anything, without destroying anything—at least, as long as there was no proof that terrorists were hiding there. He hated the easy way out. He used to squeeze his gun with all his might till it hurt, till his fingers turned white: "Don't shoot! Don't shoot! I see a kid between those people, there. And there are women and old people. Don't shoot!"

What he said wasn't always understood. Everybody did not always agree with him. There were arguments. There were attempts to convince him that protecting your own life was no less important a value than saving somebody else's. He never gave in, and argued that especially in a war such as this one, in Gaza, the human being inside each of us faced the supreme test: here it would come out whether you were a human being, or something else. He demanded not to give in to the easy solution, not to shoot into a crowd. He influenced everybody with that great spirit of his, with that spirit of a whole human being. He showed the way through this broad expanse where there are no clear orders and everyone must decide for himself how to behave. He was a wonderful example.

Yoram: We had a lot of talks about Gaza. I asked Gal, "After all these problems and doubts and all our sacrifices—doesn't that make you hate the Arabs over there?" He got very excited: "No! Certainly not! No hatred. Yoram, I think I understand our responsibility in the Strip. We aren't here as conquerors, not even as police. We must build a common foundation for our life together with them. And that can't be done with hatred!"

Whenever something like the incident with the Arab woman before the cave happens (several such events actually took place) it brings a renewed wave of doubt and debate in its wake. Some always say at such times that we act like aesthetes, and that it results in superfluous sacrifices. Soldiers and officers then begin to ask their superiors and themselves: Why shouldn't we open fire immediately, in such cases, and let the Arab terrorists bear responsibility for the lives of the women behind whose skirts they hide? In the final analysis, we did find a tactical-professional solution to the problem, one that maintains our purity of arms, our decency without endangering our soldiers. This solution calls for surrounding the area around the cave or house within the range of light arms, using loudspeakers to warn the Arabs, in Arabic, to come out of the cave or house and to lay down their arms, if any armed terrorists are present. After the time given for clearing the dwelling has elapsed— usually fifteen or thirty minutes—the order is given to shoot with bazookas, recoilless rifles, or tank cannons.

In this way a technical-tactical solution has been found for cases of this sort, outside built-up areas, and the tactical means used conform to demands of ethics and conscience without endangering the lives of our people. Still, this does not provide an answer to the problem in its entirety. What about searches in built-up areas and inside houses where suddenly somebody jumps through a door or comes out from under a bed with an automatic weapon, or somebody throws a grenade at you from a window or a roof, and the area is full of indifferent, but hostile,

212

Arabs? What are I.D.F. soldiers to do when a terrorist comes out of some door, holding an automatic rifle and pushing a woman or child in front of him? Doesn't that pose a first-class moral dilemma? How are people supposed to practice restraint and not shoot back, no matter who gets hurt, even old people, women, children, infants?

One of the I.D.F.'s best units was conducting a search when they ran into an armed terrorist who came out of one of the houses, holding two Arab children in front of him. The platoon leader at the head of his men was shocked and for a moment he didn't fire his gun. That same moment, a burst of fire was opened from another direction by a second terrorist and the young officer fell, wounded. The marauder meanwhile made his escape, leaving the two children behind; he was caught only much later, when the unit continued its detailed search mission. A few days later the same unit ran into a similar situation and one of the sergeants immediately opened fire, killing a terrorist together with the children he had used for a shield. During the debriefing, this sergeant said that he had shot because of the previous experience. The officer in command of the unit told him that the I.D.F., despite the precedent, preferred the type of commander who is momentarily shocked and hesitates for an instant when he finds women and children facing his gun, rather than the one who knows no restraint and has no difficulty shooting at women and children. In other words, a soldier of the State of Israel cannot permit himself what a criminal would do. In this instance, the commander even reprimanded his sergeant and brought him before a court-martial. In another instance the I.D.F. radio broadcast an interview with the young officer who had been wounded, but said that in spite of everything he did not regret the momentary "weak" hesitation. The very fact that the I.D.F. radio gave prominence to this approach indicates that this is also the humane approach, at least theoretically, of the I.D.F. itself.

The above examples clearly demonstrate that moral considerations and questions are part of the lives of Israel's oc-

213

cupation forces. If this tension-producing process of questioning continues over a prolonged period of time, it must be resolved in one of the following ways:

1. In the direction of an extreme uncompromising and humanistic ethic, which leads to severe feelings of guilt and the loss of the soldier's identification with the political and ideological goals for which he labors in the occupied areas;

2. In the direction of racist nationalism, which would be expressed in the gradual development of hate and contempt for Arabs as Arabs. Such an ideology could become the rigid shell that would protect and silence the soldier's conscience, justifying anything that is done against Arabs, no matter what.

Our assumption that purity of arms is the norm we desire for our soldiers' conduct also states that that norm by itself is an expression of high moral standards. Departure from this norm to what claims to be "more moral" is liable to result in opposition to all the objectives of the State of Israel and of the I.D.F.—as was the case with Giora Neuman who refused to be inducted into the service in 1972. Such deviation can, of course, also result in lesser degrees of alienation of the individual soldier: he can object to participation in the activities of the occupying forces, or else it can bring him to a state of mental exhaustion approaching complete apathy, such as Yigal Lev lets his physician, Dr. Livni, express.

> "This is a stupid game. I'm sick of playing make-believe. I make believe that I'm in charge, that I give orders. I make believe that I'm in control of this town, blow up houses, arrest suspects and finally I make believe that I get killed . . . . By the way, that's the last stage of the game, but after that one doesn't return to reality."[10]

Is this not a turn toward a morality that has gone to the point of accepting one's own liquidation?

214

There can be no doubt that the turning toward extreme and consummate humanism can endanger the I.D.F.'s ability to function, but experience has proven that the proportions of this danger are extremely small and that it does not constitute a phenomenon that really endangers the operative capacity and the efficiency of the defense forces. The importance of this phenomenon is not in any current danger to Israel's defensive capability but rather in the fact that its few current manifestations do suggest what is liable to happen in the future if more and more people stop identifying with the objectives of our struggle, of the I.D.F., and of the State of Israel.

Every nation's political leadership must pay heed to such phenomena when they first make their appearance; for if they spread—both in terms of the number of unconvinced individuals and in terms of the degree of alienation from the objectives of the war of each individual—it will become impossible to achieve certain strategic and political objectives. The world already has experienced things of this type. The attitude of most Americans to the Vietnam war, since 1966, should be studied and conclusions drawn from it.

Deviation toward a nationalist-racist direction is much more common, because it offers an ideological justification for simple, quick, and violent solutions on the technocratic level. Such often seem to be the most effective, at least in the short run. Some of these were described in the above quotations.

The external expression of this deviation can be found in a growing hate and contempt for the Arab nation, ultimately developing into real racism and the increasing conviction that the Arabs are inferior. This deviation too is well expressed in Yigal Lev's book, in the following discussion between the doctor and two young soldiers, concerning Arab people.

> Hoomi, from a kibbutz in the North, said: "But doctor, you didn't work with them the way we do. They . . . they're not human beings; they stink. They're ass kissers. They . . . they . . . how can I explain it to you?"

215

Livni spoke sadly: "They're human beings, just like us. They also hurt when they're hit. They also bleed when they're wounded . . . . They . . . ."

Zviki, a spoiled brat from North Tel Aviv who had turned into a rough-and-ready man, tried to make things clear.

"Doctor, you're dealing in theories. Wait and see what you'll say after you sit here seven days, after you deal with their informers day after day, with their ass lickers, with their betrayals. It's like . . . like some kind of poison gas that you don't even know is there before it chokes you. They're not human beings just like us. They're something different altogether. You won't understand that until you've been with them a year, or a year and a half, like we have . . . ."

. . . They're not human beings like us. How could it happen that youngsters of eighteen, nineteen speak with such quiet conviction about other human beings?

Dr. Livni broke his silence: "That's their armor. How can a kid of nineteen be expected to do all the filthy things he has to do, and how will he explain to himself why he's stuck in this business? Why does he have to push people around, arrest them, question them? They have to grow some armor plate around themselves, so they won't always be asking questions, not all of which have an answer. Not human beings—that's their armor."[11]

All the above quotations indicate that hate is increasing and that it penetrates our consciousness. All the quotations indicate that Jewish Israeli soldiers are making their peace with the perpetration of inhumane acts towards the Arab enemy and civilian population, justifying it as an extreme requirement of national defense.

Among the adherents of the extreme nationalist-racist trend there are those who find their support in religious faith, and in the claim that God Almighty himself had granted the Jewish people a prior claim on this country. Others convince themselves that our claim to this land is preeminent because it

216

is the only one we have, whereas the Arabs have other countries. Others, again, take the racist approach that the Arabs and Palestinians are naturally or historically inferior. A last group simply argues that our own vital interest comes first: if anybody has to pay for that, it is better that the Arabs do so with their blood and property, rather than we.

This nationalist-racist deviation gains important support at times from the political and military leadership of the State of Israel; at other times that same leadership tries to fight this tendency—whenever there is some case of "exceptional conduct" that is somehow publicized. The support may be direct, or indirect, or—at times—even unintentional.

The leadership orders or approves blowing up the houses of the terrorists' families, in direct contravention of Israel's Criminal Code, and this while we argue that these are no more than common criminals; the leadership allows or encourages removal by force of villagers and Bedouin from their land, as was the case in the Rafiah area in early 1972; the leadership allows wells to be blocked or blown up; the leadership permits spraying chemicals on Arab fields, in order to clear them for settlement or military training areas, such as happened at Akraba, near Nablus, in June 1972. It seems that this leadership considers only the military, economic, and political benefits to be derived from any action carried out in its name, and that from the point of view of Israel's purely Machiavellian interests. Even if these considerations prove to have been right, at least in the short run (and one can't be certain that their long-term results also will be good), *does this same leadership not consider how such action affects the moral decline of the soldiers ordered to carry them out?* Does anybody even think about all our civilians and soldiers, for whom the information received about these acts through press, radio, television, and the soldiers' grapevine constitutes the government's stamp of approval for the nationalist-racist deviation? At the moment when the conscience must decide, such as in the cases described above, the government's authority helps to determine the decision. Hasn't the time come for the political and military leadership of Israel to give more weight to the moral and humane considerations when it must make decisions? This can be done through the promulgation of rules and regulations, by preventive education, and through the severe punishment of top ranks—be they political or military—who give a hand to exceptional behavior.

All this would encourage and help all persons in command in the security forces to insist on the principle of purity of arms and to engage in a constant ideological struggle against nationalist-racist enmity taking over the Jewish people's consciousness in this country. This consideration is of such vital importance that it justifiably could even dictate a change in certain political, economic, and military decisions, adapting them to the demands of human morality. Need more be said?

The most disturbing element in the nationalist-racist deviation is that the number of its adherents may increase as the Jewish-Arab armed conflict continues, and it is likely to continue at least during the near future. The terrifying element is that this process acts upon the Zionist movement, in similar way to its effects on other national movements, after they have won their objectives. What, then, is unique about the national movement of the Jewish people?

From the earliest days of Zionism we deeply and sincerely believed that our movement based itself on ideals of justice, in the fullest sense of the concept. Most of us really believed that in the final analysis Jews and Arabs could live in this country side by side, through some kind of political coexistence, and that the development of one national movement did not exclude the existence of the other. We believed—because we were educated on these principles—that true Zionism signified the crystallization of social justice within the Jewish people reestablishing itself in the land of Israel, and that the foundations of this movement posited political, economic, and social justice to Arab neighbors who already lived in that country.

However, our belief in justice was not enough. In the face of the conflicts developing between us and the British mandate au-

218

thorities and the Arab national movement, we were forced to conclude during the 1920s and 1930s that "it is not enough to be right, we must also be strong!" For two generations we have managed to carry out the commandment "be strong," to the point where we now are the strongest state in the entire Middle East, militarily and economically.

The Arab national movement—at present, as in the past, the main enemy of the Zionist movement and of the State of Israel—is helpless before Israel's military power. At this very moment in history when our movement's physical power is apparent to all, some of us are losing our sense of proportion and argue that since we are strong it is incumbent on us to take our "heritage" by brute force. Some philosophers and writers—as well as poets and journalists from all parts of the political spectrum—have begun, only a few years after the Six Day War, to preach openly the idealization of what most of us still call exceptional conduct; they have claimed that the way of expropriation, robbery, and injustice are the highway that the Zionist movement should travel.

At this time we face the dilemma whether we should follow the untrammeled instincts of the strong or whether we should try and maintain the very principles of justice and morality in which we believed when we were still weak. The Six Day War and all the subsequent wars of attrition have proven to anybody with eyes to see that we are much stronger than the Arab world around us. Will we now conduct ourselves the way most nations would, under these circumstances, or will we deliberately force ouselves not to neglect either in our internal affairs or toward our Arab opponents that very justice and morality that lit our way during the Zionist movement's early years?

The most serious challenge before the State of Israel at this time is how to remain just and moral, inwardly and outwardly, and that especially at a time when we are strong and tempted to use force and to act unjustly. The way this challenge is met will, in the final analysis, determine just how Jewish the State of Israel really is.

1. *The Seventh Day: Soldiers Talk About the Six Day War* (London, 1970); original Hebrew edition, *Siah Lohamim* (Tel-Aviv, 1967).

2. My lecture was later also published in *Maarahot*, no. 29 (August, 1970), in *Shdemot*, no. 39 (Fall 1970), and in *New Outlook* no. 139 (February, 1973).

3. Yigel Lev, *Ha-Milhamah Ohevet Gevarim Tzeirim* [War Likes Young Men] (Tel Aviv: Bitan Publishers, 1972). All quotations used by permission of the publisher (author's translation).

4. Ibid., pp. 67–69.

5. Ibid., pp. 31–38.

6. Ibid., pp. 58–59.

7. Ibid., pp. 135–36.

8. Ibid., p, 110.

9. *Friends Tell About Gal Avinoam* (Ma'ariv Supplement, 7 January 1971).

10. Lev, *Ha-Milhamah Ohevet Gevarim Tzeirim*, p. 111.

11. Ibid., pp. 34–35.

A Response to Meir Pa'il

THE DISCUSSION WAS OPENED by Milton Himmelfarb who served as respondent. Himmelfarb stressed the difference between the moral problems that Pa'il was considering and those which concern Jews in the Diaspora. Jews who are living only as individuals within a larger society have, at most, the moral problems of individuals. These tend to be relatively trivial. By comparison with them the issues that face Jews living in Israel have scope and grandeur. The moral concerns that Pa'il presented are "infinitely difficult, infinitely serious, perhaps infinitely insoluble, and wonderfully noble." They make us aware of the difference in quality, as well as in problems, of Jewish life in Israel as compared to Jewish life in America. As Himmelfarb put it, it might be compared to the mother of a crippled child listening to the complaints of another mother. Her boy is a holy terror. He is always running around, playing football, or doing other things that might cause him injury. The mother of the crippled child says to herself, "I wish I had your worries." We American Jews may well wish that we lived on a scale of such moral tension that we had to confront the noble moral concerns of our brothers in Israel. If they are more crushing than our own, they are also more elevating, and far more significant.

Himmelfarb also cautioned against the danger of sentimentalizing and romanticizing the moral issues, a danger that could have serious practical consequences. We need not make judgments of the moral values of Arabic culture, but we must be prepared without sentimentality to deal with the practical threats that those values pose for us. Even if we take cultural relativism as our position, we must still deal with the effects of various cultures on ourselves. I need not make judgments about the moral superiority or inferiority of a tribe of head-hunters, but I cannot ignore the fact that they may take my head. If our opponent permits women to carry grenades and allows the use of infants as shields, then we have no choice but to make the practical response that the circumstances require. To moralize, or to invoke our own sentiments about the special place of women and children, means in such circumstances to pay with our lives and the lives of others. Himmelfarb called for balance between genuine concern with the very great moral issues that had been raised by Pa'il and the demands of survival. To survive without moral concern would be to live in a way unworthy of Jews. To sacrifice even survival to exaggerated moralistic sentimentality borders on idiocy.

Similar views were expressed by Milan Sprecher. "I believe," he said, "that the moral anxieties which Pa'il expressed are based on an incomplete picture. The enemy with whom we are dealing today is no longer that 'charming little thief' of an earlier time. As a result, we are no longer acting, but necessarily reacting. The expressions of moral disgust with the Arabs that were voiced by some of the characters in Yigal Lev's stories should not be construed as self-righteous or smug. They are, rather, expressions of honest astonishment and perplexity at values which are so alien to us. What would be most troubling to us is a situation in which an Israeli soldier would face the Sheikh's callous disregard for human life and not react to it with moral disgust."

Sprecher went on to argue that the ideal of "purity of arms" is not a moral absolute. It is the policy to be rigorously followed so long as it can be carried out without excessive danger to our own lives. But, "if there is a situation in which it is impossible to observe the policy of purity of arms without excessive danger, then that policy is no longer appropriate. To follow such a policy under these conditions is not a matter of self-sacrifice but of suicide, and in our moral system suicide has no proper place." Those who behave in this way are considered by Sprecher to fall into the category of *hasid-shoteh,* the pious fool, and while admiring his piety we ought not imitate his foolishness. The excessive compassion of such a pious fool only turns out in the end to be cruelty to the innocent victims of his foolishness.

Sprecher concluded with an expression of basic agreement with Pa'il that we must come to know the Arabs and their culture far more thoroughly than we do now. He urged that Israeli education would concentrate on teaching our children to hate the evil acts but not the evil-doers, an ideal that is admittedly difficult to achieve.

It was to this, in part, that Uriel Simon reacted when he characterized Pa'il's position as one of "fear of sin," and he expressed distress that true fear of sin should be treated with such exaggerated irony that it is confused with foolish piety. Simon stressed that Israel is today a nation that has much power, and the problem is, therefore, to know when and how to restrain that power.

Simon expressed the belief that "the greatest moral danger which threatens us is the tendency to take our opponents as our moral yardstick. This is a danger that every child can understand. We teach our children that just because a neighbor throws rocks at us does not mean that we must throw rocks back at him, though it may be necessary to respond in some fashion. However, if he lies, it certainly does not follow that we are also required to lie. Our morality is based on an independent structure of values that we cherish, not on the simple common denominator of 'measure-for-measure' response. It is difficult to maintain such an independent morality in a military situation, just as it is difficult in an economic situation. If all the merchants in the neighborhood use false weights and measures, it imposes a special burden on the merchant who gives true weight and measure. It may be difficult for him to survive in a Darwinian world. It may be very difficult, indeed, but this commitment to values is what distinguishes the moral man from the immoral world. In a military situation this is both more difficult and more dangerous, but we must still be guided by the principle that we should determine our behavior by our own moral standards and values, and not by reaction to the Arab rejection of our morality. Above all we must avoid the danger of self-righteousness, of the conviction that we are morally sound and, therefore, have no need to cultivate within ourselves the fear of sin."

Moshe Greenberg introduced some new notes into the discussion. First, he pointed out that we misunderstand the Arab attitudes and their self-image. It is widely thought by Israelis that although Israel feels that its very existence is threatened by the conflict with the Arabs, the other side has no such feeling about its situation. A reading of Arabic literature reveals, according to Greenberg, that there is a deep feeling among the Arabs that their very existence is at stake. "They do not fear total extermination or being pushed into the sea. They do feel that they are threatened with serious social disintegration. They fear the loss of their own self-image, of their own life-style. Arabic literature exhibits anxiety that their society may begin to view itself as decadent as it clashes with a highly organized technological society that has invaded its part of the world." Greenberg also pointed to another problem area. According to him, young people in Israel are beginning to question the validity and moral soundness of the whole Zionist enterprise. They are asking whether there can be ultimate justification for the very existence of Israel as an independent state in the Arab Middle East. This phenomenon is appearing now only at the edges of Israeli society, but one must consider its implications, and ask what it bodes for the future of Israel.

Eliakim Rubenstein called for a realistic appraisal of the military and political realities that confront Israel, and suggested that to moralize under such dangerous conditions was only self-defeating. Arab literature only underscores the depth of their hatred toward Israel and the Jews, a hatred that threatens the very existence of Israel and the Jewish people. Thus Rubenstein points out that the education of even the youngest Arab child is geared to generating hatred for Israel and the Jews. When Israeli forces captured Gaza in 1967 they found the schoolrooms filled with anti-Semitic caricatures, and they found standard textbooks that taught arithmetic to little children with examples such as, "If you kill five Jews and then five more Jews, what will be the sum of the Jews you have killed?" He asks that we consider what the realistic dangers are from such an enemy. "It is true that we are guilty of some moral errors in this conflict, but these errors are occasional and peripheral. We need to consider them in the total context, in proportion to the whole range of our activities, and these proportions are to our credit. We have conducted ourselves in a way that is morally superior to others, surely to our enemies. Above all, we have no ideology of hatred for the Arab, though we are sometimes guilty of degrading the Arabs by the ugly habit of identifying every case of poor workmanship or irresponsible behavior as 'Arabic' in quality. Yet, while acknowledging our own failures, we must always remember what things would be like if the circumstances were reversed, if the Arabs had superior social organization and technological capacity. If they had the power that Israel has now, the Israelis would long since have been totally annihilated. While sharing Pa'il's moral concerns, we must not lose sight of these chilling realities."

To illustrate the nature of the moral dilemmas, the moral sensitivities, and the moral failures of the Israeli forces, Israel Harel cited cases from a book he is about to publish based on authenticated documents and records. An Israeli soldier is in occupied East Jerusalem during the battle. He is making a house-to-house search and finds himself in a house where he sees the school books of a teenage Arab girl, including her school notebooks that she wrote in English. "I saw a mar-

225

velously neat geometry notebook and a number of physics books. I was deeply affected because these are my own favorite subjects. It was then that I began to look at the whole matter in a somewhat different light. Here we had broken into a private dwelling, and suddenly I began to think about the girl who lived there, who had fled from her home. She had all the usual school materials, books, a pen, a writing pad. I wrote her a note in English in which I explained that we were terribly sorry for all the damage that we had done to her home, but it was not something that we had wanted and it was not our fault. I promised her that after the war was over I would come to her house with a bouquet of flowers instead of a bouquet of hand grenades."

A second soldier, who lived in Europe during the Hitler years, is facing a family that is terrified of the Israeli occupiers. The father, mother, two daughters, and a son are trembling before their captors. "At that moment I recalled vividly when the Germans entered our house and threw us out. It was in Romania, and I was only four years old, but the picture is permanently imprinted on my memory. The Germans broke in, destroyed everything, and drove us into the street. As I stood before our Arab victims, the two pictures merged in my mind—the picture of myself as a little boy driven out of his home by the Germans, and the picture in which I am a soldier driving others out of their homes." He tells how he reassured the Arabs, urged them to take whatever they needed from the house, and promised them that they would be safe. "I did not want them to feel what I felt when I was a child."

Harel also reported instances of looting by Israelis after the 1967 war, but noted the deep shame that was felt by the responsible elements of the army and the general population. Essentially, he was showing that although there were surely moral failures on the part of many Israelis, civilians and soldiers, there was also a deep sense of moral responsibility toward the vanquished Arabs and even toward their property.

Among the points that Harold Fisch raised was his failure to understand why such stress was laid by Pa'il on the fact that the

226

Arabs confronted Israeli soldiers with the agonizing problem of having to face women and children as antagonists. Fisch argued that this special concern for women is a vestige of medieval notions of chivalry, but is hardly sensible under the conditions of modern warfare. "When one throws a hand grenade or drops a bomb, the explosion which follows makes no distinctions among its victims between men, women and children." Similarly, it hardly matters if the thrower of the grenade or he who shields that thrower is a woman or a child. In war such distinctions are untenable, and to introduce them as moral considerations is unsound and self-defeating. "The moral problem is not whether to enter the battle or not; this is not the moral choice which is open to us. The choice is not even whether we should remain in Israel, or not. This is no longer an open issue. The only issue is how to carry on the battle, how to remain in our land under conditions which force us into war, how under these conditions to do what must be done and still be true to our Jewish heritage."

David Sidorsky denied that there is here any special moral problem at all, or any specifically Jewish-Zionist problem. Basically, he sees the situation as one in which what is required is prudent behavior, behavior that is planned so as to reach our goals with a maximum of effectiveness and a minimum of injury and suffering to any person. In his view it is a mistake to see the situation of the Israelis as involving unusually complex or insoluble moral dilemmas. The moral answers are known. All that is required is that the issues be understood clearly, the options assessed skillfully, and the practical decision will emerge almost by itself.

ZVI YARON

Religion and Morality in Israel
And in the Dispersion

THE CRISIS OF RELIGION in modern times has given
rise to a bewildering proliferation of theories that seek to interpret Judaism in contemporary terms. These theories have in-
undated the Jewish religion with so many interpretations that
it seems to have been drained of all significant content. The
sheer abundance of exegesis has driven religion to a position
where it can mean so many different things that its rhetoric
tends to blur the substance, and since most interpretations
feature ethics rather prominently it is difficult to disentangle the
interlocking strands and come to grips with the issues of religion and morality.

Much of the ambiguity is due to the propensity to cling
strenuously to traditional nomenclature while freely rejecting
traditional patterns of thought. This phenomenon is not limited
to the religious movements in modern Judaism. It is widespread
even in self-proclaimed secular schools of thought. The apparent paradox is clearly due to the desire to preserve the
format and the mold of tradition although free rein is given to
change in contents. It is the result of the tension between immu-
tability and change, of the urge to revolutionize without
obliterating the past. This tension obscures the meanings of
words and their theological implications. The relationship of religion and ethics in contemporary life is thus overlaid by mul-

tiple definitions, explanations, and theories that frustrate attempts to analyze the problem.

The search for contemporary exegesis is not new in Judaism.[1] What is new is the acute awareness of the novelty of this exegesis and its revolutionary character. Judaism would have long ago been petrified it it had not undergone continous interpretation. In the past the process of interpretation did not arouse the kind of misgiving or downright suspicion that attend modern attempts at exegesis. For exegesis was then an integral and vital part of the religious and traditional life, whereas in our times there is a distinct division between the traditional exegesis, which assumes the unchangeable sanctity of texts and laws, and revolutionary interpretation, which consciously aims at changes in meaning and practice of the traditional texts and laws.

The historical consciousness of the implications of contemporary interpretation has thus given rise to a sharp polarization. Reformers and revolutionaries as well as conservatives and orthodox are alive to historical changes, and both poles tend therefore to exacerbate their differences. Against the declared intention made by the former to alter Judaism radically, the orthodox strenuously try to preserve a timeless and unchanging Judaism.

However, this polarization is dislocated by a process that may be described as a "preservative revolution." With the exception of the movement of deliberate assimilation and the consequent obliteration of all Jewish identity, most modern reformist and revolutionary Jewish cultural, social, and political movements insist upon the traditional ancestry of their innovations. The preservative character of the revolution is particularly marked in the ideology and practice of all the nonreligious sections of the Zionist movements. But even religious Orthodox Zionists have not escaped the tension between the urge to change and the yearning to preserve the hallowed tradition. For Zionism itself carries this built-in tension: It

229

wants to change Jewish life in order to preserve its continuity. The Zionist begins with a critique of Jewish life in the Diaspora, and continues with a program of a radical revolution that involves politics, culture, society, and above all the personal life of the Zionist who carries out in person the Zionist program. But all the criticism and rebellion and change are intended to preserve and revive the continuous existence of the Jewish people. Even when some Zionist ideology emphasizes "the birth of a new nation" it is quite obvious that behind this passionate vision the intention is to restore and revive and assure the uninterrupted continuity. The revolutionary character in Zionism is thus bound up with the preservative element.

The continuous tension between change and tradition is not merely an expression of the conservatism of rebels who want to temper their revolutionary zeal with a sprinkling of tradition. In Zionism this tension is inherent; it is an integral and unavoidable part of all the varieties of Zionist ideology. For Zionism is inherently both revolution and preservation, and every Zionist has to face two questions: (a) how much change is necessary in order to achieve preservation; (b) how much preservation is ideally important in order to justify change.

The inherent tension in the preservative revolution of Zionism is the key for understanding the historical exegesis that accompanies the thrust for change. There are numerous varieties in this exegesis, but what is evident in most of them is the desire to represent change as a revival of essential Judaism. Almost no one is satisfied with a new interpretation until it is shown to have always been the true essence of Judaism. The result is a "retroactive exegesis" that tries to reexplain the Jewish heritage from its beginnings.

What distinguishes modern Jewish thinking, whether religious or professedly secular, is its persistent search for the essence of Judaism. Despite Franz Rosenzweig's criticism[2] of the reductionism inherent in the search for *Das Wesen des Judentums* (the essence of Judaism), most Jewish thinking has continued to be dominated by the urge to discover the

230

"essence." This is shared by secular, liberal religious, and orthodox thinkers. Even the new orthodox "theology of Halakha" is in effect an attempt to reduce Judaism to what is supposed to be its underlying principle, to the exclusion of everything else. In this it is not unlike Buber's search for the hidden Judaism—and even Ahad Ha'am's decidedly secular emphasis on *Mussar Hayahadut* (the ethics of Judaism). Since rigid orthodoxy is confronted by a revolution that views itself as a revival of essential Judaism, the demarcation lines appear to be both clear-cut and blurred. On the one hand, the retroactive exegesis is invariably marked by an almost exclusive emphasis on ethics. At the opposite end there is the assertion that the Halakha is the quiddity of Judaism. Thus there appears to be an extreme polarization between the position that Judaism is ethics and the view that Judaism consists of Halakha. But in fact the situation is marked more by ambivalence than by clear division, and this ambivalence affects in particular the issue of religion and ethics. By postulating theories of essence, the apparent polarization is conducive to a confusing theoretical situation, in which it appears that we are called upon to choose between Halakha or ethics.[3] On the nonorthodox side, the exclusive preoccupation with "values" as the essence of Judaism considerably increases the polarity between religion and ethics. At the humanistic-ethical end there is often a sense of surfeit of moralistic rhetoric. The perfunctory platitudes sometimes induce a revulsion against what seems to have degenerated into sanctimoniousness.

Against this background it is extremely difficult to evaluate today the relationship of religion and ethics. The modern decline of religion and the concomitant search for the essence of Judaism have undermined the unity of religion and ethics. And yet, from the point of view of Judaism—as it is expressed both in theory and in life—there can be no doubt that there is a profound, intrinsic, and abiding interrelationship between religion and ethics.

Philosophers have always explored the nature of the good and

231

its connection with God, but Jewish life was always conducted in the firm belief that God cannot act unjustly (Gen. 18:25) and that only through justice and loving-kindness can man "walk in the way of God" (Mic. 6:8). The living reality in Judaism has always been that religion is unthinkable without ethics and ethics are intrinsically intertwined with religion. The theological question in the religion-and-ethics issue is what Emil Brunner has called the "*Anknüpfungspunkt,*" the point of contact between God's revelation and the human situation. But whatever interpretation may be suggested to this problem, Judaism as a religion of faith in Torah and *Mitzvot* would make no sense without the assumption that there is indeed a relationship between God and man. The following passage illustrates the intrinsic connection between religious piety and morality as it was set forth by Rabbi Abraham I. Kook.

> Piety is not a value in itself and it should not be counted among man's abilities and virtues. Left to itself piety may pull man and mankind down to the abyss, and it may equally raise them as high as heavens. But just because it has no value in itself, it is capable of receiving all the lights and of containing all the abilities.
>
> Each human faculty comes into its own, and then remains invulnerable, only through its relation to piety—which contains all.
>
> The ideal piety is therefore achieved not so much by preoccupation with itself as by filling it with knowledge and ability, with Torah and religious deeds, with every virtue, with every manifestation of strength and courage, glory and splendour.
>
> Piety is the most profound kind of wisdom, when it is based on the innermost view of the world. It provides a solid basis for all science and for all Torah study, whether it concerns the holy or the profane.
>
> When the profane looks for a solid basis it is bound to realize that without piety science merely hovers over the surface of concepts, and that without piety science is not really wisdom.
>
> Piety should on no account push aside the natural sense of morality, for it would then no longer remain pure piety. The crite-

rion of pure piety is that the natural morality, which is inherent in man's nature, steadily improves as a result of a person's piety, over and above what it would have been without his piety.

But if there were a kind of piety without whose influence life would have been better both for individuals and the community, and owing to whose influence the power for doing good were weakened—that would be the wrong kind of piety.[4]

Rabbi Kook rejects the idea that there can be a dichotomy between the divine and the morally good. In his view morality consists not only of the relationships between men; it is an inner drive toward the good, and morality is accordingly an expression of man's striving for holiness and nearness to God.[5] His theological position on this question expresses in a radical manner what is really a Jewish traditional position.

Rabbi Kook's position is unequivocal, but discussion on religion and ethics in the contemporary Jewish situation must take into account the ambiguities and tensions that are inherent in modern Jewish thinking. And it is against this background of tension between the traditional view of religion and ethics and the modern ambiguities, that we should project the analysis of the issues arising out of the existence of the State of Israel and the contemporary Diaspora.

IN THE DIASPORA

The problem of religion and ethics in the Diaspora has undergone three important changes in recent times.

1. The modern crisis of religion has given rise to an increasing emphasis on moral values as representing the essence of Judaism. This interpretation of Judaism is aesthetically pleasing and morally soothing, but its well-meant formulations seem to be so all-embracing that they fail to be relevant in significantly influencing life.[6]

2. At the same time modern Jewish life has witnessed a movement that has tried to give social and political expression to the moral teachings of Judaism. Since the Emancipation Jews have

been prominently active in socialist and liberal movements. In America the question of the "Jewishness" of Jewish involvement in liberalism is now debated.[7] But what is significantly Diaspora in both the early enthusiastic participation in socialism and liberalism and in the current mood of disenchantment, is the fact that the issues of morality are clearly related to the fact that the Jews are a minority community within a Gentile nation and state. The issue of the relationship between Judaism and ethics is bound to be dealt with in the Diaspora in the context of the Diaspora situation of the Jewish community. Unless Jews are willing to merge their identity completely they continue to measure their involvement in social and political parties and movements by the criterion of the position of the Jewish community.

And yet, despite the continued Diaspora character of the problem there can be no doubt that the very fact of Jewish involvement in social and political issues constitutes a significant change. Although the framework continues to be Diaspora, the nature of the ethical issues and their connection with Judaism is decidedly new. Ethics are no longer confined to the circumscribed set of personal relationships within the Jewish community. What in the past could be described as "between man and his fellow" has now become "betweeen man and society" (in Hebrew the difference is brought out by the juxtaposition of *havero*, his fellow, and *hevra*, the society). This change indicates the Jewish involvement in social and political issues. The previous emphasis upon personal piety, mercy, kindness (*gemilut hasadim*) is now assuming wider proportions. Instead of helping a particular known number of persons, the aim is now to improve the structures and policies of the economy in order to eliminate the existing poverty. In the past the ideal was the prevention of poverty. Maimonides describes eight degrees of charity and sets up as the highest degree the kind of assistance that provides employment to the poor and thus prevents poverty.[8] But in modern times the ideal of prevention of poverty implies far more than an ideally high degree of charity.

ZVI YARON

Assisting the needy is now seen in terms of social, economic, and political aims that are intended to improve the *society* of men.

This shift in emphasis necessarily tends to widen the scope of involvement far beyond the Jewish community. If Judaism connotes ethics then the ethical values inevitably require a contemporary application to the social, economic, and political problems that beset the states and the nations, even the whole wide world in which the Jewish Diaspora-communities are living freely and able to participate in decision-making. And yet, despite the general non-Jewish character of these issues, to the Diaspora Jews it is the Jewish aspect that dominates their thinking and influences the extent and the manner of their involvement. This Jewishness is expressed intellectually in the attempt to relate the new and general, political and social ideals to the Jewish roots of religion-and-ethics.[9]

3. The existence of the State of Israel has profoundly affected all aspects of Jewish life in the Diaspora. Israel is now undoubtedly a focal point not only for fervent Zionists and enthusiastic supporters of Israel but quite obviously also for the Jewish opponents of Israel. For even its most bitter antagonists do not ignore Israel. They are emotionally and intellectually compelled to explain their opposition, because the existence of a Jewish state is a fact that is replete with a multitude of meanings and connotations for every Jew who is unwilling or unable to deny his Jewishness. It is the fact of Israel's centripetal force in Jewish life that is probably the cause for the extremely harsh criticism voiced by some of Israel's Jewish opponents.

Israel's role in the life of the Diaspora communities has in recent years become a growing countervailing force to the previously described tendency of total participation in general social and political movements. Much of the prevailing disenchantment among many American Jews with the liberals and radicals stems from the shock that has come from realizing that leftist politics can be combined with uncouth hatred of Israel. But what is of decisive significance for the purpose of this

235

analysis is not whether Jews now tend more to liberalism or conservatism but that the State of Israel plays an important and explicit role in these issues. This means that Israel has by now become a crucial factor in the considerations of Diaspora Jews in their thinking on the contemporary Judaism-ethics issue.

The role of Israel is intrinsically connected with the new awareness that the Jewish people are continually facing threats to their very survival. The dangers that face Israel were dramatically brought into focus during the anxious days of waiting before the Six Day War in 1967. At the same time, Jews in the Diaspora have in recent years begun to face squarely the horrible implications of the Nazi holocaust. This does not mean that American Jews accept the Jewish Defense League's theory that a holocaust is threatening American Jewry. But there are decidedly clear indications[10] that the issue of survival has become an influential element in the political and social ideas of Jews in the Diaspora. The obvious corollary of this trend is that the Judaism-and-ethics issues, in their contemporary social application, will increasingly be influenced by the awareness that the "survival" factor and the role of Israel are an essential part of the Jewish view of social problems. And this implies a stronger emphasis on the connection between the theoretical principles of ethics and the fact of the existence of the Jewish people both in dispersion and in the Jewish state.

IN ISRAEL

The consideration of the role of Israel in the theory and practice of Judaism-and-ethics in the Diaspora should be helpful in probing the character of the problem in Israel. The outstanding feature of ethical issues in Israel, as opposed to the Diaspora, is their "uncomplex" nature. This similarity is expressive of the Zionist aim to normalize the conditions of the life of the Jewish people. The effect of normalization upon ethics is that in Israel we now have new Jewish moral problems.

236

The new problems have arisen from the fact that the Jewish community constitutes the main component of the State of Israel. A random list of these new Jewish moral problems that exist only in the State of Israel would include the following subjects: internal policy, foreign policy, social and economic policies, welfare, education and culture, labor, employment, social security, equality, law making, law observance, war and defense, the treatment of minority communities, police, prisons, taxation—and the list can be extended almost indefinitely to include every possible public problem that is likely to arise in a modern state, and which requires a moral decision. What is important in an analysis of the relationship between religion and ethics, is the revolutionary fact that these problems are now *Jewish*. Over against the essential Diaspora character of issues affecting Jews outside Israel, the new moral problems concerning Israel have a "normal" state quality. For instance, the moral question of waging war is not a new problem for states and peoples, but it is new and revolutionary for the Jewish nation.

Normalcy has thus created problems that are old and tested from the point of view of any normal state but are novel when considered in the context of the new Jewish state. For throughout the many centuries of Diaspora life Jews were not faced with the necessity to decide in matters of state. The fundamental question is therefore how the traditional ethical teachings of Judaism can guide Jews in deciding upon the new state problems. The traditional Jewish moral teachings concerned the relationships within a minority community that could not even dream of intervening, as a community, in state politics. Modern developments in the Western countries opened up remarkable political possibilities, but the Jewish involvement in politics continued to retain Diaspora characteristics. It is in Israel that the question of Judaism-and-ethics is radically new. For here we have to apply traditional concepts that were evolved in Diaspora conditions to a situation in which the Jewish people run an independent state. In addition to the change from

237

"between man and his fellow" (*havero*) to the issues of society (*hevra*), the specific innovation of Israel is that we face here problems of state for which the few available precedents date from two thousand years ago.

On the basis of those precedents and other stray pronouncements in the vast literature of the Halakha various attempts were made to work out detailed guidance for the contemporary state. But the suggestion that the ancient "kingdom" precepts of that literature can be simply translated into modern "state" terminology is unconvincing. For instance, some rabbis have argued that the Halakha for the Israel army can be based on the general rule that for the sake of saving human life (*pikuah nefesh*) it is permissible to desecrate the Sabbath. But Rabbi Shlomo Goren has argued that war, army, and the Sabbath belong to a special category of the Halakha that deals with the subject of war.[11] On the larger and fundamental question of the conduct of state affairs, Rabbi Kook wrote[12] that the laws of state (*mishpetei hamelukha*) were always treated as a special and separate category that was not derived from the laws of individual conduct (*hilkhot yahid*). The rules of conduct of the state were rooted in the Torah in a general manner but the details were interpreted by each ruler in his time and with reference to the issues arising in his time. Rabbi Kook emphasizes that the laws of war are part of the *mishpetei hamelukha.*

Apart from the novelty of having to cope with the ethical problems of running a state, there is an inherent dialectic in the history of Zionism and particularly in the short history of Israel. The Zionist ideal envisioned a utopian state of justice and peace, in which the Jewish nation was to achieve the fulfillment of the moral teachings of Judaism. But the return to Eretz Israel was met with violent opposition, and since 1948 Israel was compelled to wage war in order to exist.[13] The vision was a state that would be free from inner and external strife, yet Israel is beset with hatred from outside. Israel is thus far more normal

238

than Zionism ever wished it to become. Zionist ideology was unprepared for the necessity to apply moral principles to a completely normal state. The inner tension between the utopian ideal and the stark reality has therefore caused confusion and anxiety, and there is now much heart searching and painstaking probing into these questions.

Since war has unfortunately become such an overriding necessity in Israel, it is significant that the most influential Judaism-and-ethics rule to have recently evolved in Israel is the principle of "the purity of arms" (*tohar haneshek*). This is pursued with much determination and with a great measure of success, in spite of the obvious difficulties in imposing an inner moral discipline in waging war. *Tohar haneshek* implies far more than the internationally recognized rules of war, such as the treatment of prisoners of war. It is a general rule of moral guidance for the soldier on what has to be done in fighting and on what must be absolutely ruled out. Although the *tohar haneshek* priniciple is sometimes described in sermonic terms, its significance lies in the uninterrupted probing by many commanders in applying the test of *tohar haneshek* to actual conditions of army operations.[14]

However, it should be admitted in sorrow that the purely religious contribution to the thinking on the new moral problems in Israel has been extremely poor. There is no lack of vague preaching on the greatness and splendor of Jewish ethics. But there is very little thinking on the actual problems.[15] And worse than the lack of thinking is the impression one unavoidably gets in Israel that the religious leadership is conspicuously disinterested in ethical issues that are not mentioned in traditional literature. A glaring example, which ought to cause much anxiety, is that most of the religious establishment, consisting of both rabbis and political leaders of the religious parties, has had nothing to say on the acute moral problem of Israel's rule over the Arab population in the Shechem, Hebron, and Gaza areas. There are frequent religious pronouncements on the question of the territories, but hardly a meaningful word about the people involved—apart from repeating a few biblical phrases.

It is a sad reflection on the religious establishment that it should be afflicted by moral torpidity on issues affecting live human beings whilst stirring up much excitement over autopsies on the dead. This reflects the amazing ossification of the religiosity of the established rabbinate and party leadership in Israel. It practices and preaches a religion that is deliberately shorn of theological confrontation with the present. It is the kind of religiosity that Rabbi Kook has described in Yiddish as *proste frumkeit,* a coarse piety that is keen only on finding in traditional literature the precise rule for action or abstention.[16] It avoids new questions by entrenching its piety in "religious behaviorism."[17] It faces every new problem by surrounding it with an impenetrable wall of suspicion.

Ethics are contained within the firmly circumscribed circle of the old Diaspora conditions. The traditional inherent connection between religion and ethics is firmly maintained only in the field of interpersonal relationships. But the absence of a stand on the new public questions of morality in society has given rise to a widespread impression in Israel that religion is concerned only with ritual. Although the cultural situation in Israel is diffuse and complex, the political tendency is to present the situation as polarized between orthodox-religious and secular-irreligious. This formal and official polarization has the further effect of strengthening the impression that religion is not concerned with the new moral issues that beset Israel. At the same time it appears that it is humanist-secular morality that is exploring and seeking solutions for these problems. There is thus a widening gap between the traditional complete integration of religion and ethics and the growing public view that religion is unrelated to ethics.

The tragic situation is rooted in orthodoxy's adamant rigidity and its unthinking fear of the new. It has no theology that has meaning for contemporary questions. But it has an ideology of suspicion. When it cannot reject the new, it blandly ignores its existence. The consequent deceptive divorce between religion and ethics is only one of many results arising from this enormous failure. But this may have the most serious effects upon the future of religion in Israel.

1. See Simon Rawidowicz, "On Interpretation," *Proceedings of American Academy for Jewish Research* 26 (1957): 83–126; A. J. Heschel, *God in Search of Man* (New York, 1955), pp. 273–75. The opposition to theological interpretation is sharply stated by Walter Kaufmann in his *The Faith of a Heretic* (New York, 1963), pp. 105–17.

2. In *Die Bauleute* [The Builders], first published in 1921 and later included in the posthumous *Kleinere Schriften* (1937), Rosenzweig criticizes Martin Buber for adhering to the school of thought that searches for the elusive essence of Judaism. The influential work upholding this approach to the interpretation of Judaism was Leo Baeck's *Das Wesen des Judentums,* which was first published in 1905. But the search for an all-embracing formula to encapsulate "the essence of Judaism" began in the nineteenth century and continues to this day to be a persuasive influence in Jewish thought.

3. The writings of Professor Isaiah Leibowitz appear to point in this direction, by his insistence that ethics are not an element of Halakha and that Judaism is Halakha and nothing else.

4. *Orot Hakodesh,* vol. 3, Introduction, pp. 23–27 (author's translation).

5. Cf. Paul Tillich, *Morality and Beyond* (New York, 1966), p. 20.

6. Cf. Franz Rosenzweig's "Sermonic Judaism" in N.N. Glatzer, *Franz Rosenzweig, His Life and Thought* (New York, 1953), pp. 247–50; A. J. Heschel, *God in Search of Man* (New York, 1955), p. 3.

7. See, for example, the discussion on Judaism and liberalism in the Winter 1972 issue of *Judaism;* Charles Liebman, "Toward a Theory of Jewish Liberalism," in *The Religious Situation 1969,* ed. D. R. Cutler (Boston, 1969).

8. *Mishne Torah, Matnot Aniyim* 10, 7. Maimonides' interpretation is based on Sifra's comment on Lev. 25:35: "Do not let him be reduced to poverty."

9. This analysis should not ignore, of course, the numerous Jews who are determined to exclude any kind of Jewish consideration in their political thinking and activity. However, the contemporary religion-and-ethics problem in the Jewish Diaspora affects only those Jews who affirm their Jewishness.

10. One of these indications is the remarkable popularity of Eli Wiesel's works in the American Jewish community. Another is the growing influence of Emil Fackenheim's theological writings on the Holocaust.

11. For a detailed discussion of this problem see my "Public Services on the Sabbath in Israel," *Tradition* 4 (1962).

12. Responsum 143 in *Mishpat Kohen.*

13. This dialectical tension is one of the main themes of *Siach Lochamim.*

14. The April 1972 issue of the army journal *Maarachot* carries an essay on "The War according to the View of Judaism" by the Chief Rabbi of the Army Tat-Aluf Mordechai Piron and a remarkably bold exposition of the problem by an anonymous colonel in a highly relevant situation—military security measures against terrorists in a densely populated area.

15. Significant exceptions are the discussion by Rabbi Shaul Yisraeli and Prof. Isaiah Leibowitz on the religious aspects of the reprisal carried out in 1953 against the Arab village Kibya in which civilians were killed. Leibowitz's article "After Kibya" (Hebrew) appeared in *Beterem* (1953) and was reprinted in his *Torah and Mitzvot in our Times* (Tel Aviv, 1954). Rabbi Yisraeli's essay on "The Kibya Incident in the Light of the Halakha" (Hebrew) appeared in *Ha'Torah Ve'Hamedinah,* vols. 5–6 (Tel Aviv, 1954).

16. In his *Igrot Hareiyah,* vol. 1, p. 160.

17. As described by A. J. Heschel in his *God in Search of Man,* pp. 320–35.

SIMON HERMAN

A Response to Zvi Yaron

I WANT TO SAY AT THE OUTSET that the paper by
Zvi Yaron is one with which I so fully agree that all I am going
to do is here and there supplement it, and here and there translate his more philosophical terminology into the more mundane
social-psychological terminology that I use.

I would make one first obvious point. Yaron has been dealing
with religion and ethics, in Israel and in the Diaspora. And when
we deal with Jewish religion and ethics, in the Diaspora in particular, I think we have to take cognizance of the fact, the obvious fact, that any Jewish identity anywhere can only be
understood in its interaction with the other identity, with the
majority identity. The Jewish identity of an American Jew can
only be understood in the light of its interaction with his Ameri-
canism, which leaves its imprint on every aspect of his Jewish
identity.

And so I believe that we cannot understand fully what Jewish
religion and ethics mean in the United States and in any particular community unless we see them in relation to the norms
prevailing in the general culture. It would be an interesting exercise to trace the impact of the majority culture on our views of
what Jewish religion and ethics are in each of the cultures in
which we are located. And we would see that even the Orthodox
Establishment in the United States, in Britain, and elsewhere, is
influenced by the prevailing norms defining religion, the role of

religious leadership and the relationship between ritual and between ethics.

I may add that if we look at the rabbinate in Israel, one can hardly call it an indigenous Israeli rabbinate. Another interesting exercise would be to see what are the influences originating in the setting from which it has come, which still act on this rabbinate.

I come to a second point which I must want to state in the briefest form. Yaron speaks of the attempt on the part of affirmative Jews, as he calls them, in the Diaspora, when they participate in general social movements, liberal social movements, to find the roots of their outlook in the Jewish tradition. And here I would point out that if our approach is a survivalist one, as he states it to be, there are certain dangers even in this attempt on the part of affirmative Jews. The problem in any Diaspora Jewry, and particularly in American Jewry, is to my mind today not one of Jewish identification; particularly after the Holocaust, particularly after the Six Day War, most Jews are prepared to identify themselves as Jews. The problem is rather one of giving distinctiveness to our Jewish identity; and the sort of participation you have in the Diaspora in general social movements, even if there is an attempt to find some relation, as you say, to a Jewish heritage, to Jewish tradition, to Jewish religion and ethics, does not provide that particular distinctiveness that is necessary in terms of Jewish survival.

I come to a third point, and let me take here again the specific case of the American Jew. If we look at the identity of the American Jew, he is, in most regions of what we call the life space, an American. On certain specific limited occasions he is a Jew. In other words, being Jewish in the United States is something specific and delimited, and there is a very sharp and clear demarcation between his being American and his being Jewish.

If we turn to the majority Jewish society, which is Israel, that demarcation does not exist. There is a very considerable overlap between Jewishness and Israeliness. Being Jewish in Israel is not something specific and delimited; it pervades most regions of the life space. By the way, people coming from the outside often make this mistake—because Jewishness isn't specific and delimited here, they think it doesn't exist. Actually it is much more pervasive and can therefore be much more meaningful because it enters into so many wider regions of the life space.

When Yaron speaks of "normalization," translated into my terminology it would really mean a situation where being Jewish pervades a large, unlimited number of regions of the life space, where the strict compartmentalization between being religious and being ethical or between being Jewish and being something else does not exist. I put it forward in these terms, and I think an analysis of this kind allows for a number of derivations.

I come to a further series of points in the paper where I want to raise the relevant practical questions. When people speak here and elsewhere on religious questions, particularly on religion in Israel, you can locate them on a continuum of optimism-pessimism. Strange enough, I know that Yaron has a more optimistic outlook, but if I were to limit myself to his paper I would locate him on the more pessimistic side of that continuum. All of us who are concerned with the religious situations in Israel have a certain sense of deep concern and deep indignation about the situation as it is. I think you will find that a feeling has spread that ritual belongs to the rabbinate and to religious circles, and ethics belongs to the secular humanistic circles; that is a feeling which is spreading and much of what we see today is a reaction to the present chief rabbinate. And, although I share this concern, I think that too much criticism can on occasions be destructive. These things have to be said, and they have to be said in the proper quarters. But I think that, by focusing too much on these negative manifestations, we don't do so much practically as we could do if we were to focus on certain positive trends, and we were to try and see what could be done in practice to strengthen these positive manifestations.

I know it is difficult to influence the religious parties; I know it is difficult to influence the rabbinate, although even there the

245

election of Rabbi Goren may provide some glimmer of hope. But let us look at other foci of possible positive action, and I want to just mention a few. Thus, as a first example, I think that one cannot ignore the significant contributions made by the religious kibbutz. When we look at the religious educational system and the products of that system, let us not always point out just the negative aspects.

I happened just a few days ago to receive from a group of religious soldiers, some of them students from Yeshivat Hakotel who are at the present moment in a religious unit, the questionnaire they had completed in the study we are doing on Jewish identity. I must say that I was deeply stirred by this magnificent *mizug* (synthesis) of Jewishness and Israeliness. It was quite clear that being Jewish was for them a value system that entered deeply into all regions of their life space.

And when we think of the relations between religious and secular—and here we have a considerable body of data based on a representative sample of the high school population in Israel—on any social distance scale it is precisely the religious who feel themselves closer to the secular than the secular feel to the religious. In other words, there is a desire on the part of a considerable part of the religious sector to come nearer and to meet the secular.

As for the secular sector, although they have been dismayed by much of what the rabbinate and others have done, there are misconceptions they have about *datiim* (the religious) that can be removed. If I may just introduce a personal note, I have invited Zvi Yaron to lecture to my seminars on Jewish identity and on Zionism from year to year. The secular students have expressed their appreciation for this lecture and have indicated how it has removed for them certain of the misconceptions that they had about the religious sector. These things can be done.

When rabbis have gone out to the kibbutzim, there has been a welcome and there has been a receptivity to what they had to say. I have just had occasion to hear positive reactions to a series of programs that appeared on Israeli television—a day in the life of a rabbi in Migdal Ha'emek, a day in the life of a physicist at the Hebrew University, of a physician down at Beersheba.

I would say that, in practical terms, much more can be done by focusing on those particular aspects of the situation that give some glimmerings of light, where things can be pushed forward, rather than dwelling too sharply on the things that are amiss.

NOTES ON THE CONTRIBUTORS

HAROLD FISCH is professor of English at Bar-Ilan University in Israel. He is the author of several works of literary criticism and editor of an English translation of the Hebrew Scriptures, the Koren Jerusalem Bible. He is the chairman of the Institute for Judaism and Contemporary Thought.

MARVIN FOX was until recently the Yassenoff Professor of Philosophy and Jewish Studies at the Ohio State University. He is now the Appleman Professor of Jewish Thought at Brandeis University. His published works include many studies in general philosophy and in various areas of Jewish thought.

SIMON HERMAN is associate professor in the Department of Psychology and in the Institute for the Study of Contemporary Jewry at the Hebrew University of Jerusalem. He is the author of two recent books, *Israelis and Jews: The Continuity of an Identity* and *American Students in Israel.*

EMMANUEL LEVINAS is professor of metaphysics at the University of Paris-Sorbonne. For many years he was also director of the Ecole Normale Israélite Orientale de l'Alliance Israélite Universelle. He is the author of numerous books and articles in various areas of philosophy with particular emphasis on phenomenology. English readers will be most familiar with his book, *Totality and Infinity.*

AHARON LICHTENSTEIN is currently serving as Rosh Yeshiva of Yeshivat Har-Etzion in Alon Shevuth, Israel. In addition to his book, *Henry More: The Rational Theology of the Cambridge Platonists*, he has published a number of articles on aspects of rabbinic law and thought.

MEIR PA'IL is currently serving as a member of the Knesset, the parliament of Israel. After completing a career in the Israel Defense Forces in which he served in many key positions, he retired from military service with the rank of colonel in 1971. He received his doctorate at Tel-Aviv University and has published studies in general history, military history, and the history of the Middle East.

JAKOB J. PETUCHOWSKI is research professor of Jewish theology and liturgy at Hebrew Union College, Cincinnati. Among his books are *The Theology of Haham David Nieto, Ever Since Sinai, Heirs of The Pharisees, Prayerbook Reform in Europe*, and *Understanding Jewish Prayer*.

NACHUM L. RABINOVITCH is principal of Jews' College (University of London). He is the author of *Probability and Statistical Inference in Ancient and Medieval Jewish Literature* and *Hadar Itmar*. He also serves as associate editor of *Hadarom*, a journal for research in rabbinics.

DAVID SIDORSKY is professor of philosophy at Columbia University. In addition to his academic work and his writing in various areas of philosophy, he has been actively concerned with the quality of life in the American Jewish community. He recently edited a book on *The Future of the Jewish Community in America*.

ERNST SIMON is professor emeritus of education at the Hebrew University of Jerusalem. He has been for many years a leading figure in practically every organization concerned with the development of better Jewish-Arab relations. His many publications include books on *Ranke and Hegel, Pestalozzi's Teachings*, and studies in areas of Jewish thought and contemporary Jewish affairs.

ABNER WEISS is professor and head of the Department of Hebrew and Jewish Studies at the University of Natal, South Africa. He also serves as chief minister of the Durban United Hebrew Congregation. He has published a number of articles in the field of Jewish thought.

250

ZVI YARON is an Israeli writer and educator. He teaches at the School for Overseas Students of the Hebrew University of Jerusalem. He is also director of Information Services for the Jewish Agency in Jerusalem. His book on the philosophy of Rabbi A. I. Kook, *Mishnato shel HaRav Kook* was recently published.

INDEX OF REFERENCES

GENERAL INDEX